I0902370

BLACK AMERICA SERIES

WESTMORELAND COUNTY

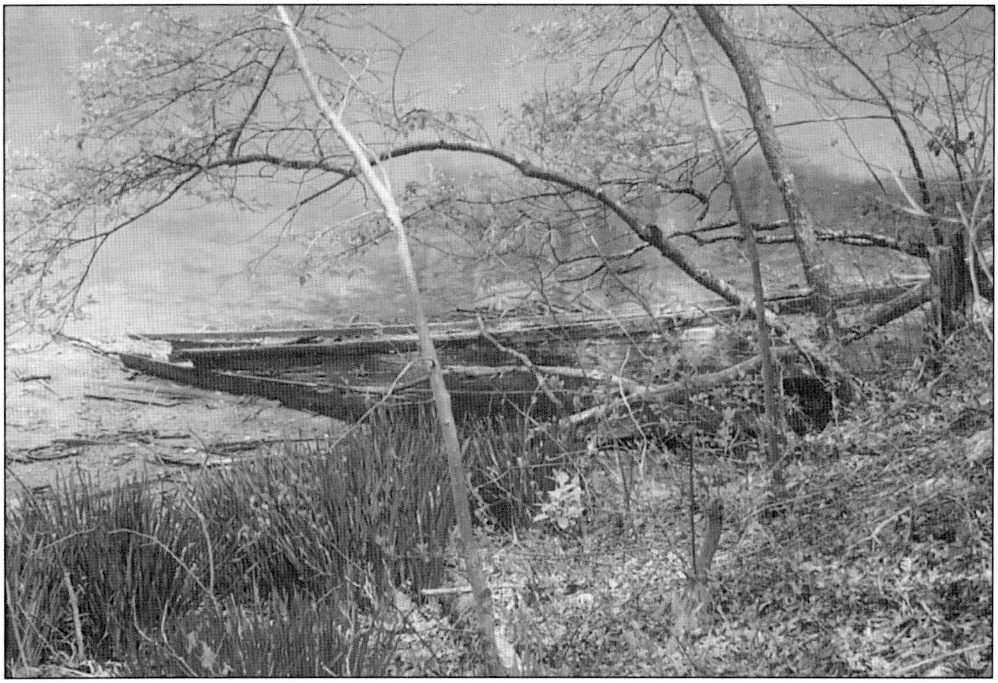

Adele Page Roane used this boat daily as a child to get from White Point to school with her young brother. For over 60 years, this small boat has remained in the waters of Westmoreland County. A remembrance of happy times gone by, it provided not only transportation, but a way of contact with the larger community and a means to secure more fish, oysters, and crabs for selling to the market and feeding their families. Its final resting place is embedded in the bank of the White Point Creek and, appropriately, surrounded by daffodils.

BLACK AMERICA SERIES

WESTMORELAND COUNTY

Cassandra Burton

ARCADIA
PUBLISHING

Copyright © 2000 by Cassandra Burton
ISBN 978-0-7385-0607-4

Published by Arcadia Publishing
Charleston, South Carolina

Printed in the United States of America

Library of Congress Catalog Card Number: 00-105231

For all general information contact Arcadia Publishing at:
Telephone 843-853-2070
Fax 843-853-0044
E-mail sales@arcadiapublishing.com
For customer service and orders:
Toll-Free 1-888-313-2665

Visit us on the Internet at www.arcadiapublishing.com

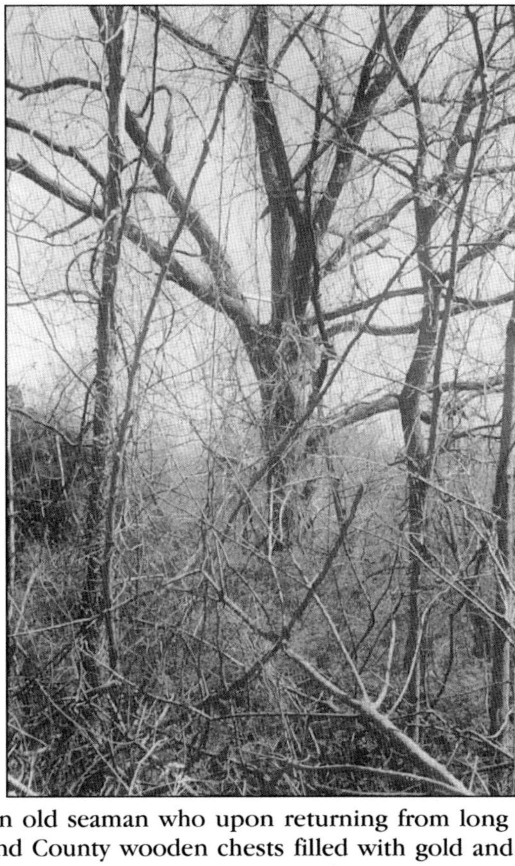

Legends abound of an old seaman who upon returning from long voyages, would bring home to Westmoreland County wooden chests filled with gold and silver coins and bury each one in the county's woods. Tales of persons finding coins in the woods for the last 200 years affirm the legend. However, many think the buried chests are today under the Potomac River's waters.

Contents

ACKNOWLEDGMENTS

This book is dedicated to those on whose backs we stand, the unsung heroes of America—to those people who have cared for, nurtured, and encouraged not only myself, but many others. To them, we say thank you.

This book is a communal effort of "born here's, come here's, been here's, and come back here's." After many working long hours, walks through the woods and cemeteries, trips researching old records, newspapers, and family documents, and hours at the Library of Virginia and the Virginia Historical Society, the author greatly appreciates all those people who have come forward to share some wonderful photographs of yesteryear.

Special thanks go to the following people: Adele, John, and Yosif Roane; my extra wheels, Lucille Ware; Lois Johnson; Joyce Wilson Jones; the "other" Lees, especially Reverend Carolyn Lee; Lola and Joseph Graham; Melanie Hall; Alease and William Lane; Calvin Jenkins; Mary and Fal Jones; Lloyd Willis; Marion Ashton; Gloria Hackett; Vernell London; Susan Roberts; Bessie Brown; Reverend Emily Tate; Reverend William B. Scott; Mark Berry; and Malachi Burton.

I would also like to recognize the many families that came forward with information, such as the Smith, Reed, Douglas, Dixon, Coates, Wright, Henderson, Fauntleroy, Henry, Fisher, and Greene families. I want to thank the writers who have come before me, such as Inez Johnson, Bernice Tate, Harrison Smith, Olie Smith, Dr. Esther Johnson, Gwen Day Pearson, Daisy Howard Douglas, and Maude Ware, for I am very appreciative of their written documentations. I would also like to thank the Westmoreland County Department of Education, George Ortman (superintendent of schools), Joyce Clayton (assistant superintendent), and the rest of the wonderful staff for all their assistance.

"Each day is a gift from God and what we do each day should be our gift back to God." May future generations know the work, deeds, customs, and accomplishments of the black citizens of Westmoreland County, upon whose backs we stand today. This book is dedicated to my grandchildren and their futures.

INTRODUCTION

Rural counties, such as Virginia's Westmoreland County, are the backbone of America. Located east of Richmond, between the Potomac and Rappahannock Rivers, the county is intersected by numerous creeks and ponds on a peninsula known as the Northern Neck. From the county's waters, there is an abundance of flounder, spots, perch, croakers (or more commonly called hardheads), crabs, and oysters, feeding not only the area's own families, but providing succulent seafood for many cities and towns, from Philadelphia to Florida, and especially nearby Washington, D.C. and Baltimore. Black members of Westmoreland County not only work the waterways, but also work in the crab and fish houses tucked in the distant corners of this 52-mile-long, 10-mile-wide community. The county's fertile fields of soybeans, milo, corn, and winter wheat provide sustenance for the American marketplace and homes. Since 1653, Westmoreland has been and continues to be a rural county, and the black community has played a prominent role in its development and success.

The black citizens of the county are very proud of their heritage and community. Many local names, such as Horn Point, White Point, Pretty Point, Cat Point, Sandy Point, Seldon Point, Hinnom, Zacata, Tucker Hill, Peckatone, Erica, Machotec Neck, Mount Holly, Hague, Acorn, Oldhams, Kremlin, McCoy's Corner, Burton's Corner, Hackett's Hill, Neenah, Templeman's Crossroads, Leedstown, Flat Iron, Baynesville, Potomac Mills, Chiltons, Lerty, Maple Grove, Campbelltown, Frog Hall, New Richmond, and Sugarland Cole's Point, are but a few of the place names that today are serviced by Kinsale, Montross, or Colonial Beach post offices; in many cases, only a small marker denotes where these smaller communities once existed.

Tucked down dirt roads and hidden from view are the black farms, such as the Lee farm, which is owned by Robert E. Lee (the patriarch of the "other" Lees of Westmoreland County); Cloverdale Farm, from the Johnson dynasty; Hull Spring, one of the many farms owned by the Dixon family; and Springfield farm, home to the Jones family. Like some of their white farming counterparts, the Reed family owned a lot of land and many farms, as did the Roanes, Weldons, and Claytons. The Ashton family's story reveals the indomitable spirit of the American farmer, who through will power and ingenuity turned from failing sheep and hog farms to raising poultry and winning national acclaim for its success.

Black businesses have and continue to exist in the county, from the days of transporting by boat and oxen to the trucking interests of today. No longer is there bus service to Richmond or Baltimore, but there are van pools transporting citizens to work to nearby cities, especially Washington, D.C.

The county hosted many special occasions for its citizens in prior years. For example, the Kinsale community showed movies during the summer months under a tent, where both blacks and whites could attend; however, at the movie theater in Montross, blacks were forced to sit upstairs, while whites sat downstairs. Of special interest, there was a floating river theater that provided entertainment for those who could afford to attend.

The black community also enjoyed events outside of Westmoreland County, such as the annual fair in Warsaw, which provided rides and games. Another big event, Emancipation Day was celebrated on April 3rd of each year in Tappahannock. Many recall what a enjoyable trip it was to cross the Rappahannock River to support and attend this celebration, which was organized and sponsored by the county's neighbors outside of the Northern Neck. The parades and activities are still well remembered by locals as a way for black residents to pay tribute to their ancestors and their struggle for freedom. Today, the Westmoreland County NAACP Chapter's Jubilee Day is celebrated, and the Emancipation Proclamation is read to participants so that future generations will not forget the price that black America has paid over the past centuries. Another popular event, the yearly Martin Luther King Prayer Breakfast is sponsored by the local churches to remember the struggle and contributions of black Americans.

The citizens of Westmoreland County acknowledge and praise the crucial role of God and the church in the black community. Religion has been the first priority in local development, and it continues to be a foundation for other developing communities. People of Westmoreland County define who they are by what church they attend. A pastor's anniversaries, church anniversaries, and assortment of local plays and pageants continue to provide a busy life for the rural citizens of this county. During August, church revivals are held, appropriately at a time when the a break is due, for the fields are growing and the gardens have produced—truly, some downtime was now at hand. In the past, new clothes were made or purchased for the nightly prayer services; many times the necessary funds came from the egg money. For those living away, this late summer event provided and still provides an opportunity to come home.

The black community of Westmoreland County has hosted a variety of pageants for its daughters, beautiful weddings, and glorious anniversary celebrations. The county's black citizens have educated and instilled in its children a value for education, for many have gone on to obtain advanced degrees. The county is especially thankful for those who have chosen to return home, giving their talents back to the community.

The black Westmorelander is bound not by blood, but a commonality to reach back and help the other up. Proudly, the county's black members have served in every battle and conflict in this country's history, ensuring future generations an opportunity to help one another and prosper.

One

Transportation and Work

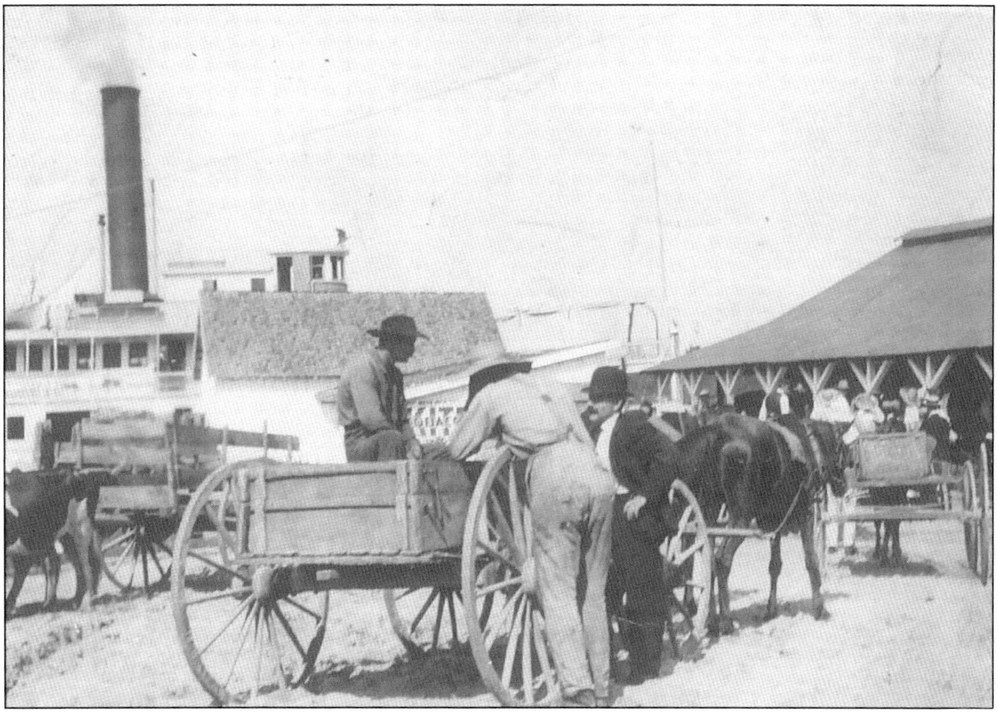

Travel to and from Westmoreland County occurred via steamship. Horses and wagons came over dirt roads to the Deep Creek pier down by the Nomini Creek, which flowed into the Potomac River and was used to take goods and persons to locations north, such as Washington, D.C. and Baltimore. (Courtesy of Jesse Coates.)

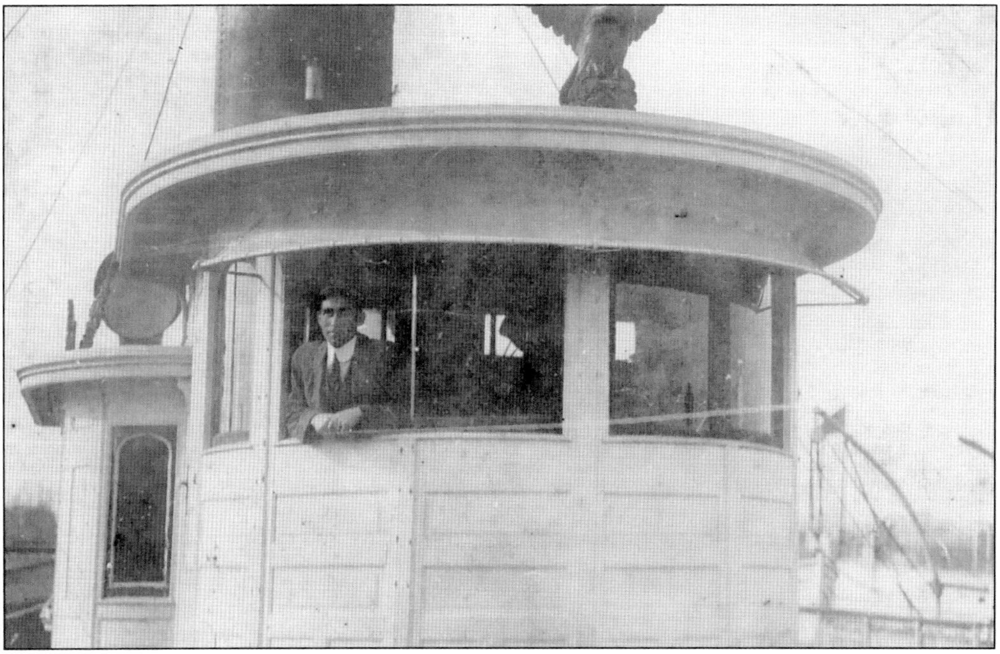

Jesse "Bud" Roby Knight is seen here in the pilot house of a ship coming into Deep Point in Westmoreland County. (Courtesy of Jesse Coates.)

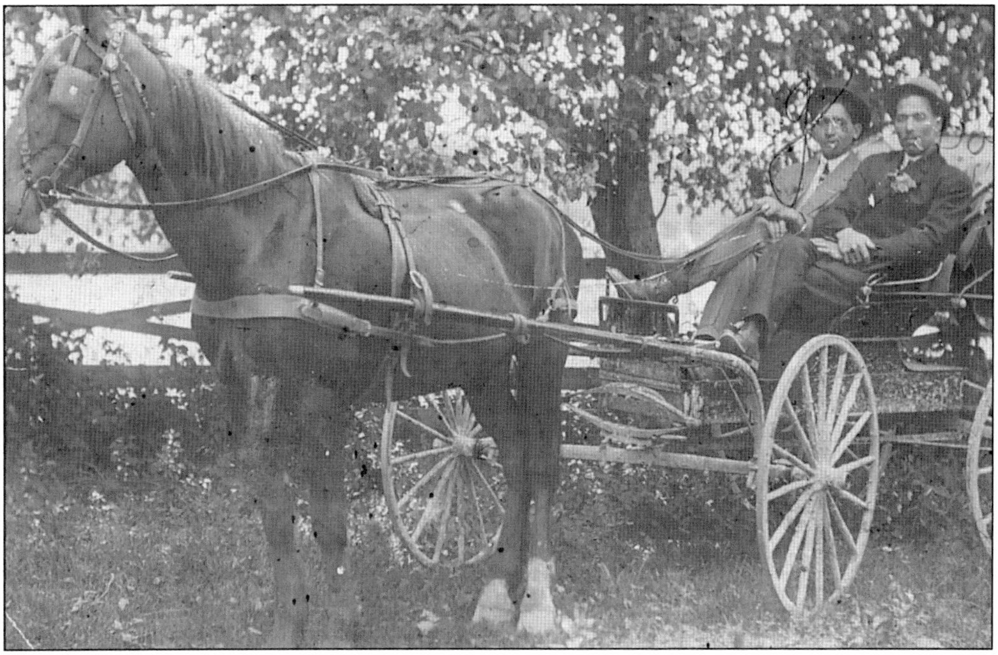

A horse and buggy provided transportation around the county before automobiles. In this view, Gelson Johnson and Dan Ware pose for a photographer on their Sunday drive. The prevalent use of wagons and horses provided a lot of work for the local blacksmith. As can be seen in this view, the county's dirt roads were typical for many of the county's rural communities. (Courtesy of Lucille Ware.)

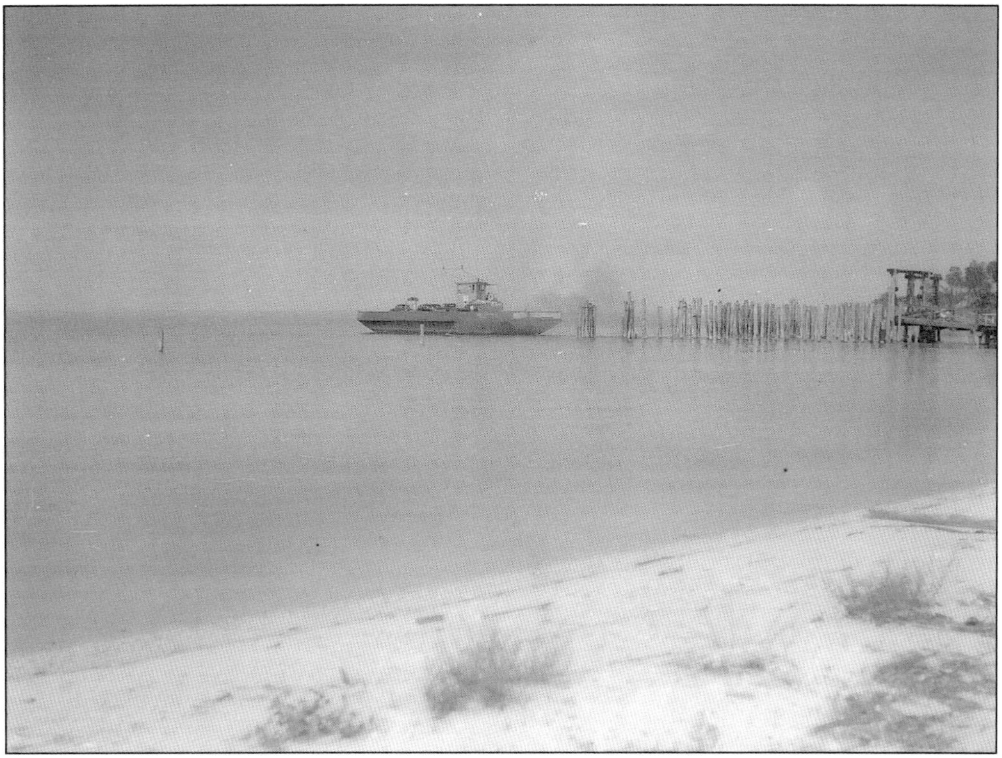

This photograph shows a ferry heading into the pier at Colonial Beach. Many tourists came to enjoy the beach and to stay in the fine Colonial Beach Hotel and guesthouses. Many early African Americans served as cooks on the ferries, and also used the ferries to leave the county for cities such as Washington, D.C. and Baltimore—places that provided much more opportunity for blacks.

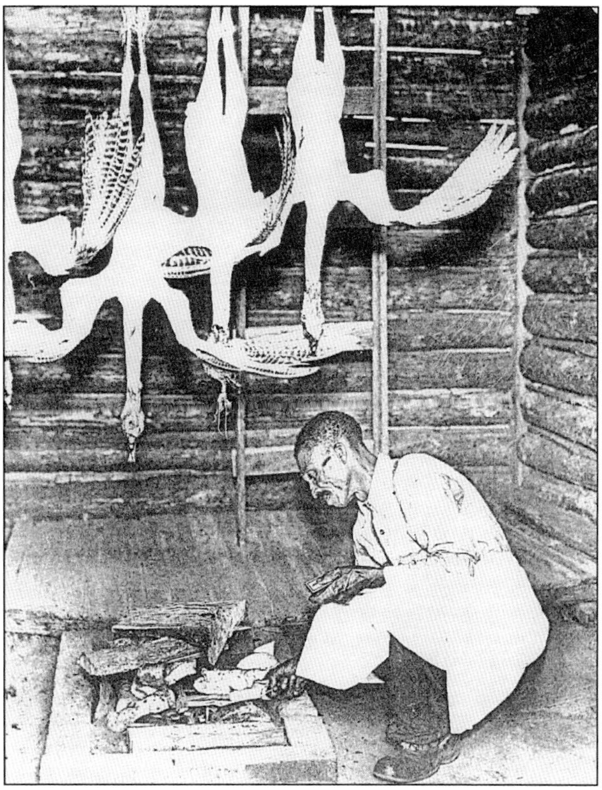

Smoking food was an important part of food preservation in the county. Mr. Wesley Payne, seen here, was a skilled craftsman in the art of cooking and preserving meat. Known to many as simply Uncle Wes, Mr. Payne was born on Stratford Hall Plantation. (Courtesy of Lois Johnson.)

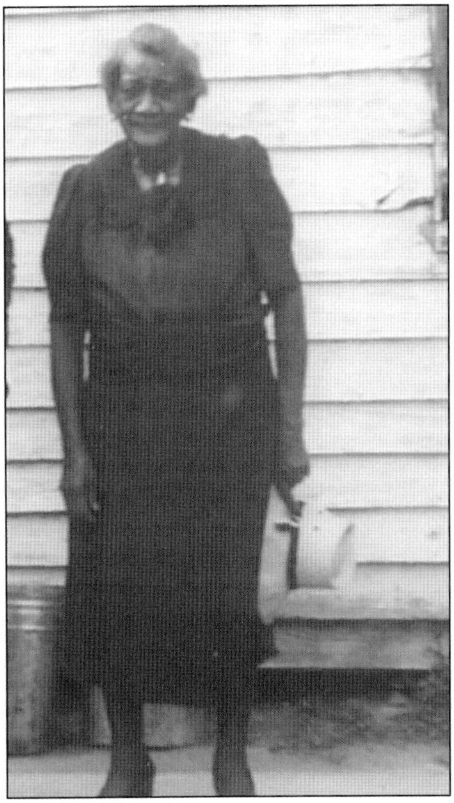

During the earlier parts of the twentieth century, local doctors would send a horse and buggy, and later a car, for Fannie Ann Taylor Nelson, known affectionately as Momma Fannie. A native of Neenah, Virginia, Ms. Nelson decided, at age 40, to become one of the few licensed midwives, black or white, receiving her certification on December 7, 1937. She had nine children, some of which were said to be "hand picked." One of her children, who was only 10 days old when her birth mother passed away, later asked why she and others of her brothers and sisters were not with their real families; Ms. Nelson answered, "Child, me and God picked you out for me." The fee for delivering a baby went slowly up over the years from a sack of potatoes or a bundle of wood to $2 (by 1960, she charged up to $10). (Courtesy of Marion Ashton.)

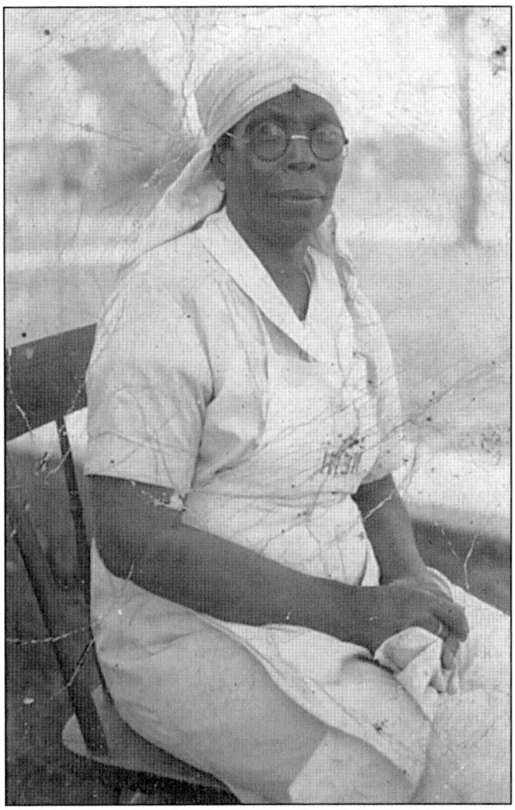

Eliza Rich Johnson, a daughter of Betsey Kelby Rich and Claiborne Rich, was a midwife in the Tucker Hill and Kinsale areas of the county. A certified midwife, she was very useful in an area that found doctors scarce due to its rural environment. (Courtesy of Eliza and Stephen Lee.)

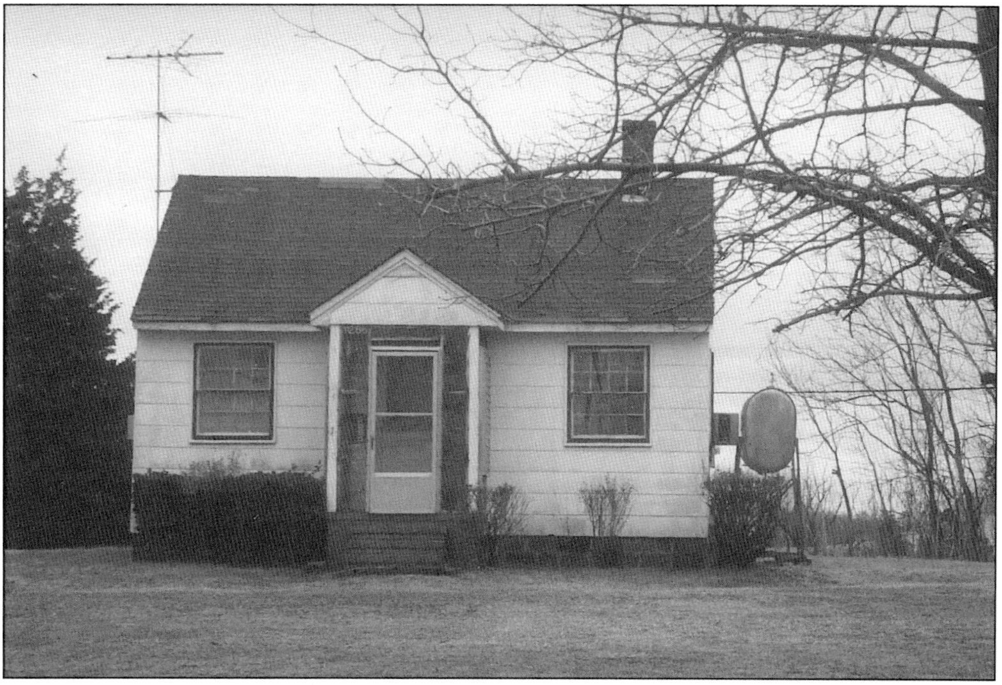

No sign is needed for the popular local establishment of Roane's Corner Barber Shop in Kinsale. Yosif Roane was the owner and barber.

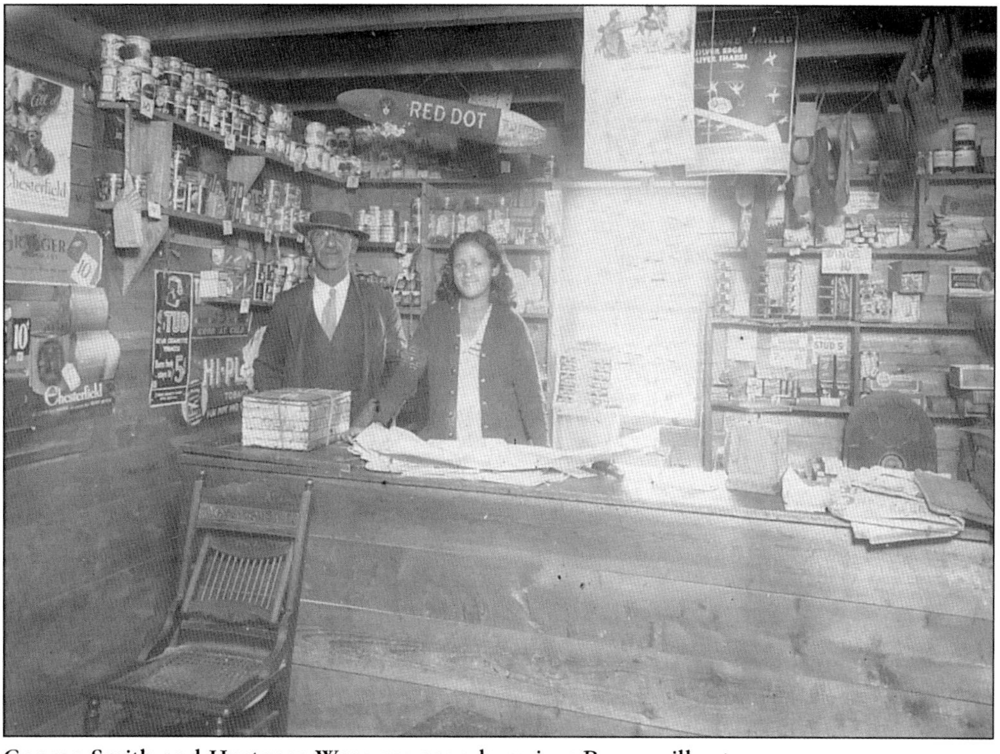

George Smith and Hortense Ware are seen here in a Baynesville store.

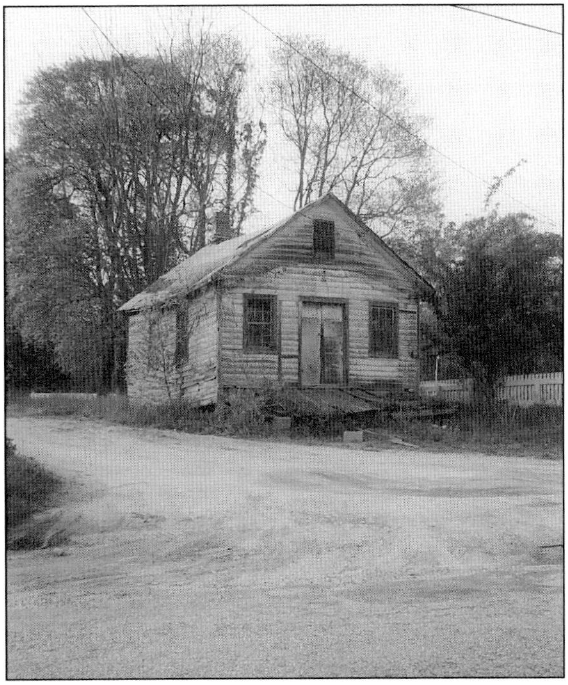

George Nelson's all-purpose store was an important part of life in the rural community of Zacata.

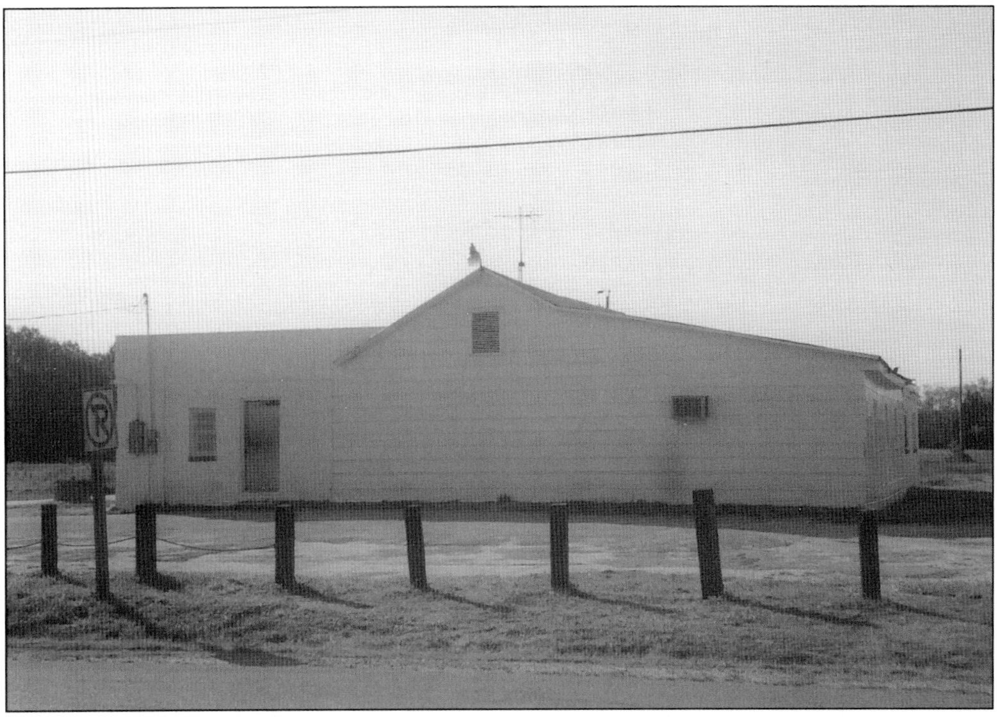

Vets Inn, a local nightclub owned by Ferman Dixon, provided entertainment for so many years that the building didn't need a name or sign on it to tell patrons where to come on the weekends to unwind. For decades, Mr. Dixon has run a black club in Westmoreland County.

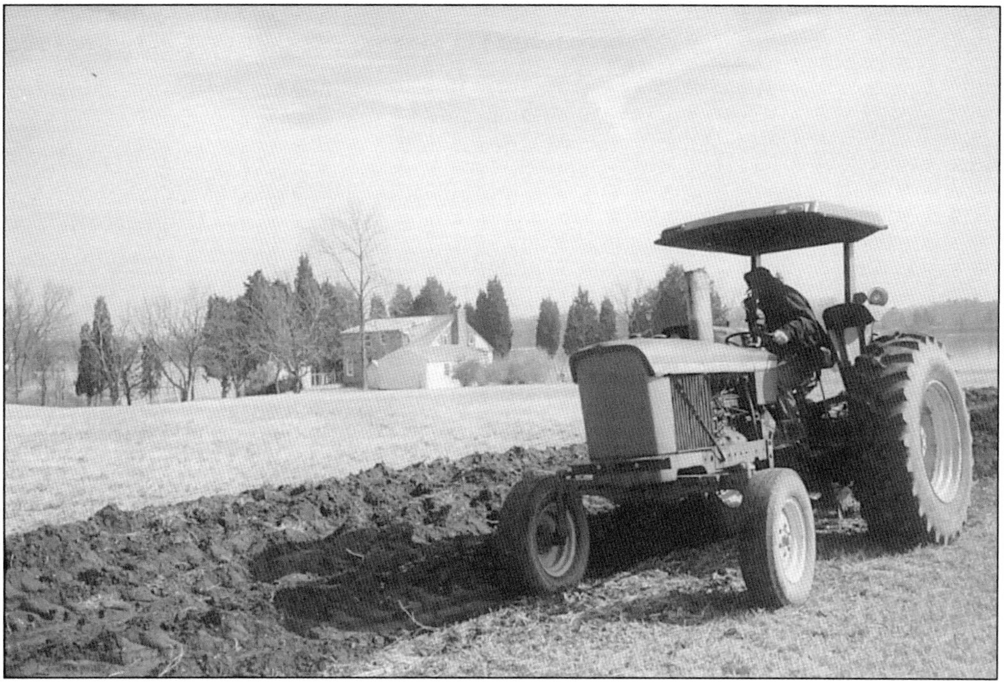

A love of earth and the joys of farming have been passed down through the generations of the Reed family. In this photograph, Robert "Billy" Reed continues to farm, like his ancestors before him.

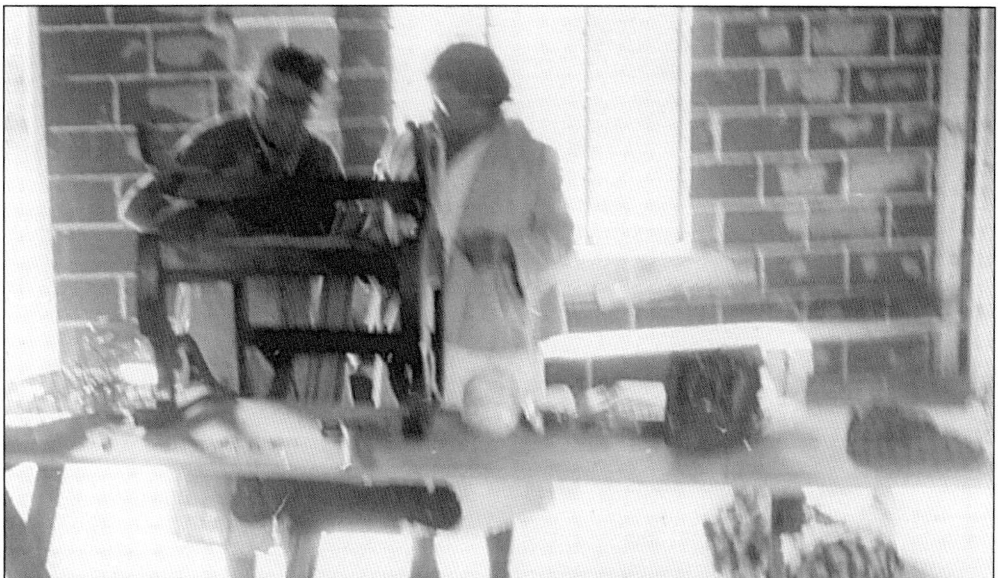

Maude and Rachel Ware are seen here reworking a chair. Possessing artistic vision and skilled hands, the county's women, as well as men, knew how to make the ordinary beautiful.

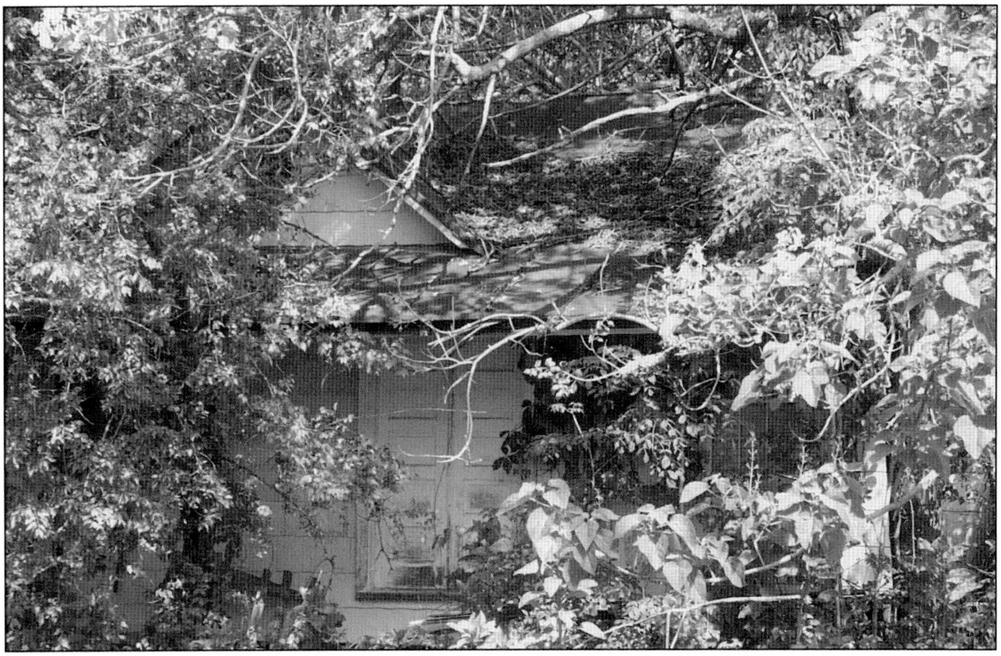

Located in Oldhams, G.H. Weldon and Son was the first black funeral home. Established in 1908, the funeral home was a joint effort of Randolph Spence, George H. Weldon, and John H. Roane. Spence and Roane sold their interests in the business, and Weldon was joined by his son, David. It operated as G.H. Weldon and Son until 1961, when the elder Weldon passed away. In 1949, Granville Fisher, a grandson of George Weldon, had also joined the business. In 1961, a new partnership was formed to include Granville Fisher Jr.

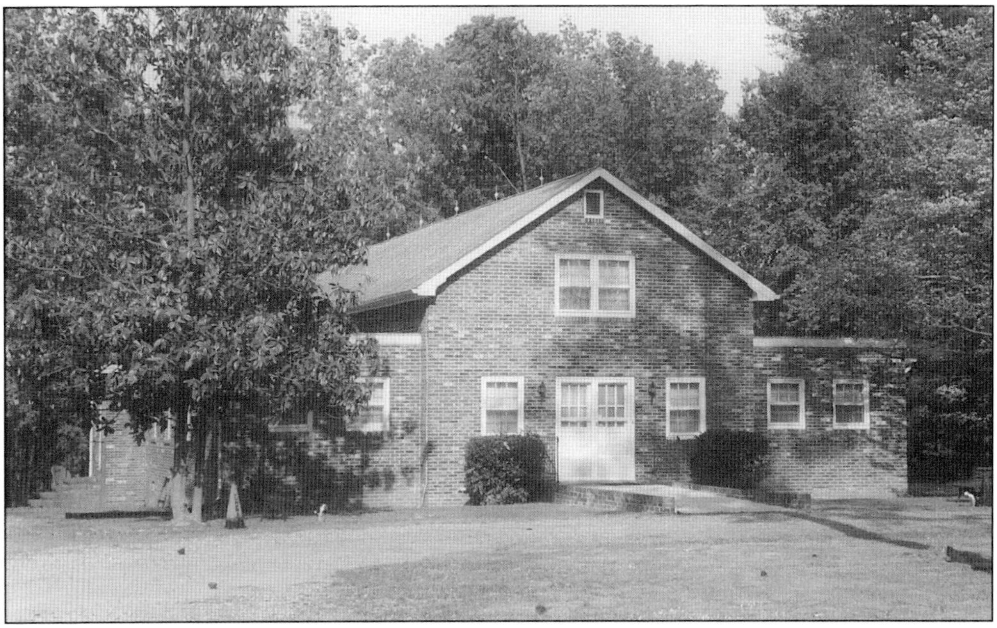

Weldon Fisher Funeral Home constructed a new building in 1970 near Nomini Grove. Granville Fisher's son, Reverend Darryl Fisher, is now the owner and manager.

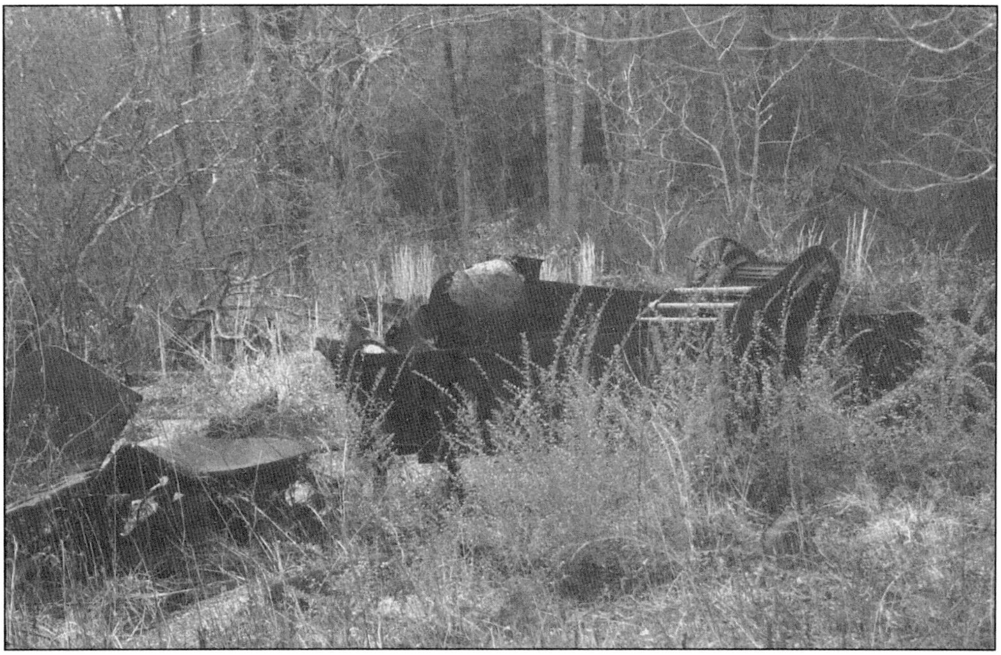

John H. Roane's tomato-canning factory is all that remains of the once-thriving business called Kremlin Packing Company. George Weldon and Tom Jones were both partners in the business.

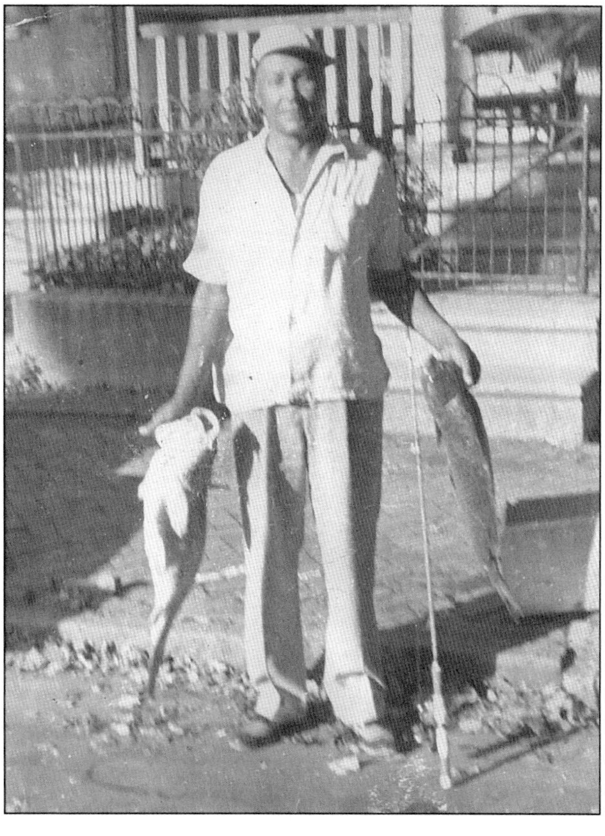

Fishing has always been a way of life and livelihood for many Westmorelanders, as can be seen in this photograph of Robert Washington and his catch.

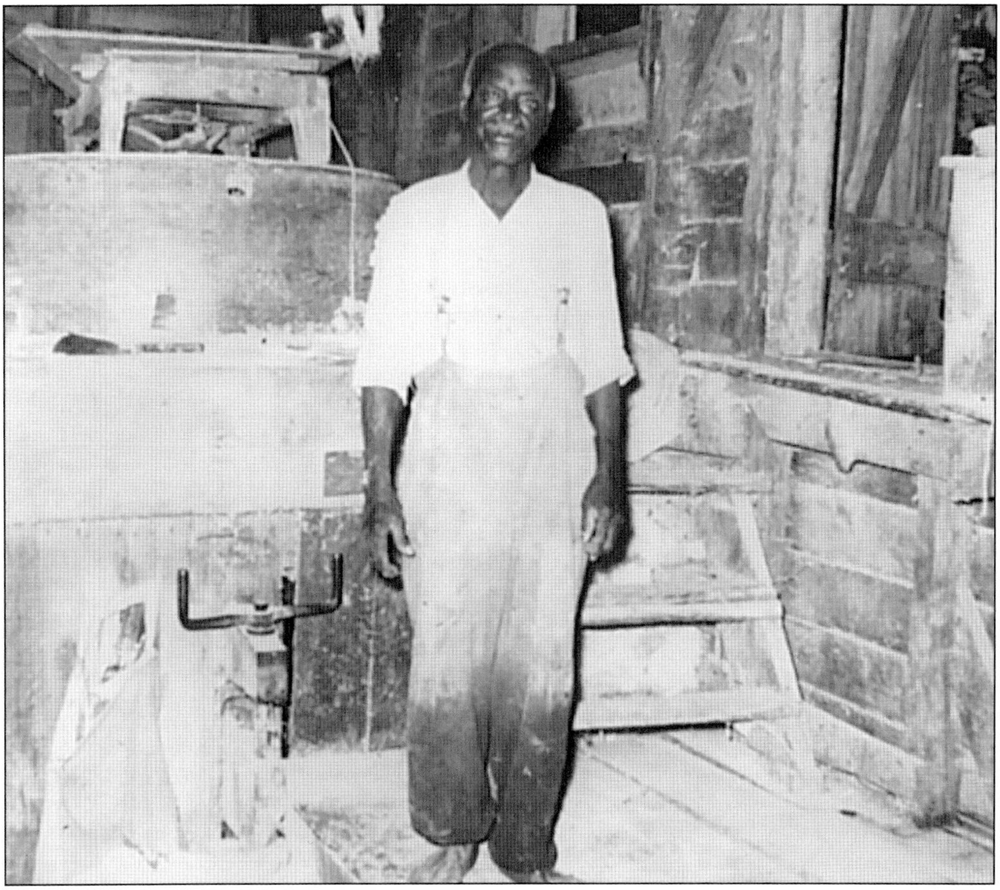

A descendant of a black man named Robert E. Lee, Frank A. Lee of Kinsale was a well-known well digger—many times digging deeper than 75 feet. He was also a truck farmer specializing in strawberries, lettuce, asparagus, eggplants, rutabagas, rhubarb, watermelons, cantaloupes, parsley, and sweet potatoes. Frank Lee was also a miller at Bailey's Grist Mill in Bailey's Hollow in Kinsale.

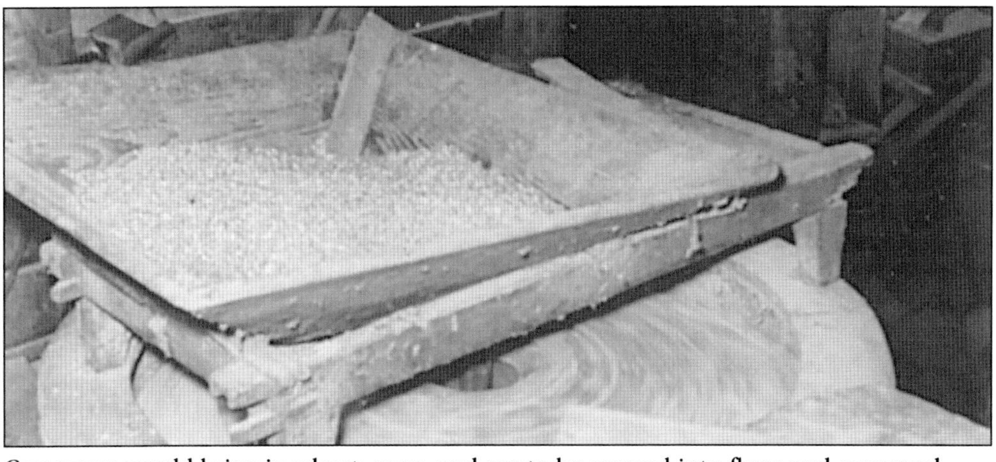

Customers would bring in wheat, corn, and rye to be ground into flour and cornmeal.

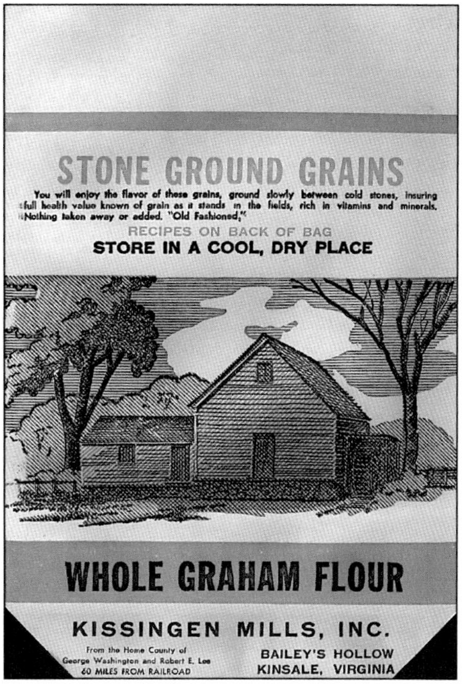

This is a whole flour bag from a local mill. Below, the following recipes were found on the back portion of the package.

A few suggestions for using WHOLE GRAIN PRODUCTS ground by slowly revolving stones - solely powered by a stream of water - retaining all the flavor and food value placed in the grain by nature - Nothing removed - Nothing added.

WHOLE WHEAT BREAD

2 tbsp. Butter or Margarine — 2 tsp. Salt
1/2 cup Molasses or Sugar — 2 cups scalded Milk
1 cake Yeast dissolved in 1/4 cup Lukewarm Water
4 1/2 to 5 cups Whole Wheat Flour

Add shortening to hot milk. Stir until well mixed, add sweetening and salt, mix. When lukewarm add disolved yeast cake and flour. Beat well. Cover and let rise until double in bulk. Again knead thoroughly and shape into loaves and put into greased bread pans. Be sure pans are only one half full. Let rise and bake at 450 F. for 15 minutes then at 350 F. until done. During this last rising and baking the bread will approximately double in bulk.

OLD FASHIONED WHOLE RYE BREAD

4 cups Whole Rye Flour — 2 cups Whole Wheat Flour
1 cup riced boiled potatoes - solidly packed
1 cake Yeast — 1 tbsp. Salt
1 tsp. Caraway Seed — 1 pint hot Potato Water

Pour potato water in mixing bowl. When lukewarm add yeast dissolved in 1/4 cup of the lukewarm liquid. Stir in rest of ingredients, knead until smooth and elastic. Let rise in warm place until bulk is doubled. Form into loaves approximately 1/2 size of pan in which to be baked and let rise. When doubled in bulk bake at 375 F. 1 hour or longer. Brush top with water.

WHOLE SOYA MUFFINS

2 cups Whole Soya Flour — 1 cup white or yellow Corn Meal
2 tsp. Baking Powder — 4 tbsp. Butter or Margarine (melted)
1 1/4 cups Milk — 2 Eggs (beaten)
1 tsp. Salt

Sift dry ingredients together. Mix beaten eggs, melted shortening and milk, then stir in dry ingredients. Bake in well greased muffin pans in hot oven 425 F. for about 15 minutes. Makes 14 muffins.

SOUTHERN SPOON BREAD

1 cup white or yellow Corn Meal — 2 1/2 cups boiling Water
2 tbsp. melted Butter or Margarine — 2 Egg Yolks slightly beaten
1 1/2 cups Buttermilk
1 tsp. Soda — 2 Egg Whites
1 tsp. Salt

Add corn meal gradually to boiling water. Cook 15 minutes in double boiler. Let cool - add butter, egg yolks and buttermilk mixed with soda. Beat 2 minutes and add egg whites beaten until stiff. Turn into buttered 2 quart baking dish. Bake 40 minutes at 425 F. Serves 8. To make with sweet milk omit soda and add 2 tablespoons baking powder.

RAISED WHOLE BUCKWHEAT CAKES

1 1/2 cups Whole Buckwheat Flour — 1/2 tsp. Salt
2 cups scalded Milk — 1/2 Yeast Cake dissolved in 1/4 cup lukewarm water

Stir to batter thin enough to pour. Let rise overnight in warm place. In morning add 1 tablespoon molasses or brown sugar and 1/4 tablespoon baking soda dissolved in 1/4 cup lukewarm water. Stir all together and cook on hot, well-greased griddle. Makes 20 to 24 cakes.

MUFFINS - GEMS

1 cup Whole Rye Flour — 1/2 tbsp. Salt
1 cup Whole Wheat Flour — 2 tsp. Sugar
1/2 cup Corn Meal (white or yellow) — 2 tbsp. melted Shortening
2 tsp. Baking Powder
2 cups Milk or Water

Mix dry ingredients, beat in melted shortening and liquid, spoon into muffin pans and bake 20 to 25 minutes at 400 F. Serves 16.

ESPECIALLY GOOD GRAHAM BREAD

1 can (14 1/4 oz. Evap. Milk) — 1 tbsp. Salt
1 2/3 cups hot Water — 1 pkg. dry Yeast
1/4 cup melted Shortening — 1/2 cup warm Water
1/3 cup Sugar — 3 cups Graham Flour
4 cups unsifted All-Purpose Flour

Mix evaporated milk with hot water, shortening, sugar and salt in a large bowl. In a separate bowl sprinkle yeast over 1/2 cup warm water to soften. Then stir yeast into milk mixture. Add graham flour and enough white flour to make a stiff dough. Mix thoroughly, cover with a clean tea towel and let rise in a warm spot (away from drafts) until Punch the dough down with your fist, transfer to a floured board and almost double in size.
knead vigorously until relatively smooth. Grease two 9 x 5 x 3 inch loaf pans. Divide dough in half and shape into 2 loaves. Place in pans and let rise, again in warm spot, for 20 to 30 minutes. No longer. Bake in a preheated 375 F. or moderate oven for 50 to 60 minutes or until bread sounds hollow when rapped with your knuckles. Remove from pans and cool.

WHOLE SOYA SALMON LOAF

1 lb. can Salmon — 1 beaten Egg
2/3 cup Whole Soya Flour — 1/2 tsp. Salt
2/3 cup whole Milk

Sift whole soya flour with salt. Combine beaten egg and milk and gradually stir into dry mixture. Break salmon into small pieces and add with juice. Bake in greased loaf pan in moderate oven - 350 F., about one hour.

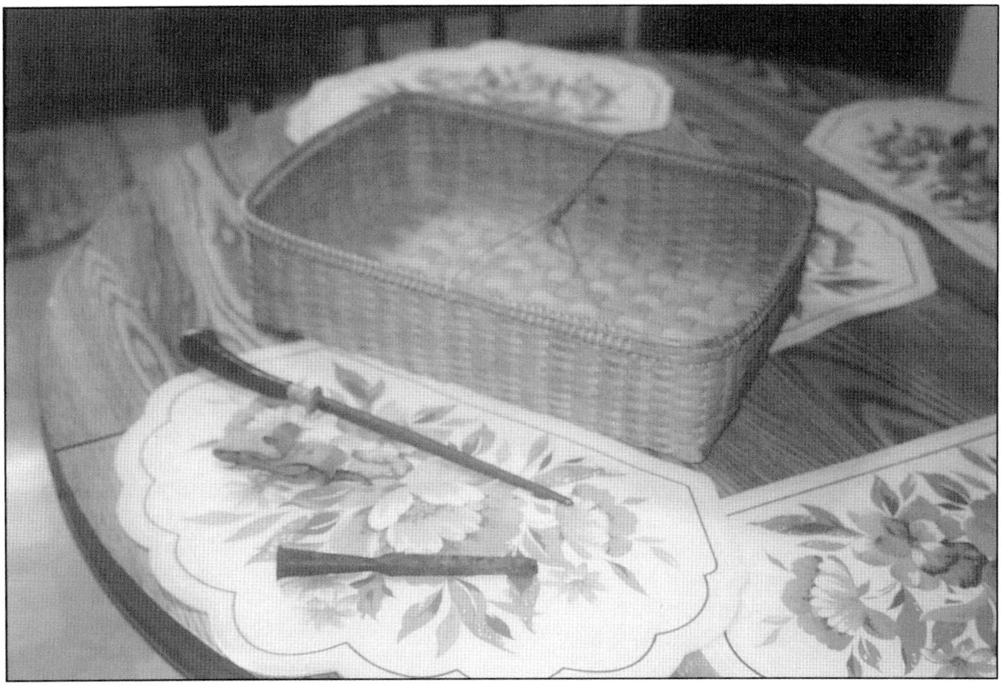

These handmade baskets were produced by the skillful William "Willy" Jones, also famous for his carpentry, of Lyells. (Courtesy of Alease and William Lane.)

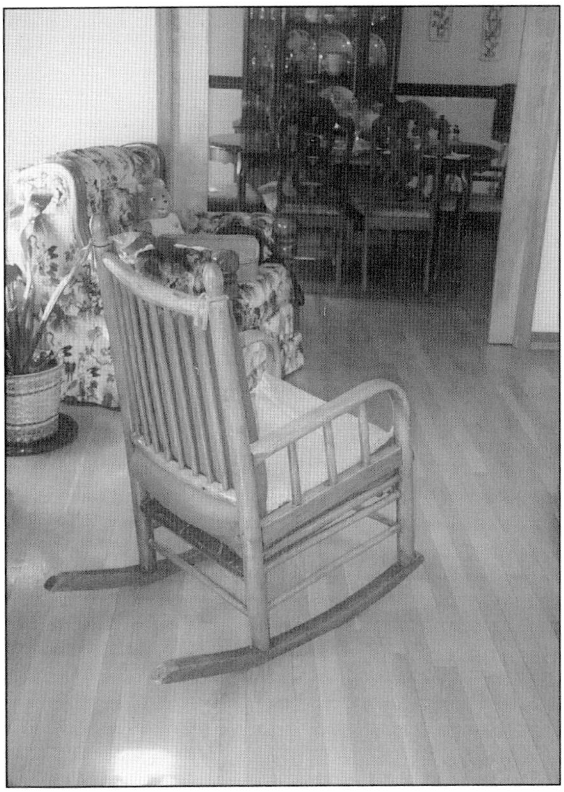

William "Willy" Jones also crafted this rocking chair. (Courtesy of Alease and William Lane.)

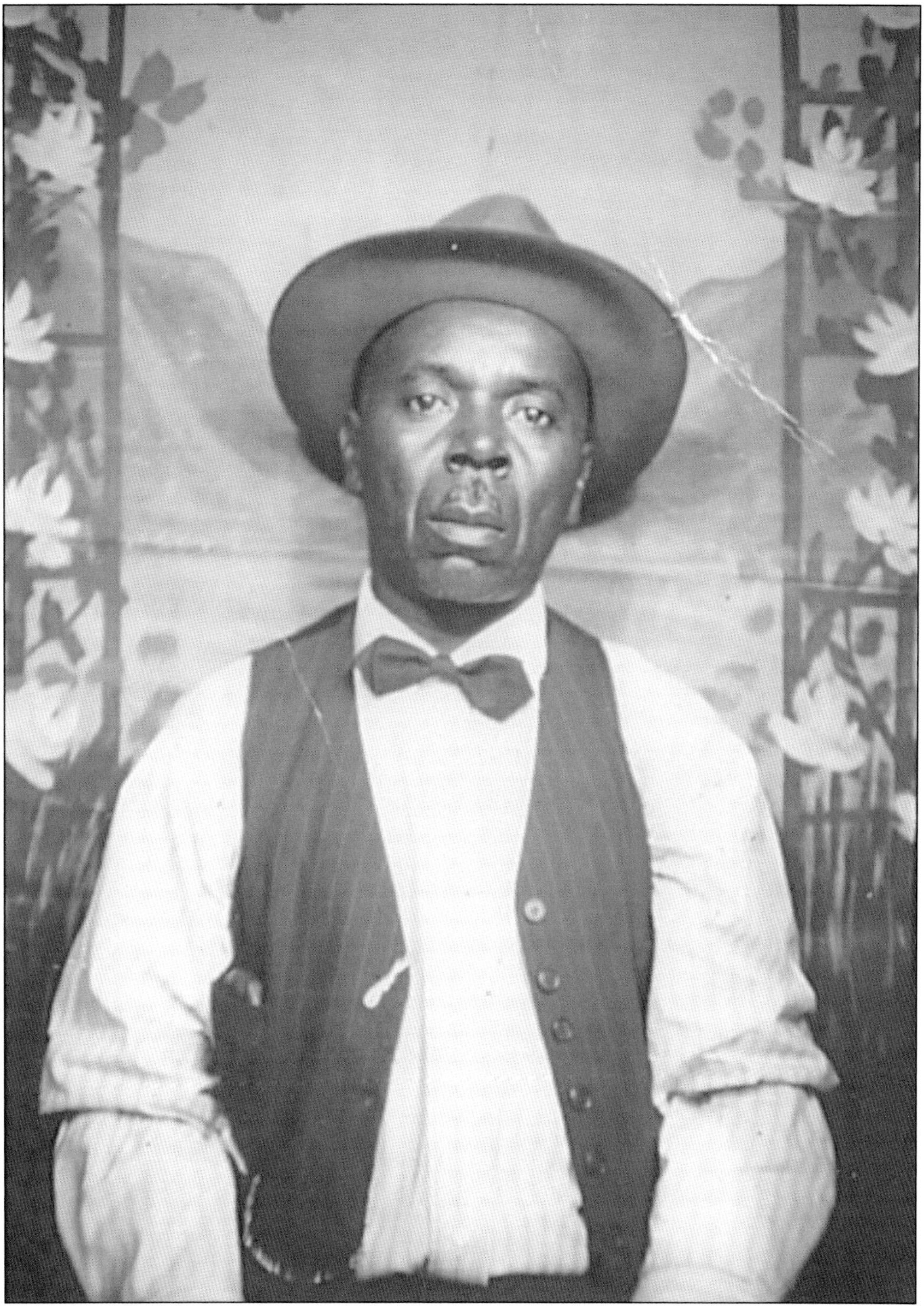

Besides being a skilled craftsman, William "Willy" Jones was also charter member of the Westmoreland Rescue Squad.

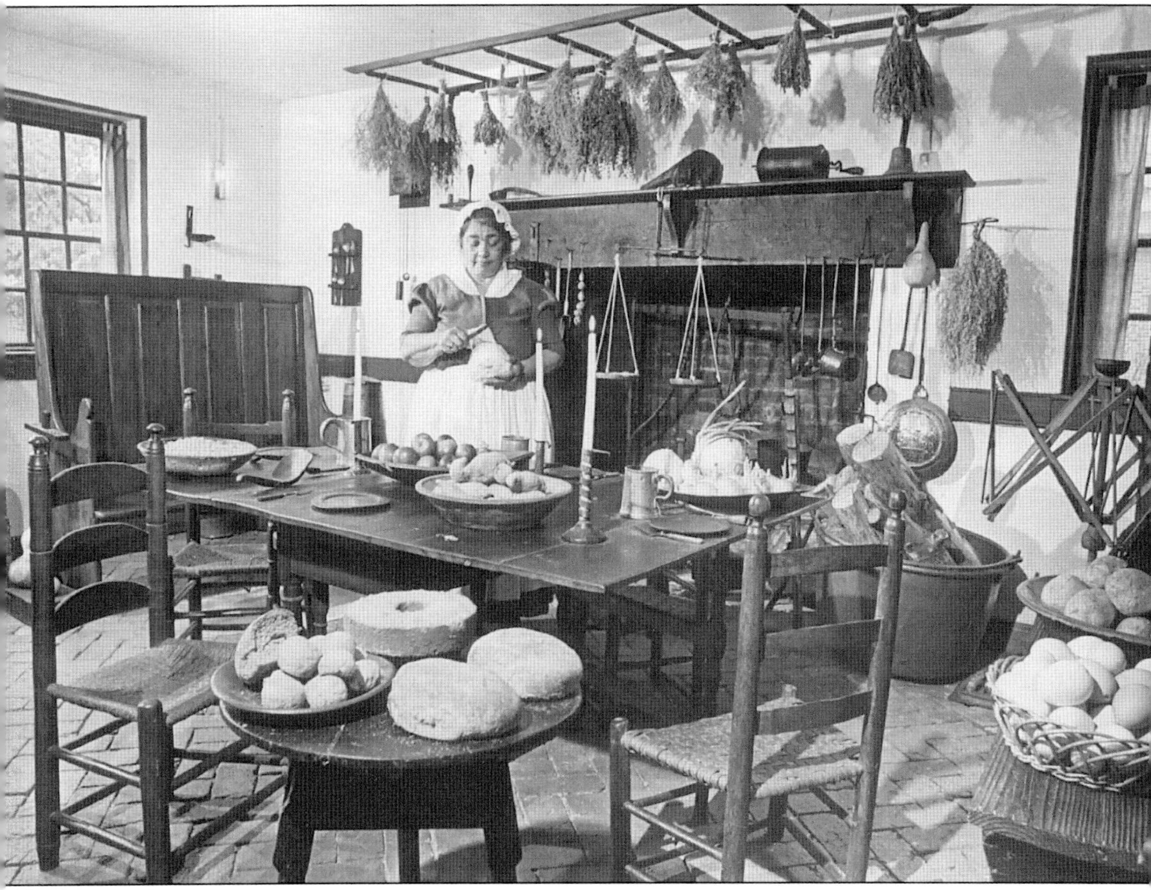

Mrs. Ida Johnson worked for the National Park Service in the kitchen house at George Washington's birthplace, giving living history demonstrations of what an eighteenth-century kitchen was like. (Courtesy of Susan Johnson Roberts.)

Betty "Bee" Smith, former owner of the Bunny Burger in Montross, also ran the Strafford Hall Plantation Dining Room for many years.

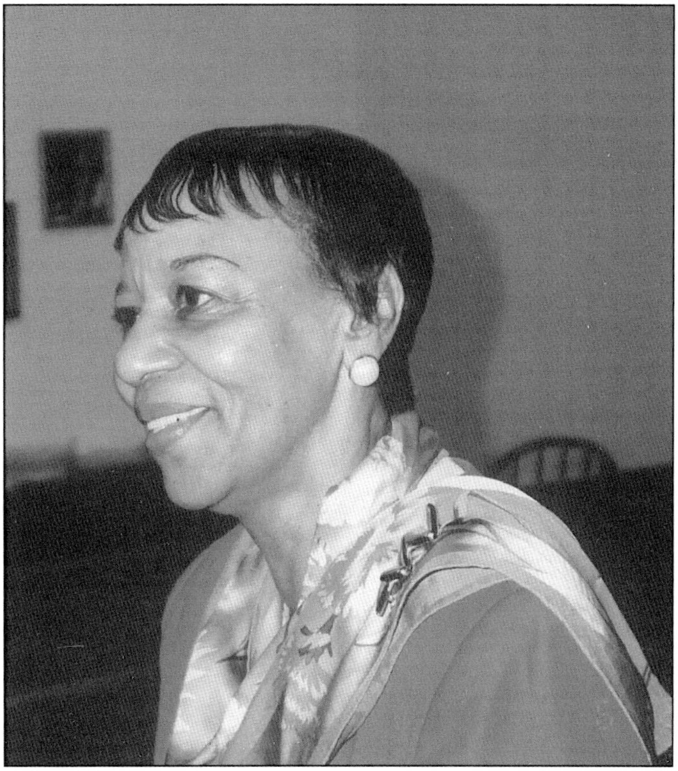

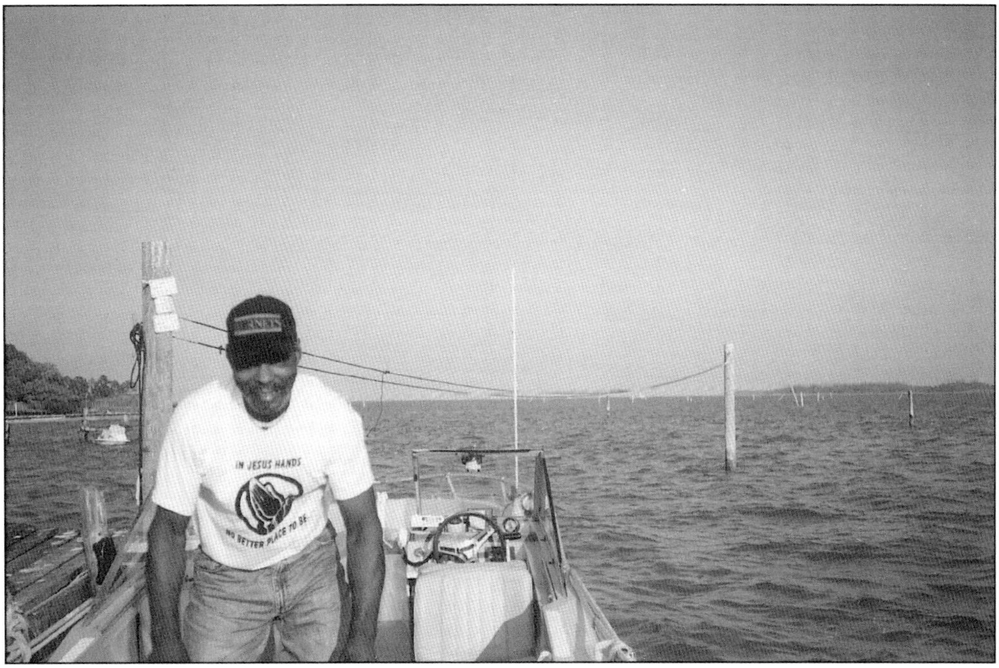

James Allen Douglas started out in his early life working on the water, but found by leaving the area and commuting home for over 30 years that he could better provide for his family. After he retires, he hopes to once again return to the water on a daily basis.

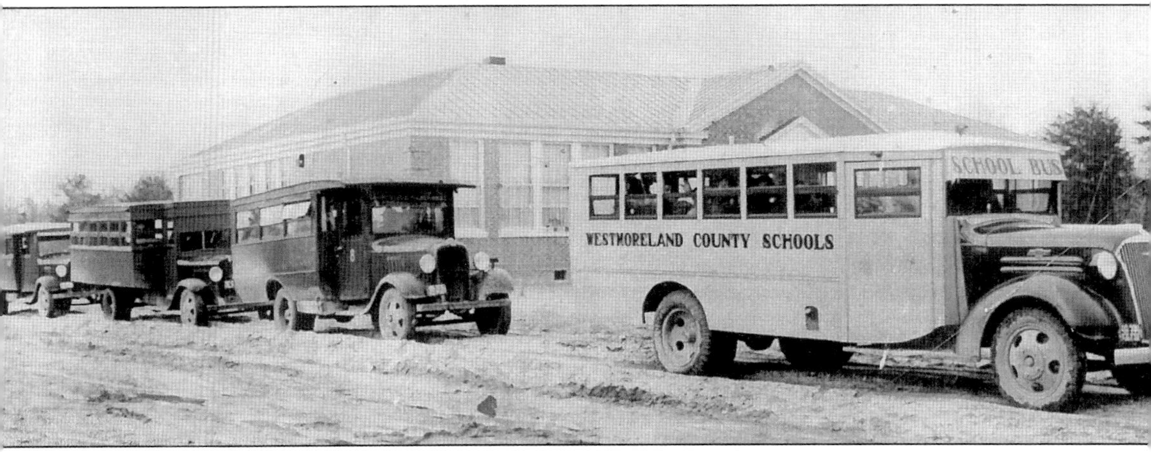

Pictured here are a few of the early county school buses. John H. Roane's school bus appears on the far right and was later driven by Willy Jones. The other school buses, from right to left, were driven by the following: Mr. Stewart, Mr. Johnson, and Mr. Watson (of Colonial Beach). (Courtesy of Gloria Hackett.)

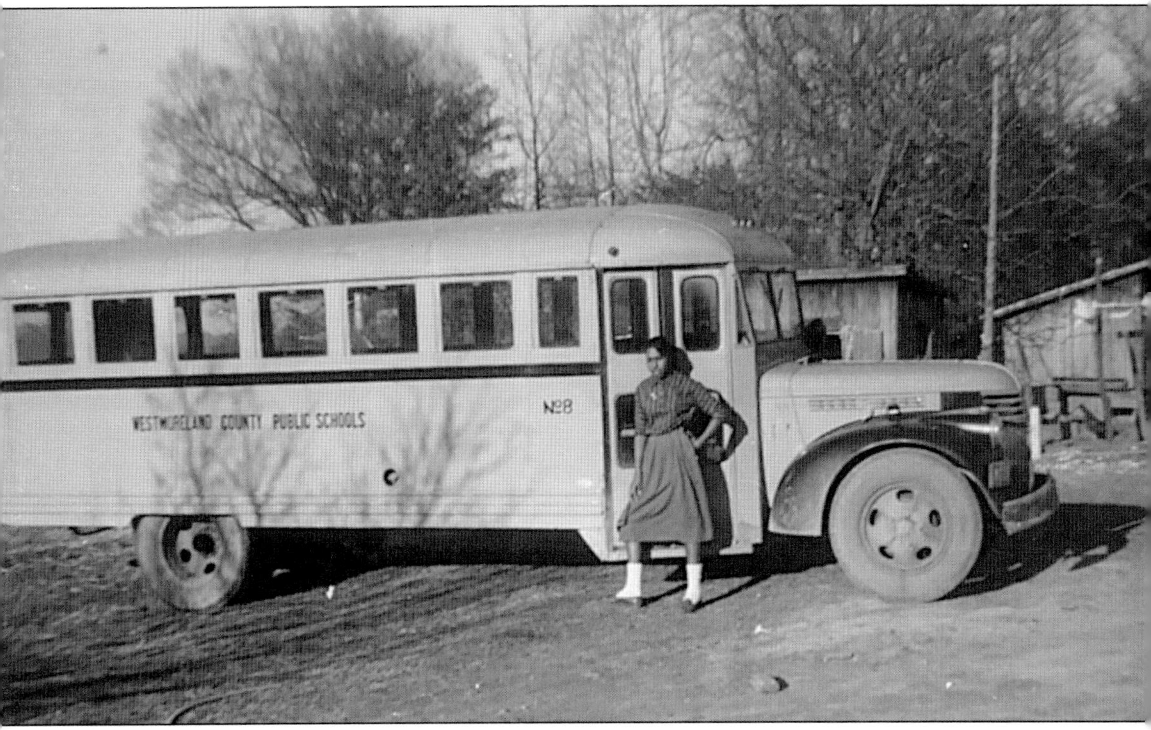

This photograph shows a 1959 county school bus. (Courtesy of the Lee family.)

Gravel Run Colored School, seen top and middle, was built in 1918.

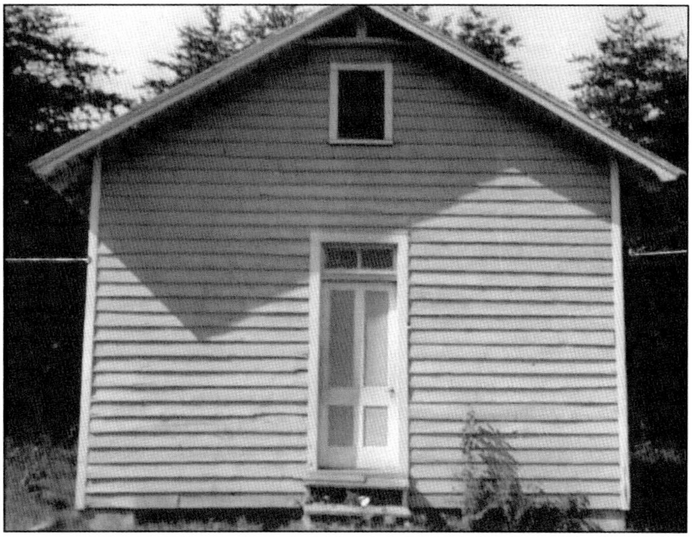

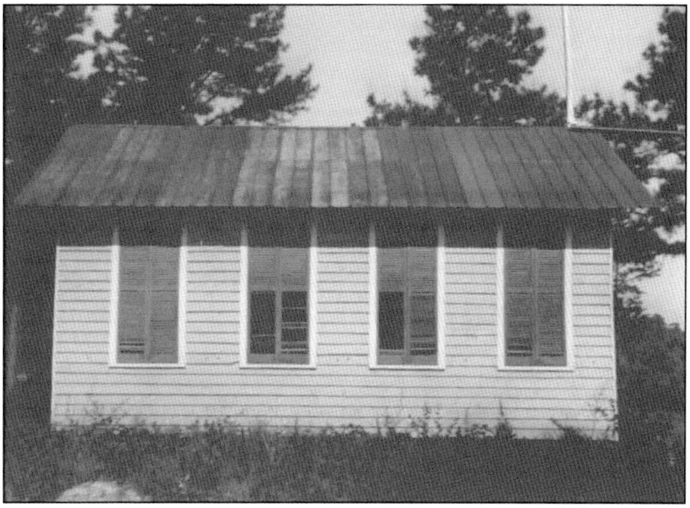

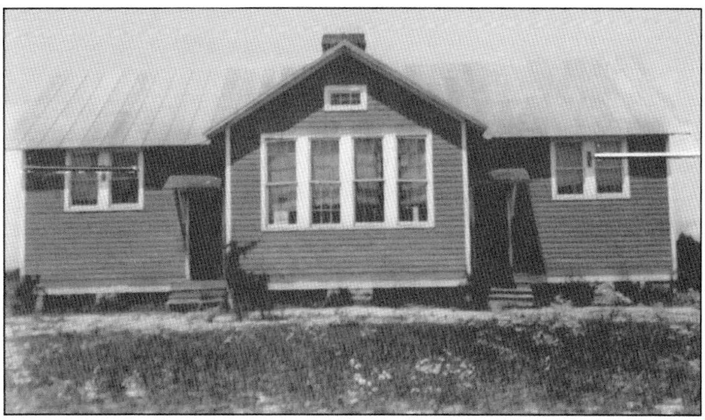

Potomac Colored School was constructed in 1925.

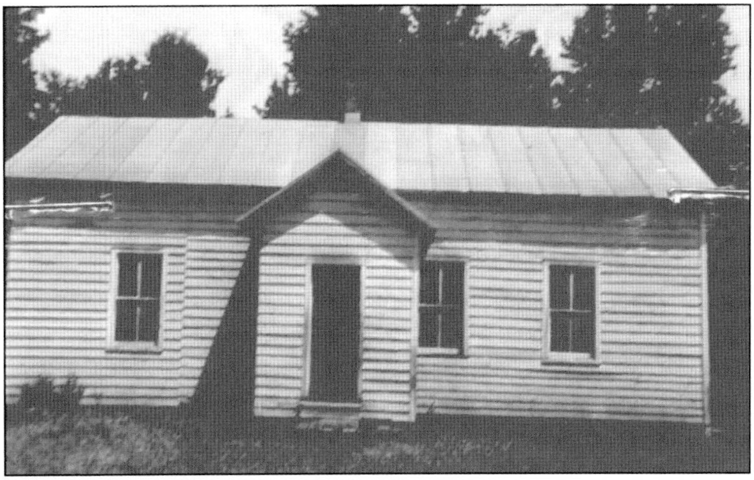

Salem Colored School was built in 1890.

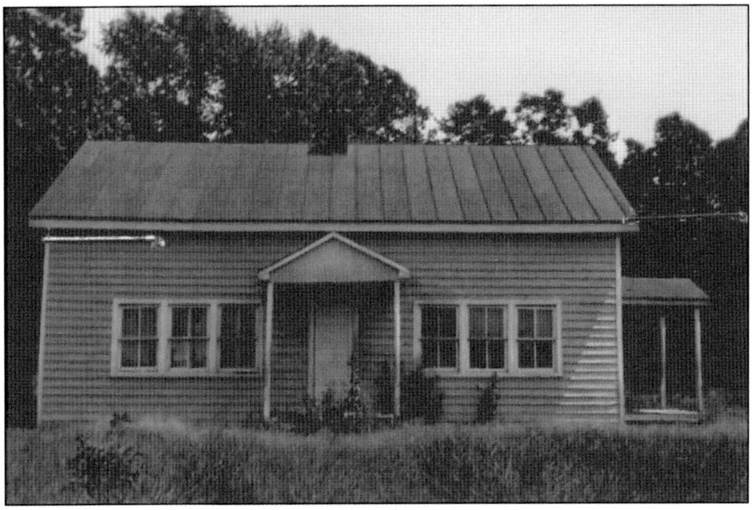

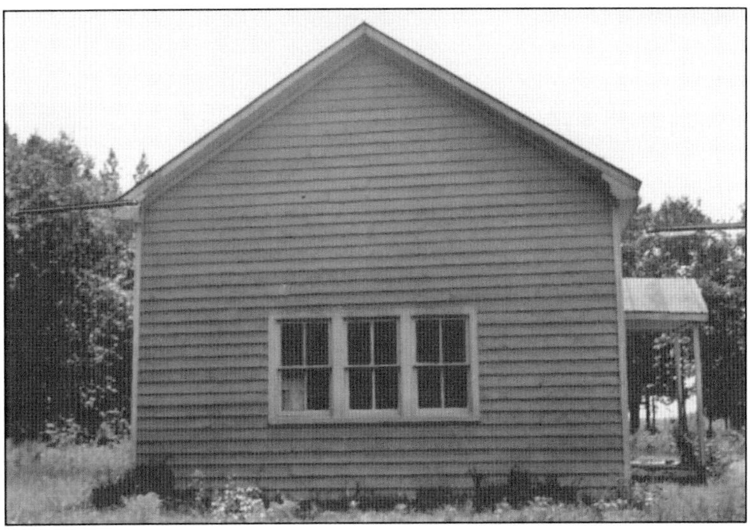

Erica Colored School, seen middle and bottom, was constructed in 1913.

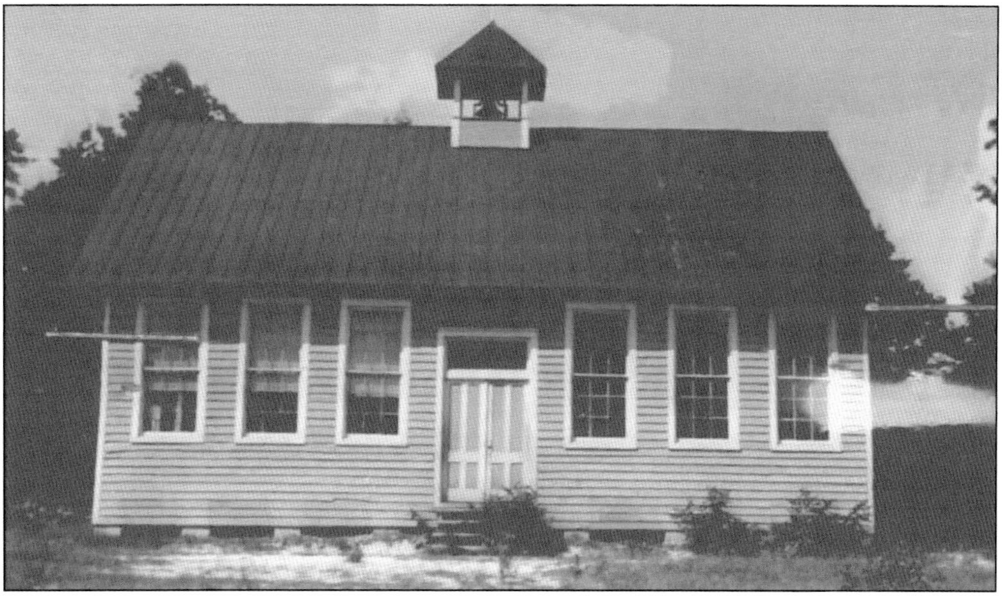

Oak Grove Colored School was constructed in 1920.

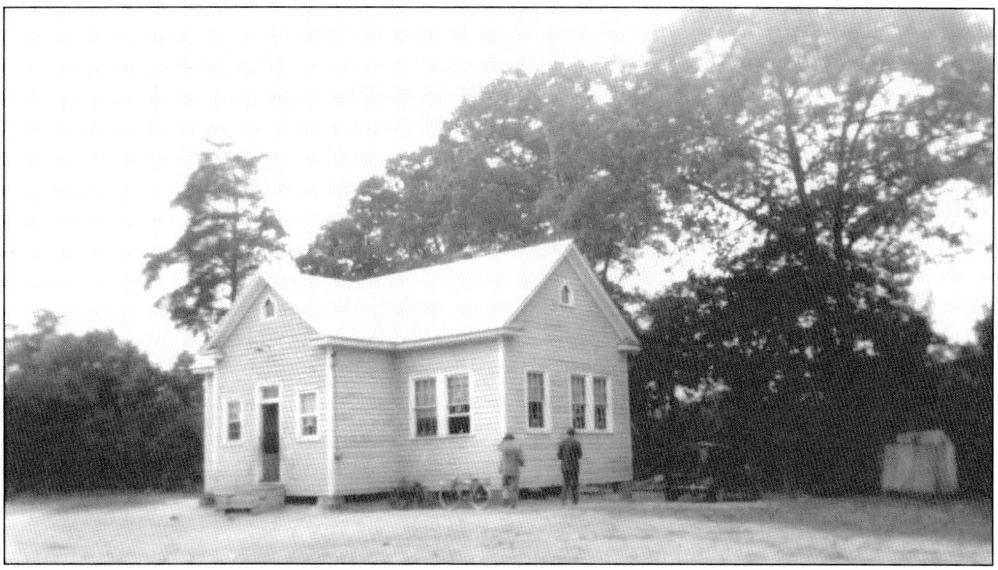

Hacketts Hill Colored School was opened to students in 1929.

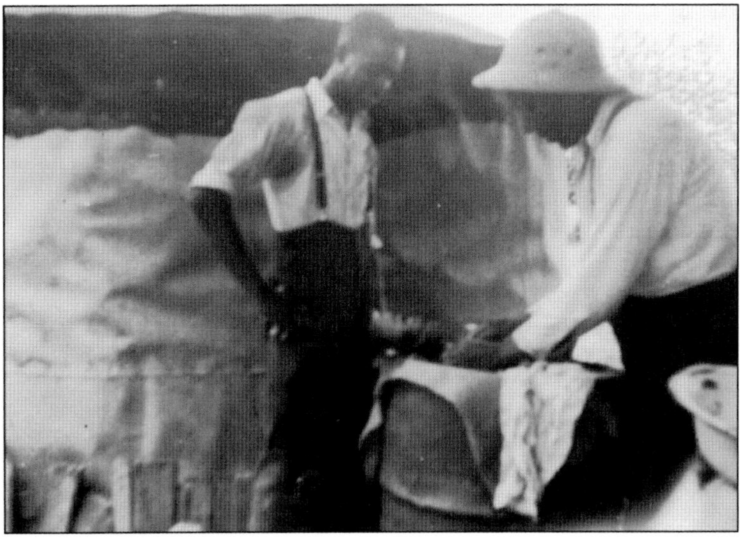

The following photographs, top and middle, document some typical rural scenes from mid-twentieth-century Westmoreland County—a time and place before automation. The top photograph shows Ferman Jenkins, a renowned community leader and farmer.

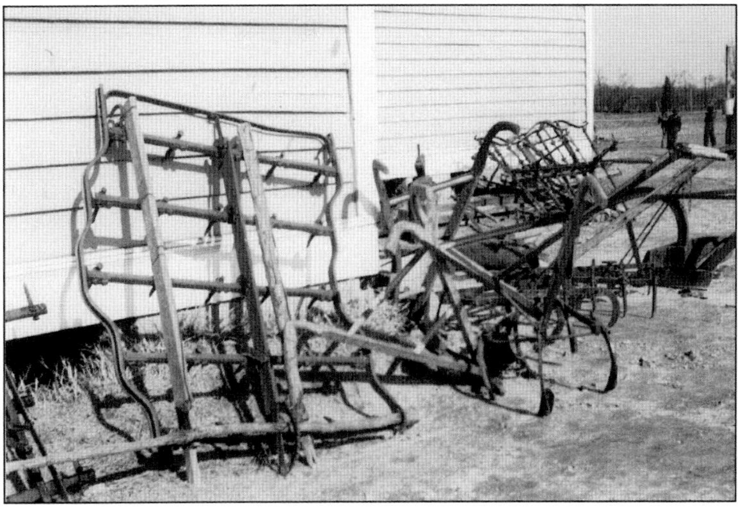

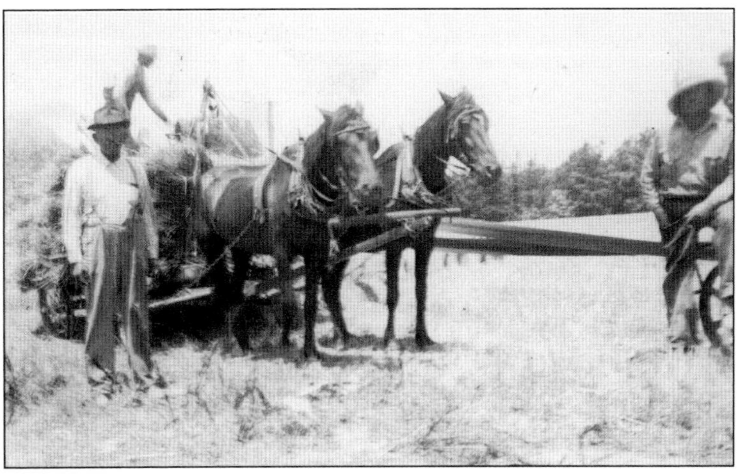

John Roane is seen here leading his horses out on the farm.

Two

Families, Homes, and Farms

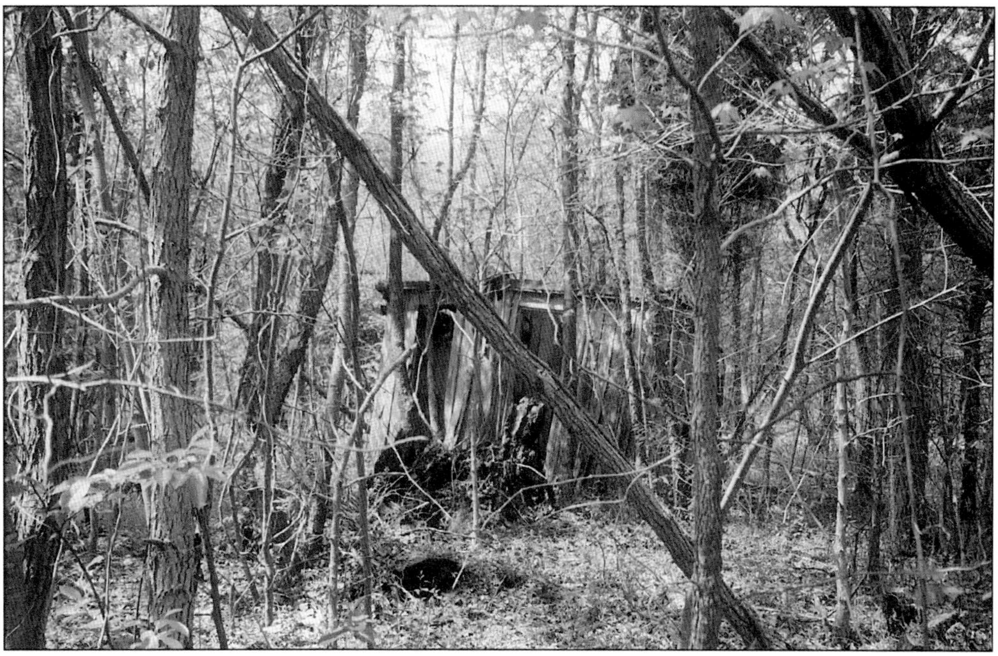

As black Americans prospered, so too did their homes' outward signs. For example, a widow who had married a new husband was able to build onto her older home and also construct this sturdy two-room outhouse (seen here), which is still standing in the woods today after years of abandonment.

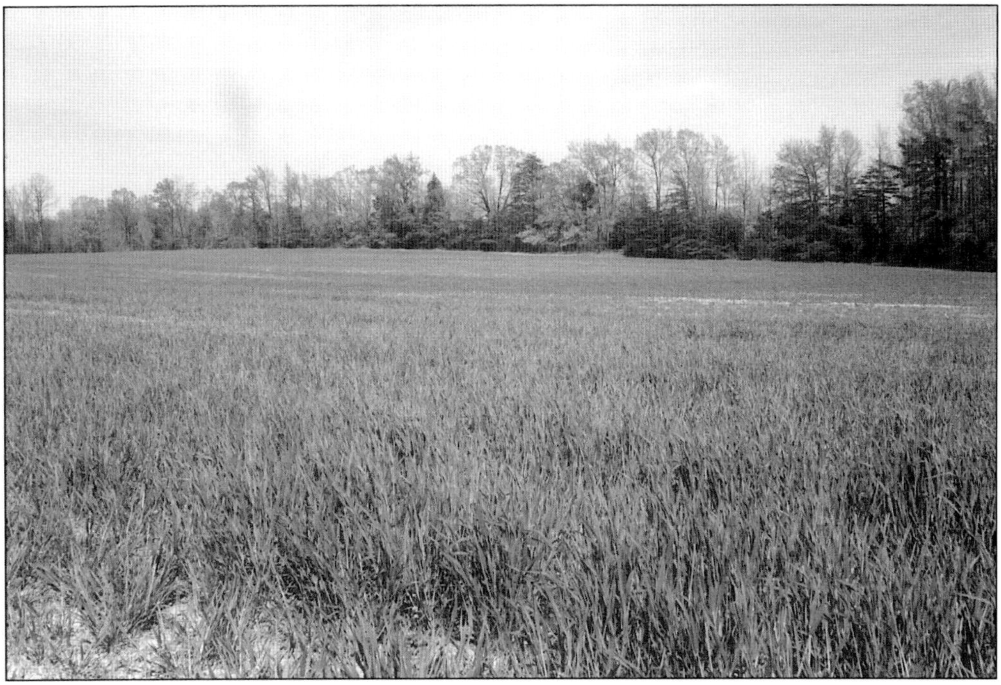

Truly an outward sign of upward mobility, these lush fields of winter wheat were the former farmland property of a black man named Robert E. Lee.

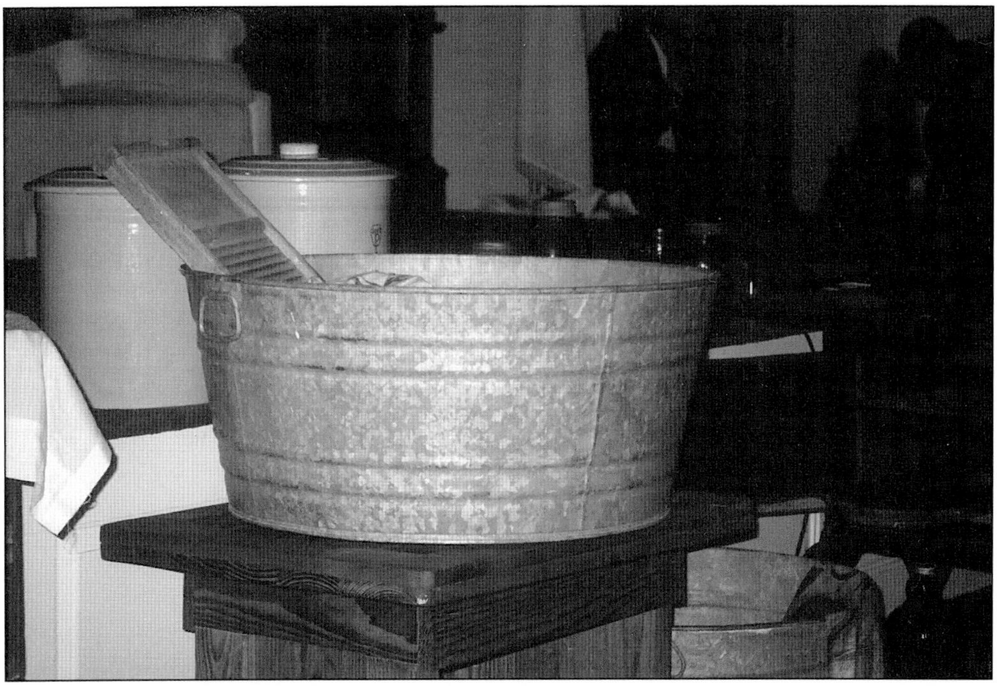

Women no longer had to wash their clothes with rocks in the creeks or rivers once they obtained a scrub board and washtub, the forerunner to today's washing machine. Clothes were then hung outside to dry.

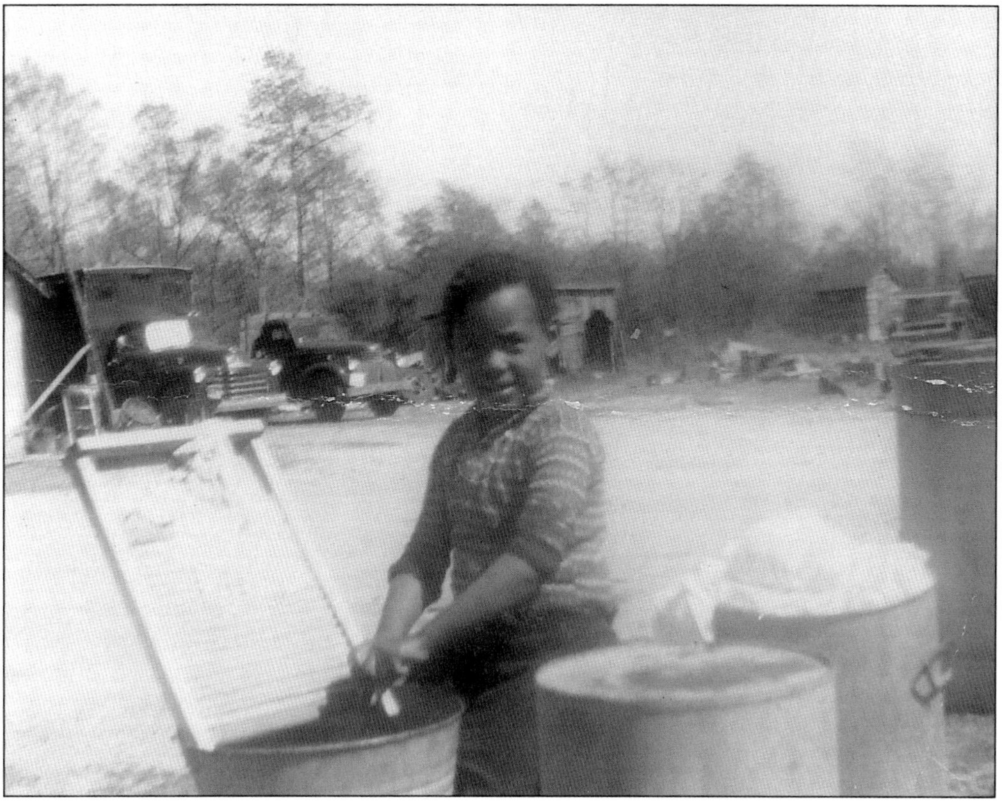

Carolyn Malinda Lee is pictured at the washtub. The trucks in the background belonged to her father, Stephen Lee, who had one of the first black seafood businesses in the county. He sold seafood from Baltimore to Florida. (Courtesy of the Lee family.)

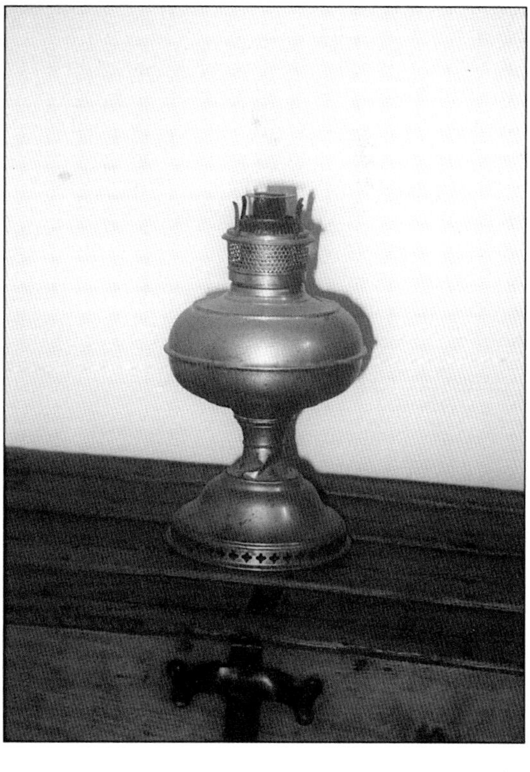

Oil lamps, both tin and glass, replaced candles as the primary source of lighting for the home.

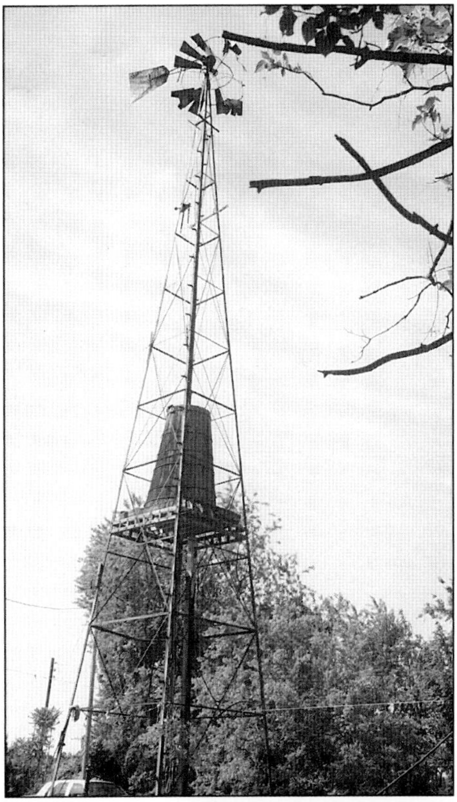

A real sign of wealth was a home with a windmill; this meant that the residence had indoor plumbing and electric lights.

William Hamlen "Ham" Johnson was born in 1857 in Caroline County, but came to Westmoreland County at age 18 to work in a sawmill. He went on to become an export dealer in lumber and walnut logs. According to the *Fredericksburg Star* newspaper, Mr. Johnson was appointed postmaster in Baynesville, Virginia, by Congressman W.A. Jones over a one-legged Confederate soldier, and the Republicans caused a ruckus. Mr. Jones made no apology for doing so and went on to state that Mr. Johnson was a man of fine address and his word were as good as his bind in business transactions. Johnson was truly a credit to his people and state, and his example should be emulated by future generations.

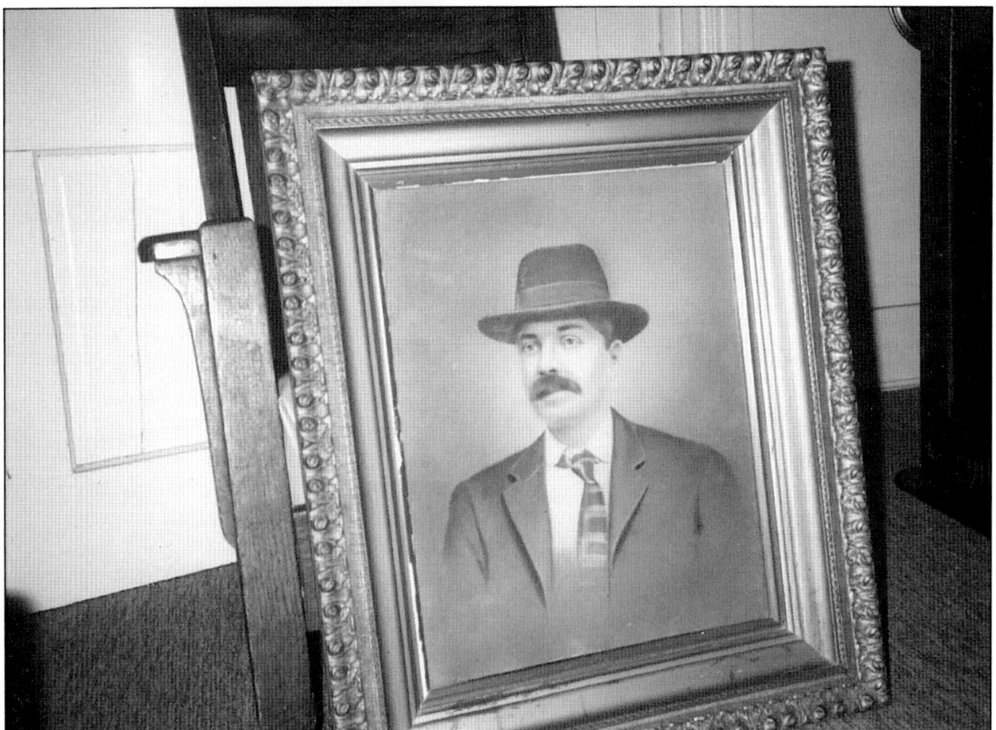

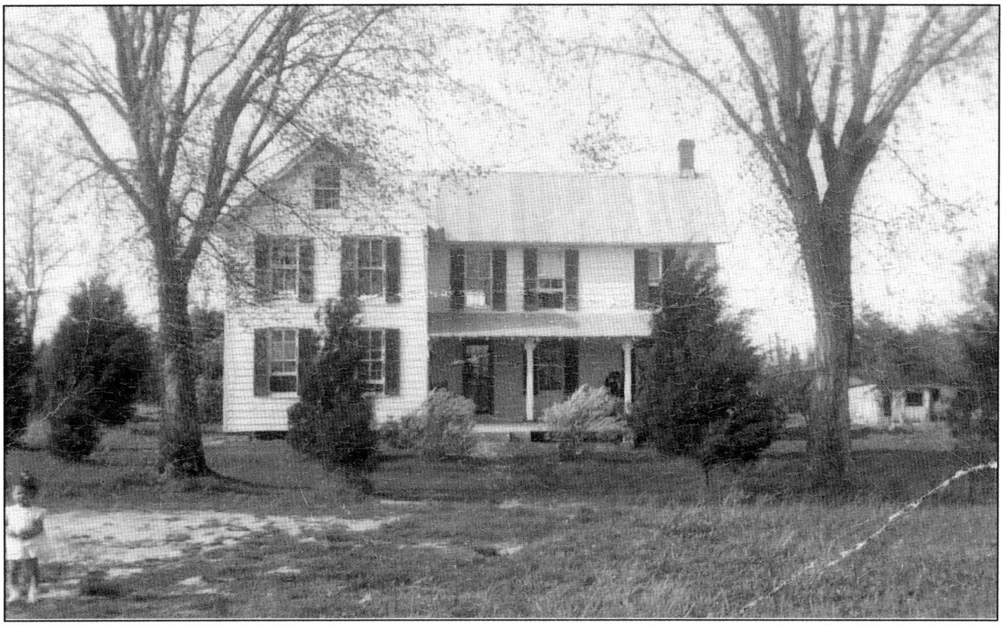

Cloverdale Farm manor house was built by Ham Johnson for his wife, Susan Howard Johnson. They had three children, Maude, Pauline, and Texana. All of the lumber for this fine home was imported. (Courtesy of Lucille Ware.)

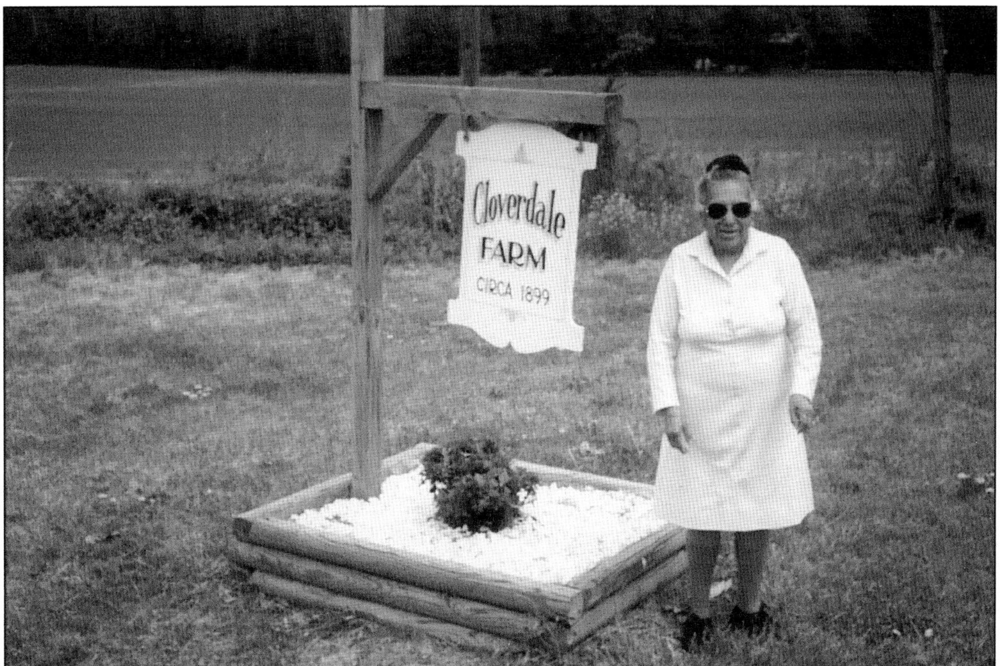

Cloverdale Farm is home today to his granddaughter, Lucille Ware.

Peter Fortune was an uncle of Lucille Ware. (Courtesy of Lucille Ware.)

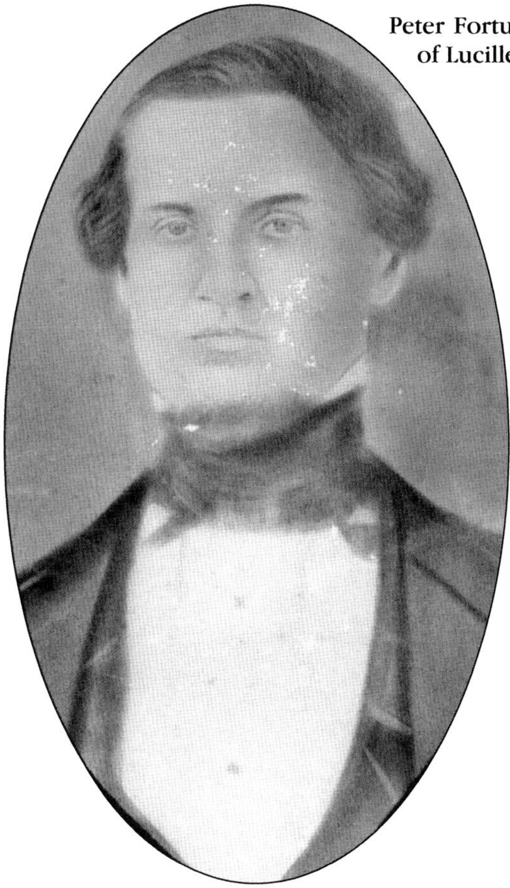

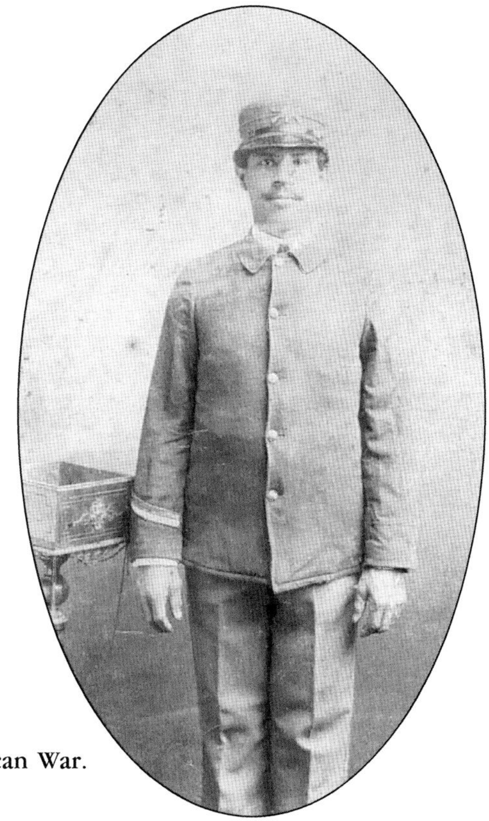

Joseph Johnson served in the Spanish-American War. (Courtesy of Lucille Ware.)

Seen here during World War I, Gibson Johnson and his wife, Jennie, pose for this portrait. (Courtesy of Lucille Ware.)

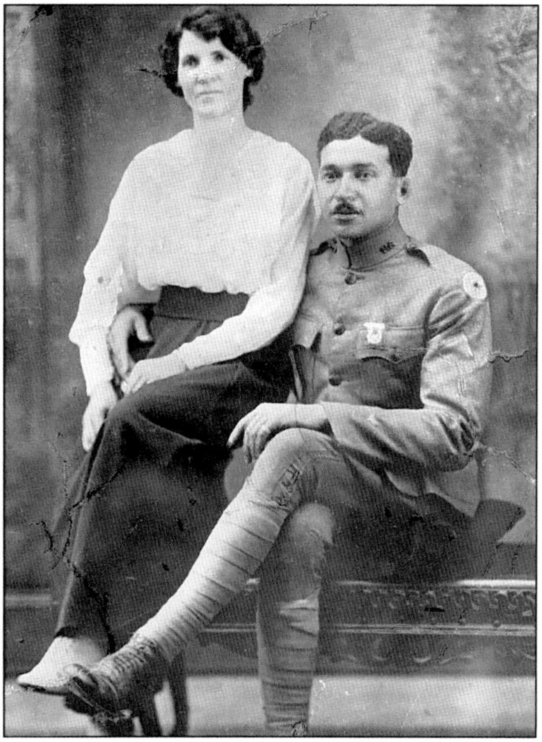

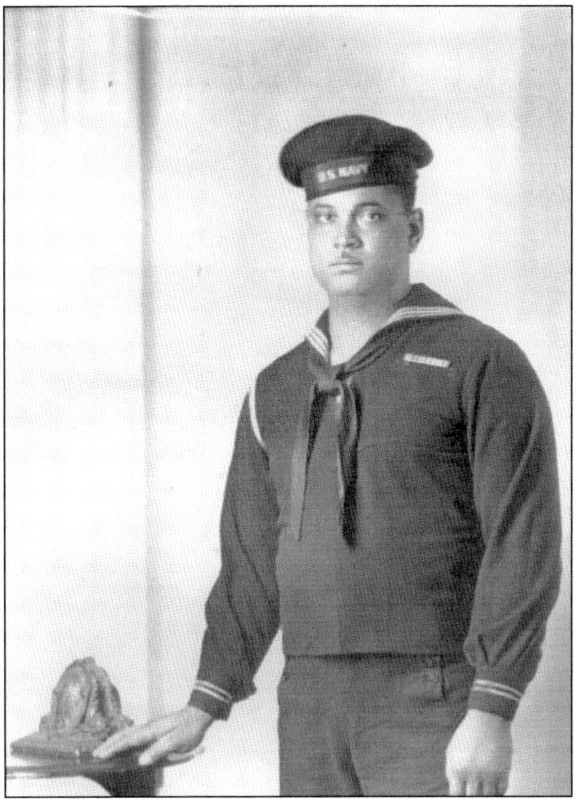

Charles Ware, of Oak Grove, served in the Navy during World War II. (Courtesy of Lucille Ware.)

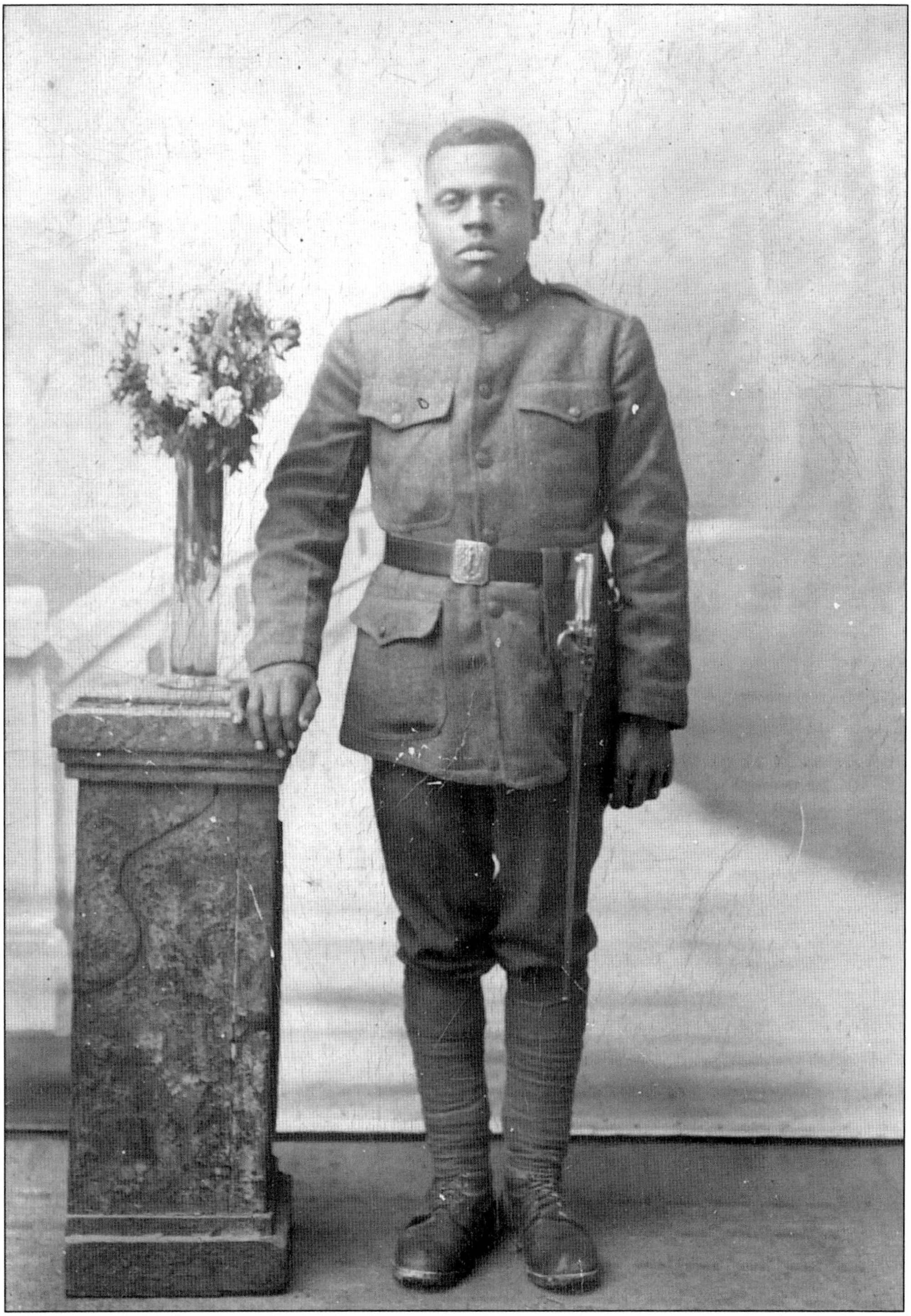

A native of Oak Grove, Dennis Johnson Jr. served in World War I. His parents, Susan and Dennis Johnson Sr., operated a sawmill, which Dennis Jr. went on to run. He also owned and worked a 200-acre farm. (Courtesy of Susan Johnson Roberts.)

Matilda Piper Smith was a slave of Westmoreland County's D. Wheelwright family. Matilda, as well as her husband, Henderson Smith, could both read and write. They are the ancestors of community leaders Queen Syetta Smith Richards, Olivette Richards Peyton, and Clinton Richards.

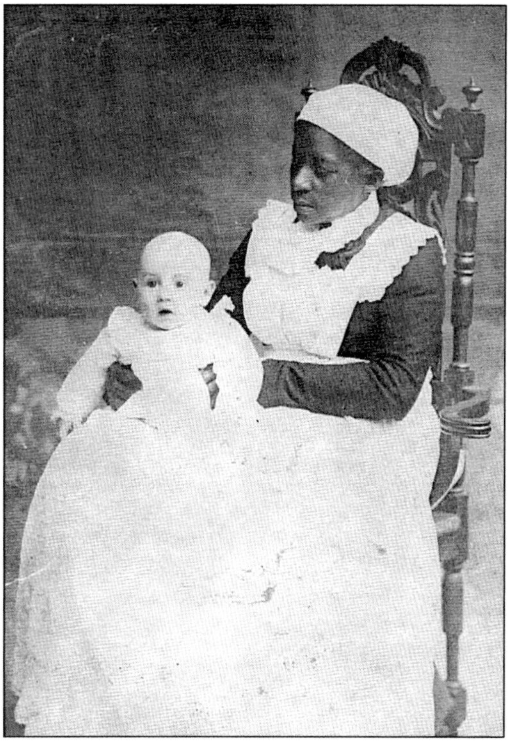

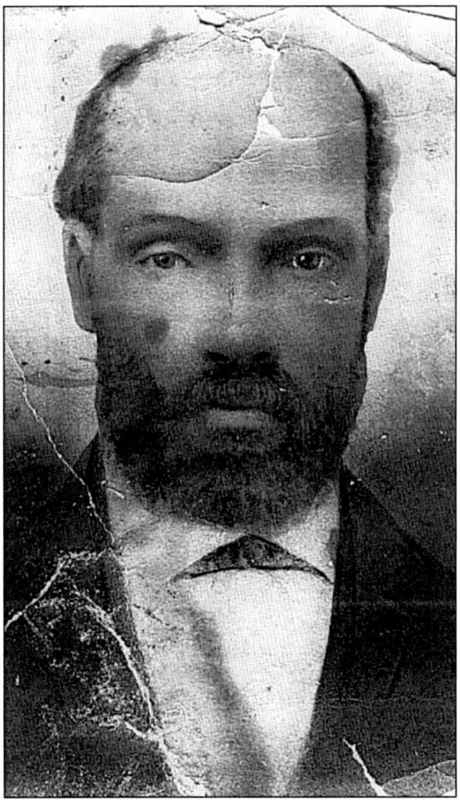

Born into slavery in 1820, Solomon Dixon was the child of Rubin and Mary Figget. He changed his name from Rubin to Solomon Dixon early in his life. On December 30, 1840, he married Emily Thompson, and they had 16 children; on December 20, 1868, he married Barbara Ann Thompson, and they had 16 more children—for a total of 32 children! The names of his known children are as follows: (by his first wife, Emily Thompson) Susan (1840), James (1846), Solomon Jr. (1846), Frances (1848), Cephus Noah (1850), Lewis (1855), and Robert (1860); (by his second wife, Barbara Ann Thompson) John Warren (1870), Mary M. (1871), Lucia (1873), Joseph S. (1875), Coro O. (1876), Bettie (1879), Hugh B. (1886), General Putman Dixon, Rosa, Benjamin D., George, and Sophia (1897). Said to be a quiet Christian man who worked hard, Dixon acquired two well-stocked farms and considerable property. According to his obituary on November 26, 1897, in the *Northern Neck News*, he was a big supporter of the Republican party. He is buried on his farm in Hague, Virginia. (Courtesy of Mary Dixon Jones and Lloyd Willis.)

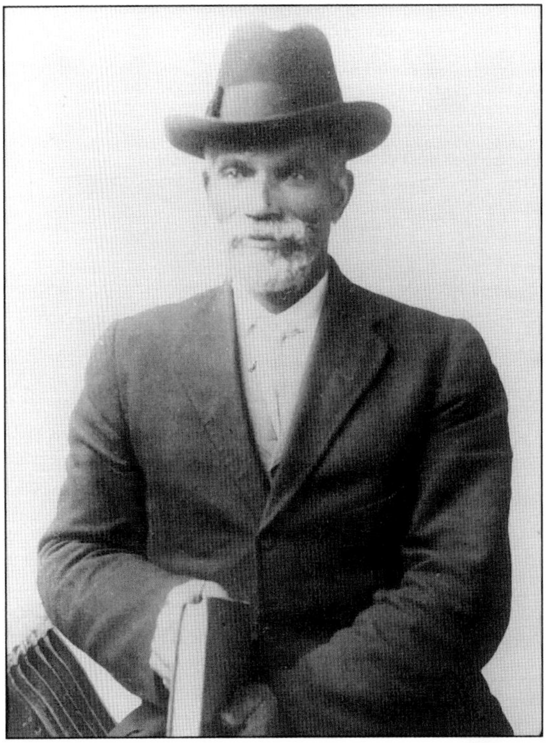

Cephus Noah Dixon was born in 1850.

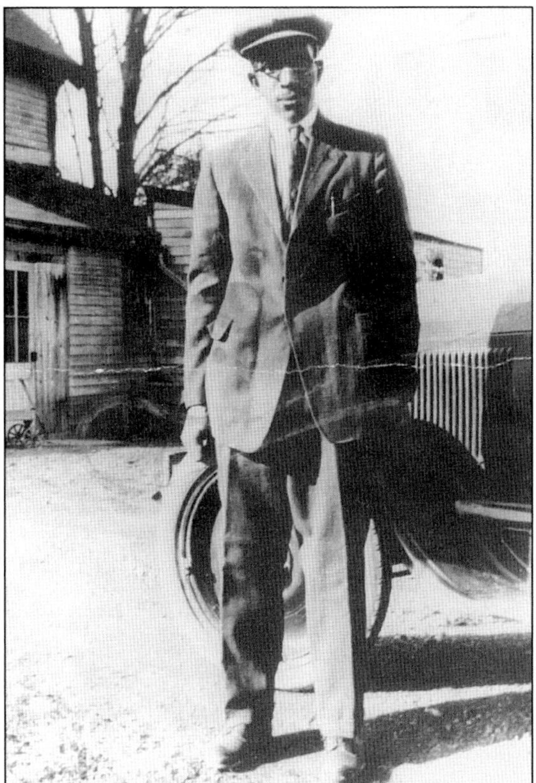

David Solomon Dixon was the son of Cephus Noah Dixon.

This early-twentieth-century photograph shows an early Dixon family member. (Courtesy of Mary Dixon Jones.)

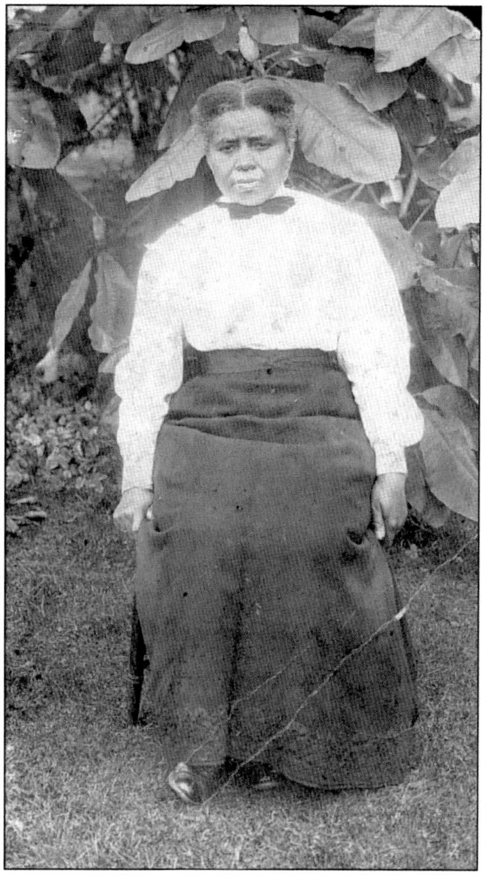

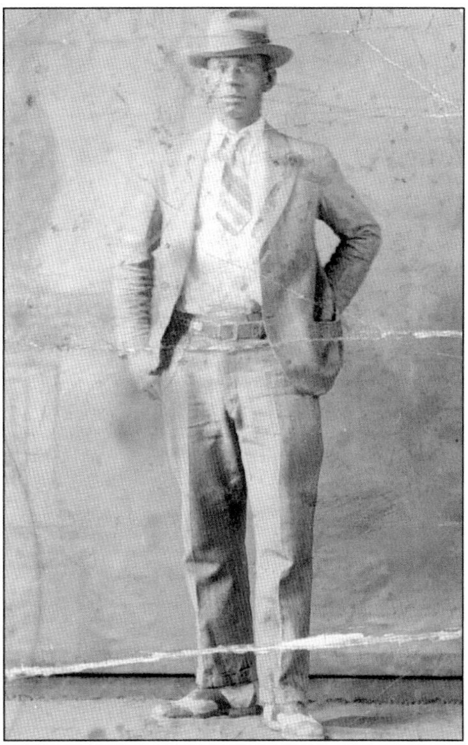

This early-twentieth-century photograph also shows an early Dixon family member. (Courtesy of Mary Dixon Jones.)

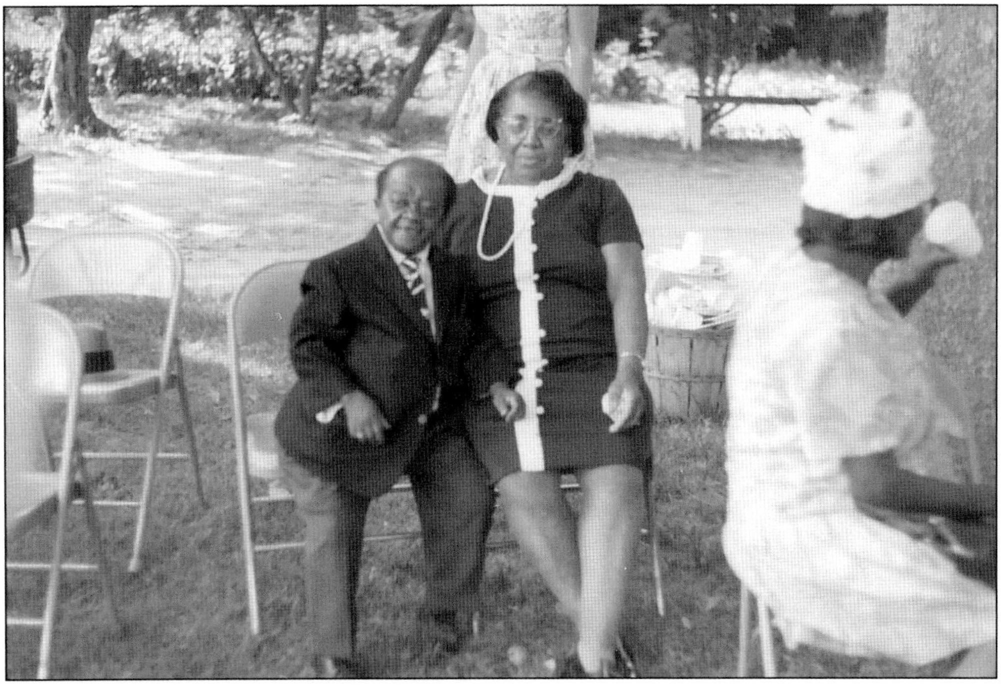

Webster Montique, left, was involved in a floating theater show that traveled the waterways each summer. (Courtesy of Mary Jones.)

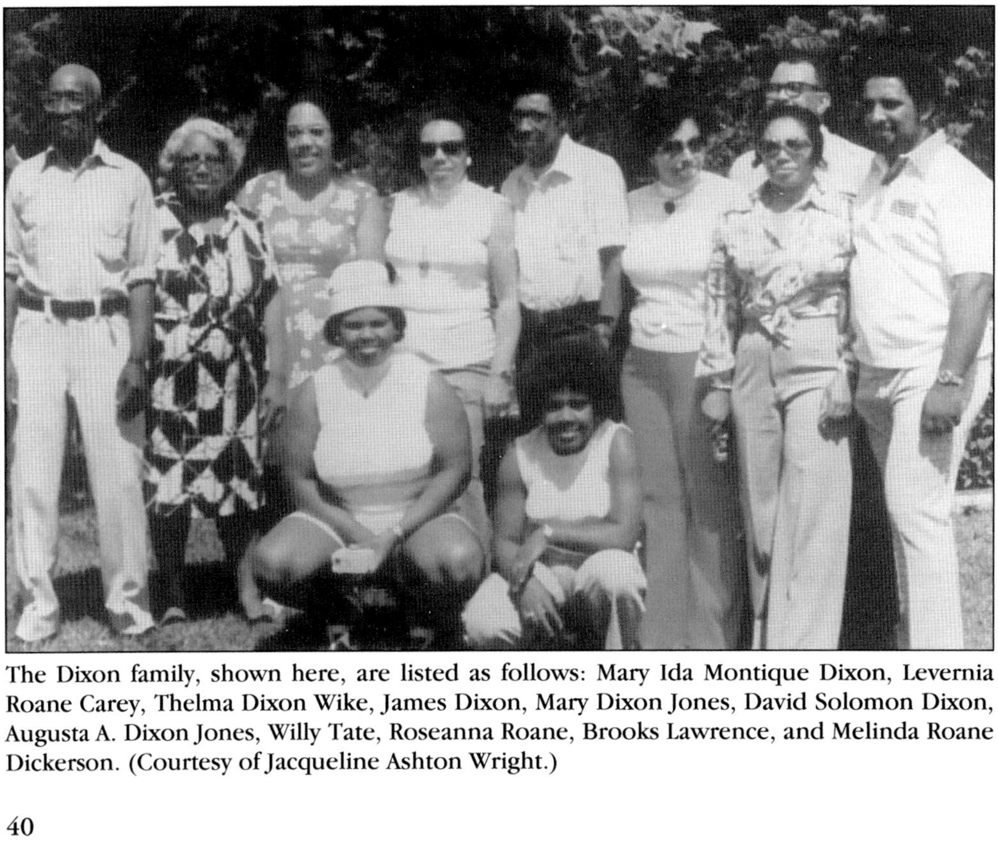

The Dixon family, shown here, are listed as follows: Mary Ida Montique Dixon, Levernia Roane Carey, Thelma Dixon Wike, James Dixon, Mary Dixon Jones, David Solomon Dixon, Augusta A. Dixon Jones, Willy Tate, Roseanna Roane, Brooks Lawrence, and Melinda Roane Dickerson. (Courtesy of Jacqueline Ashton Wright.)

Pictured here is Abraham Montique.

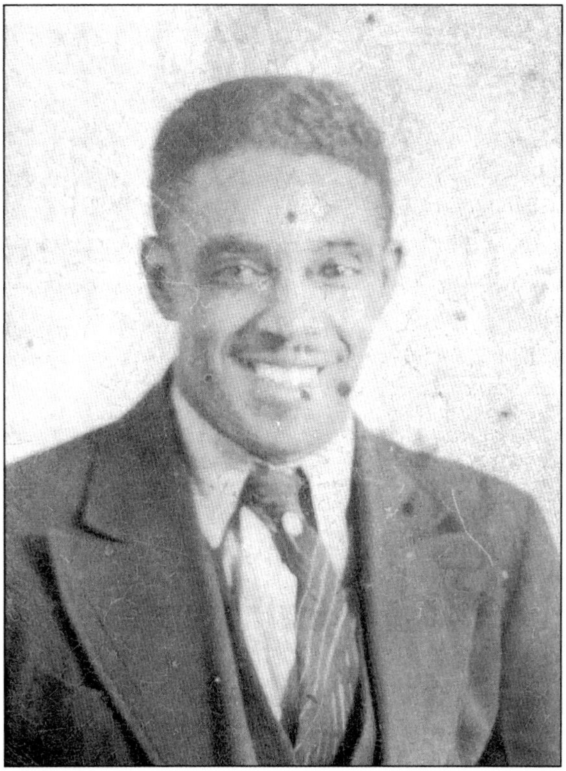

Mary Ida Montique Dixon, Tate Roane, and an unidentified friend pose for this photograph.

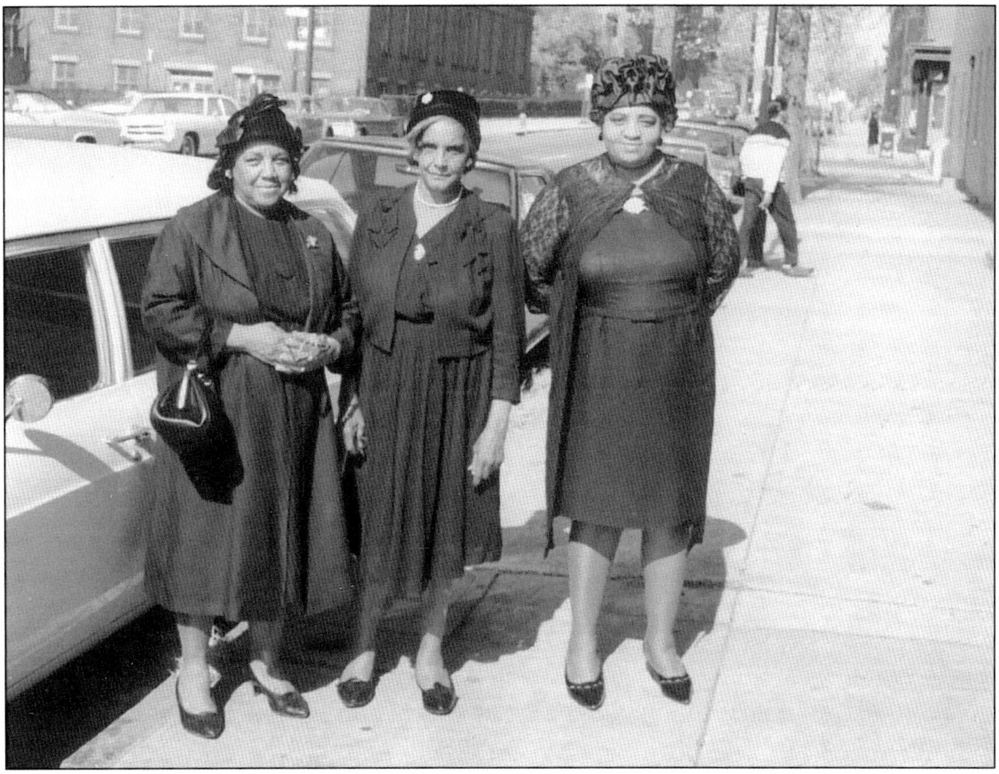

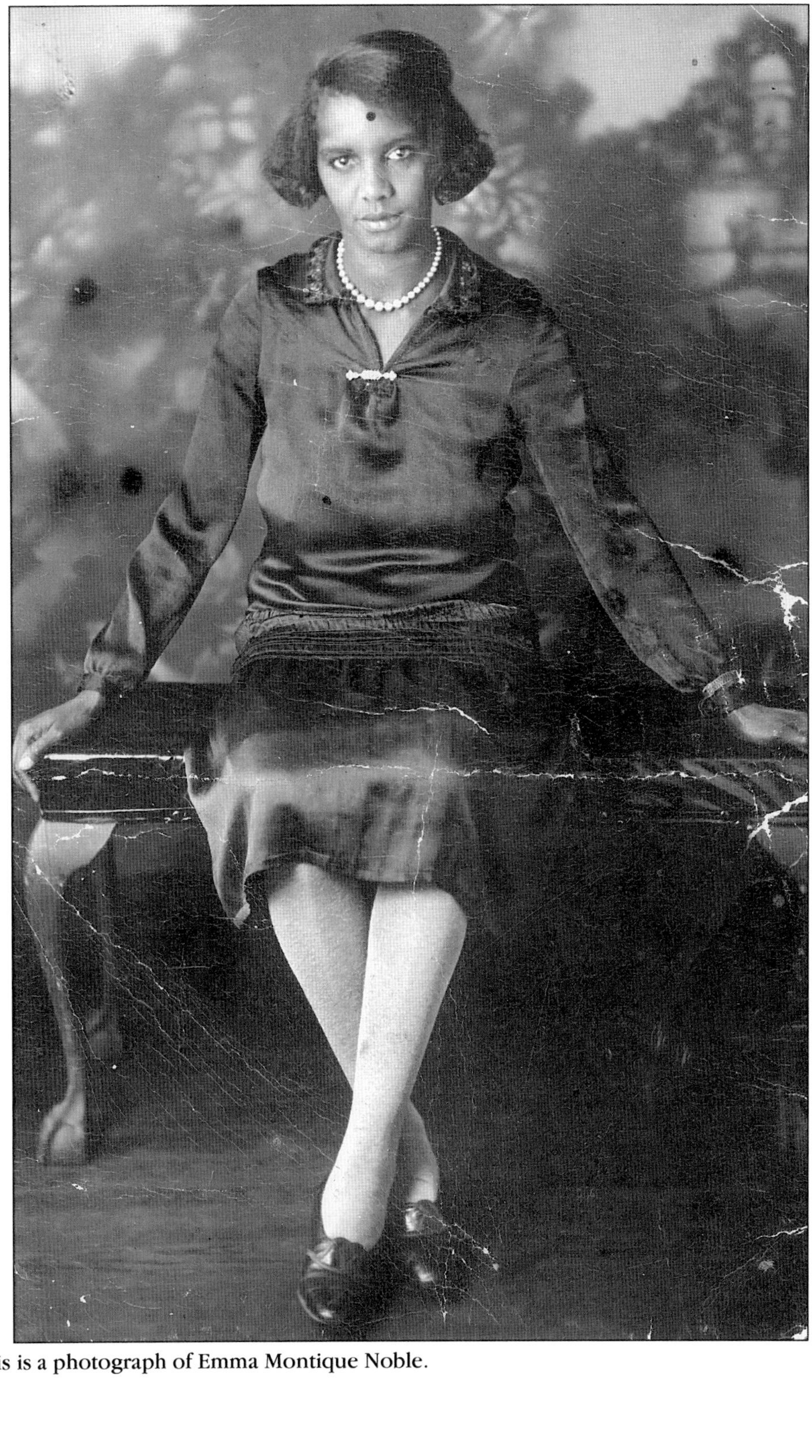

This is a photograph of Emma Montique Noble.

This portrait shows a young Ada Montique.

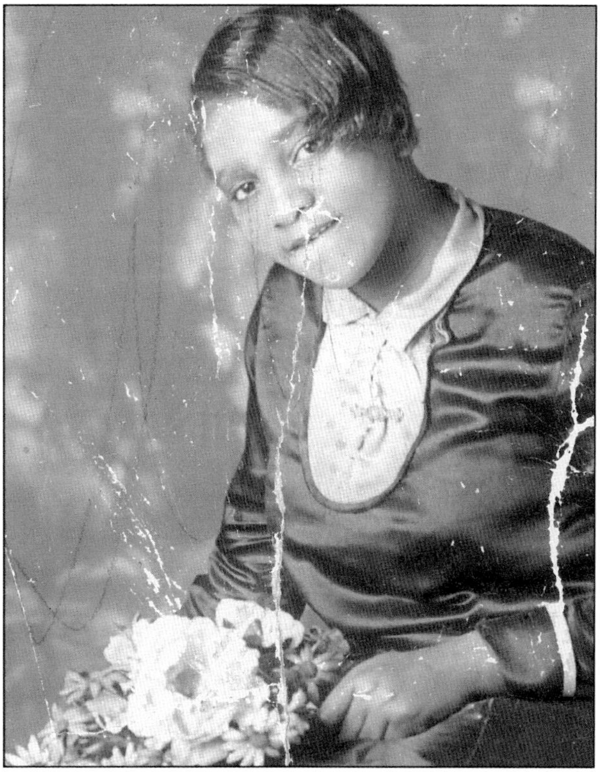

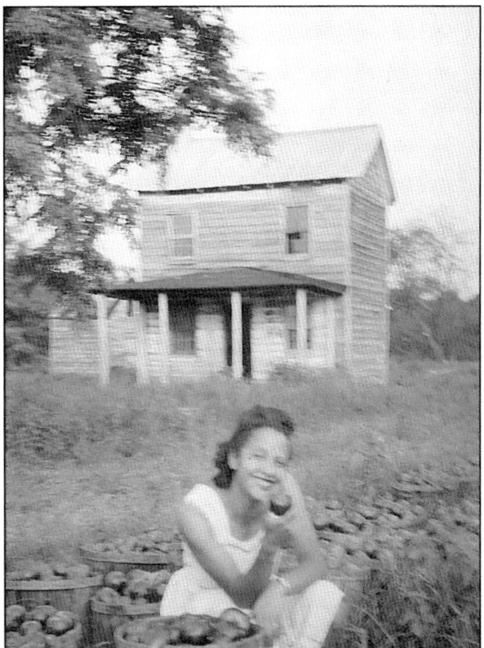

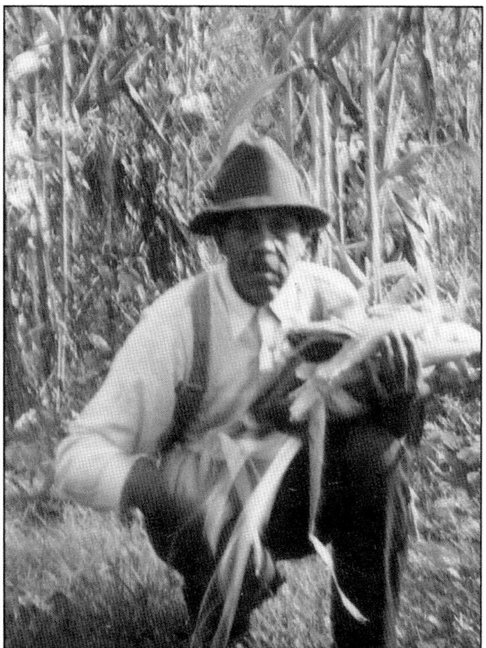

Left: Marie Ashton, in front of her mother's house, is picking tomatoes. *Right*: Jerry Ashton is seen here picking corn.

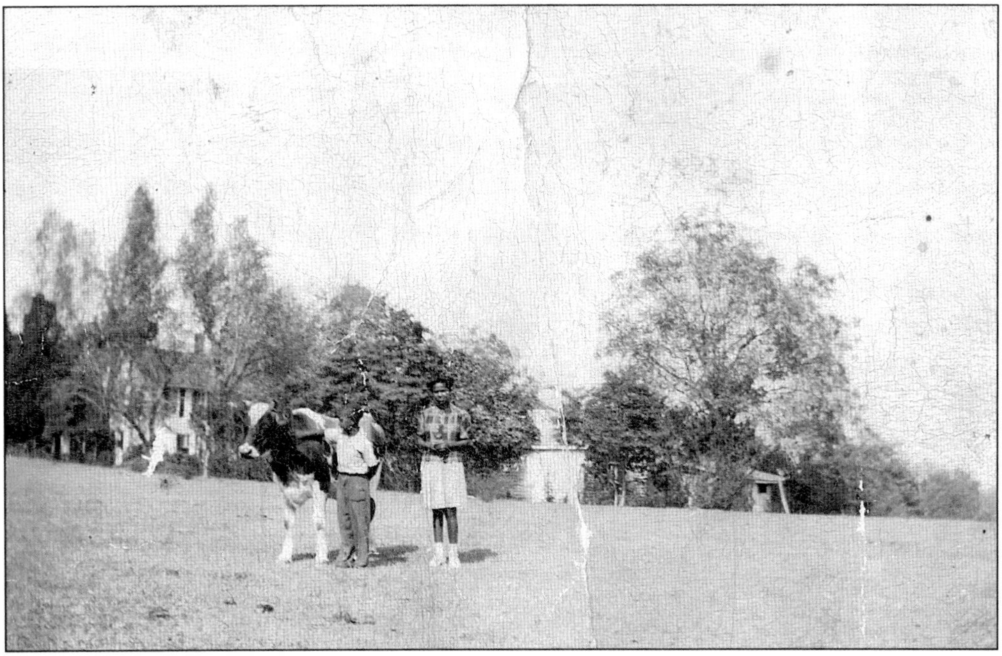

This photograph captures the Miller Farm in Hague. (Courtesy of Pauline Miller Smith.)

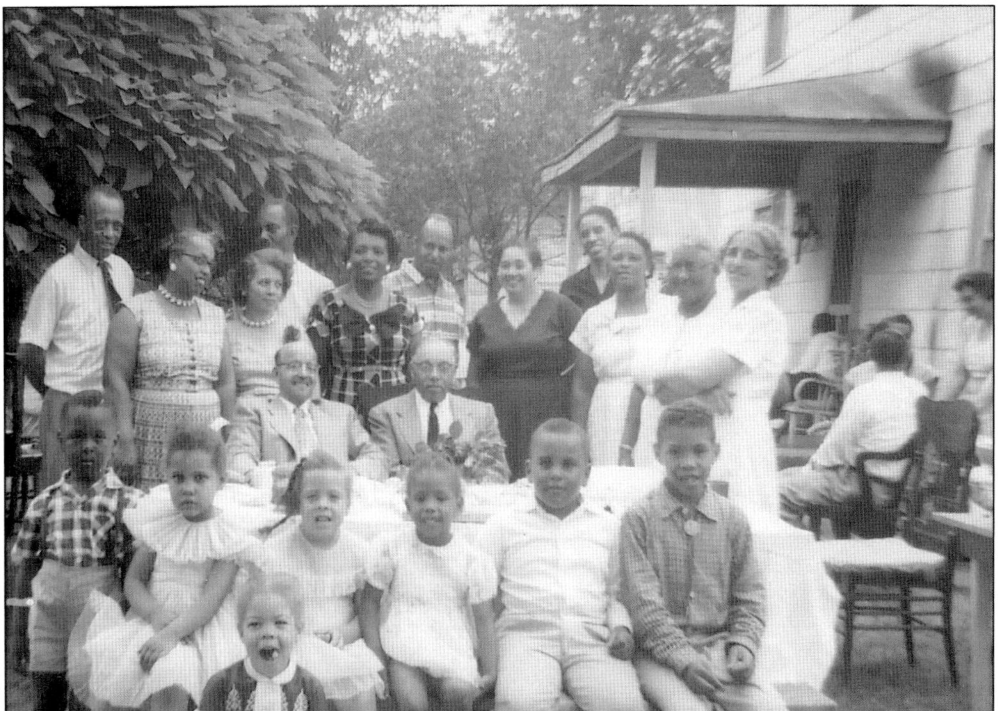

This group photograph shows the Hacketts at a family reunion *c.* 1959. (Courtesy of Melanie Hall.)

This portrait shows Susan Hackett. (Courtesy of Melanie Hall.)

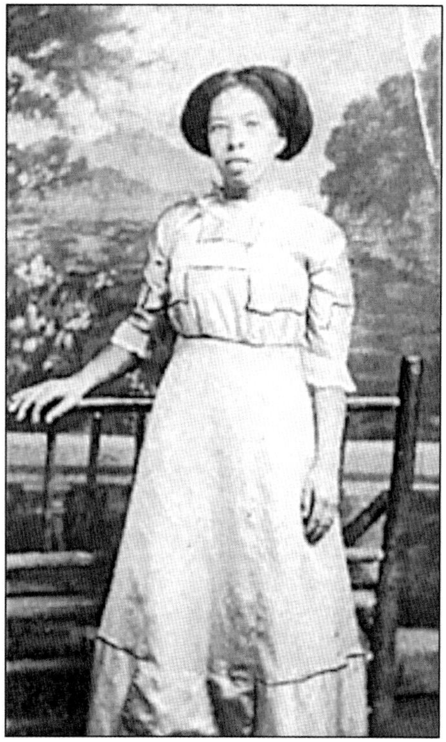

Bob Goodes, Peter Hackett, and Rany Roane pose for this photograph at a homecoming at the Potomac Baptist Church in Hague. (Courtesy of Melanie Hall.)

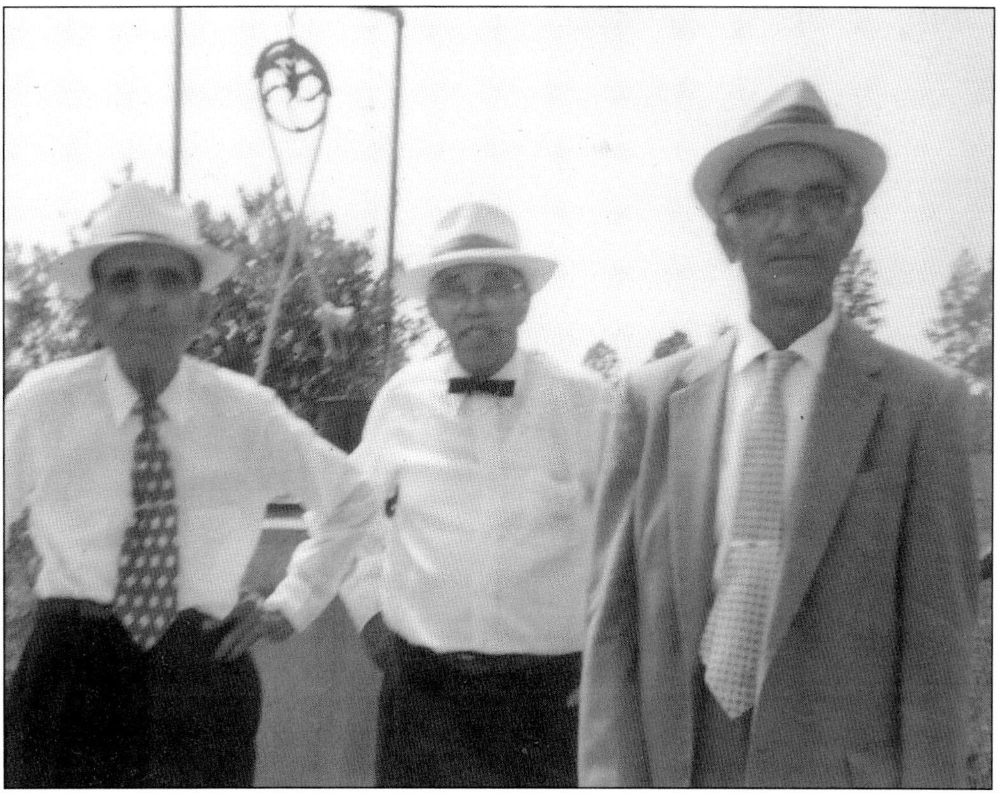

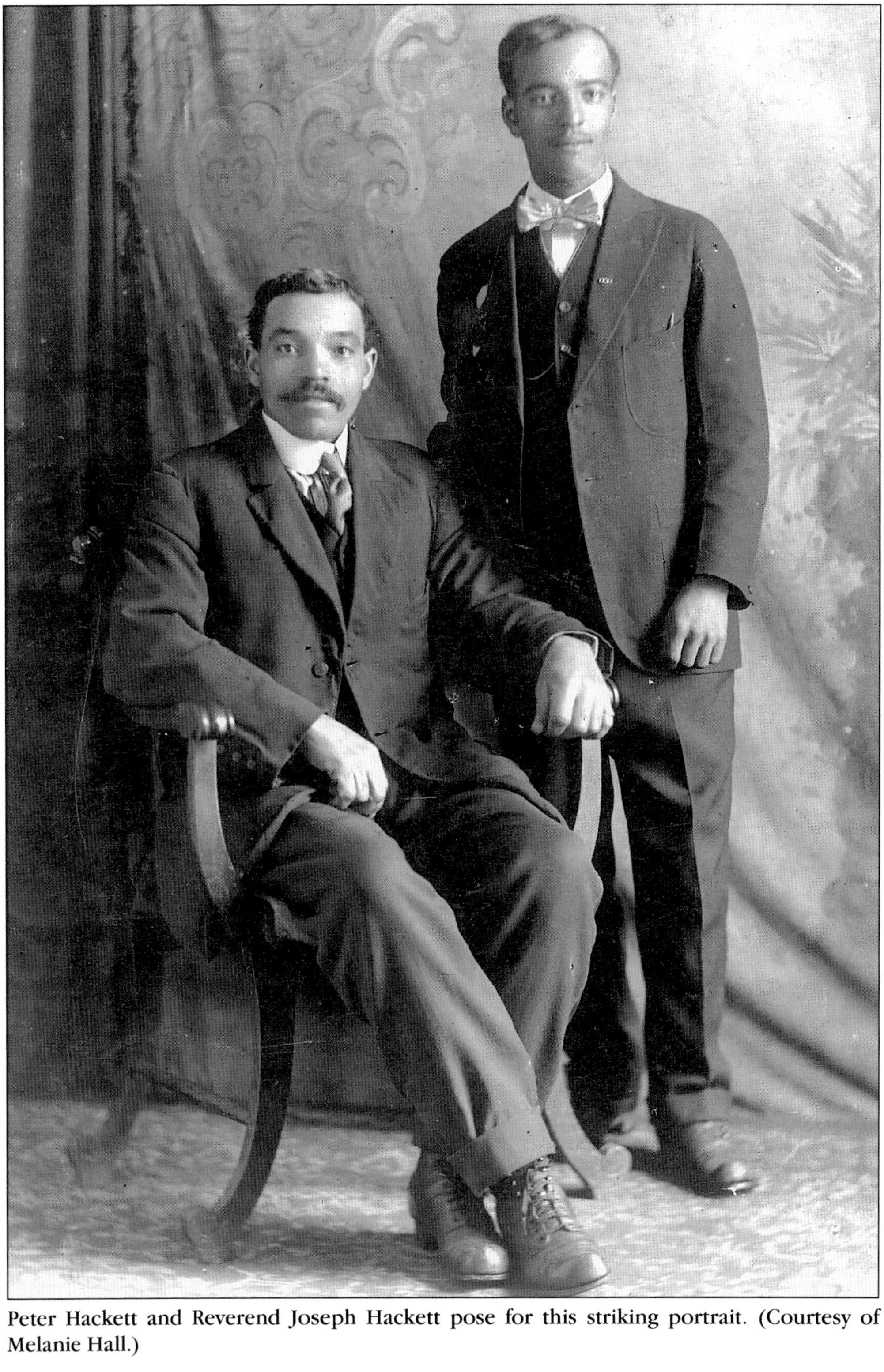

Peter Hackett and Reverend Joseph Hackett pose for this striking portrait. (Courtesy of Melanie Hall.)

Pictured here with his family is James Hackett, for whom Hacketts Hill School was named. (Courtesy of Melanie Hall.)

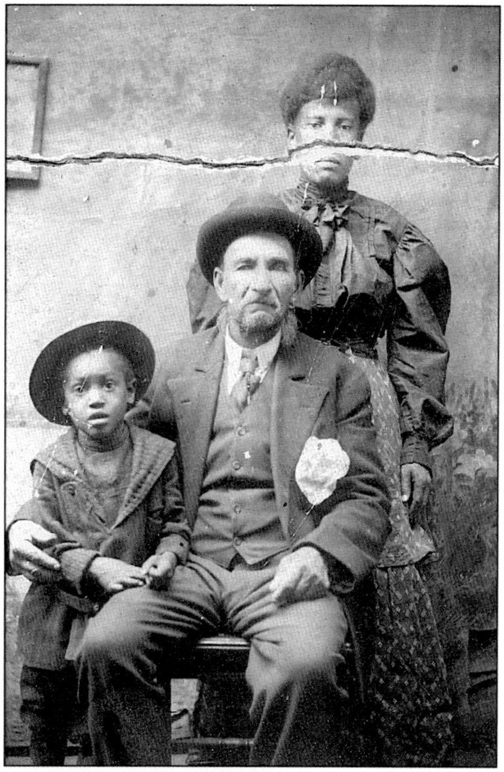

Susan Hackett Newman, center, proudly poses with her child, Ellsworth.

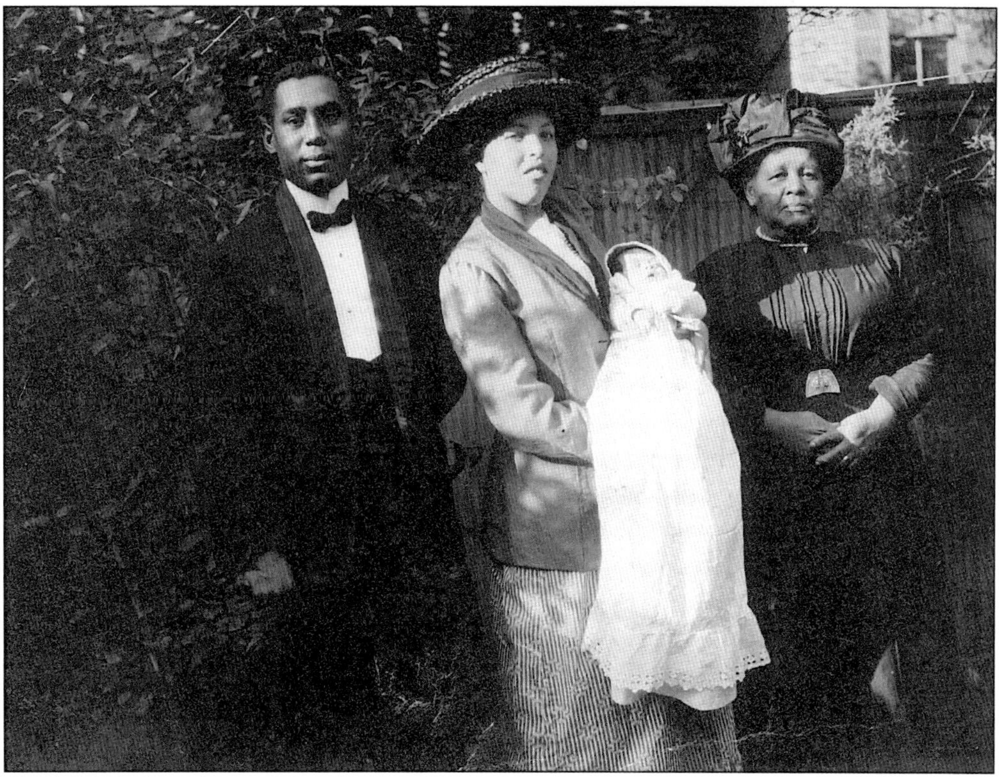

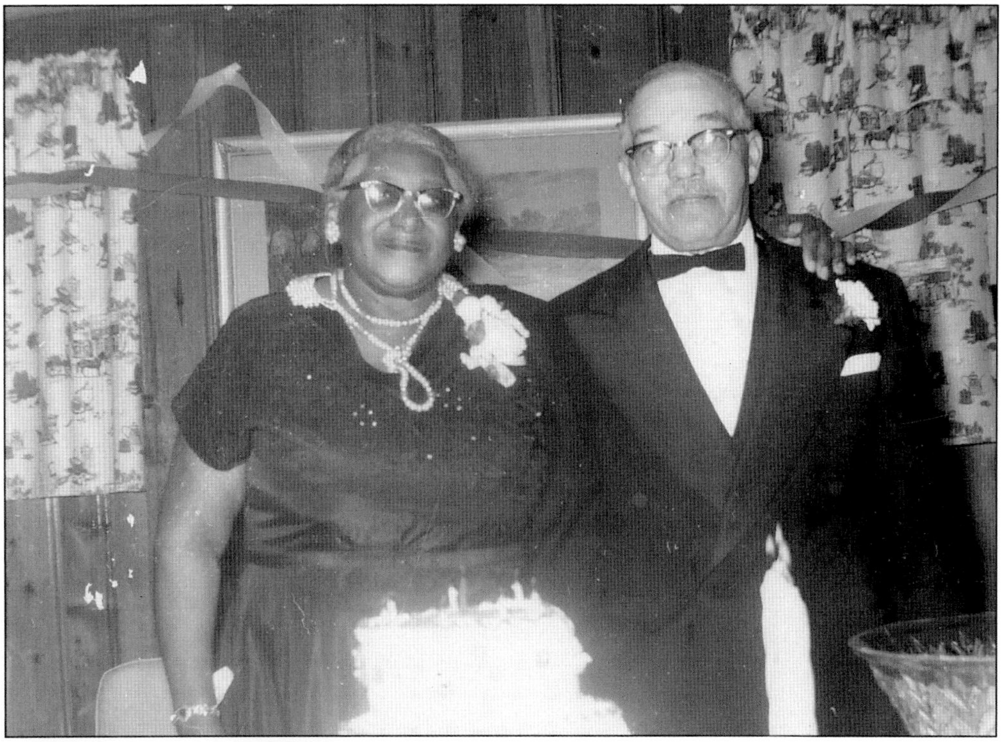

Peter Hackett is seen here with his wife, Jenette Hackett.

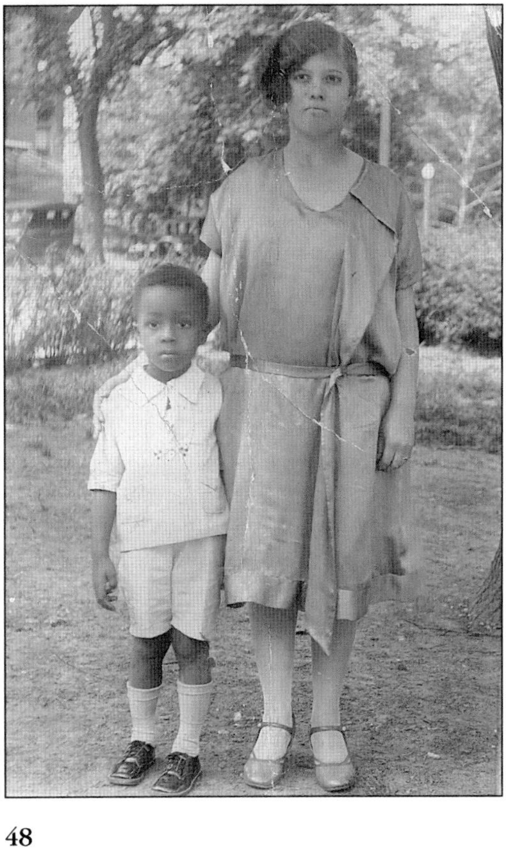

In this *c*. 1929 photograph, Helen Ashton Greene, right, poses with Oscar Morrison. (Courtesy of Melanie Hall.)

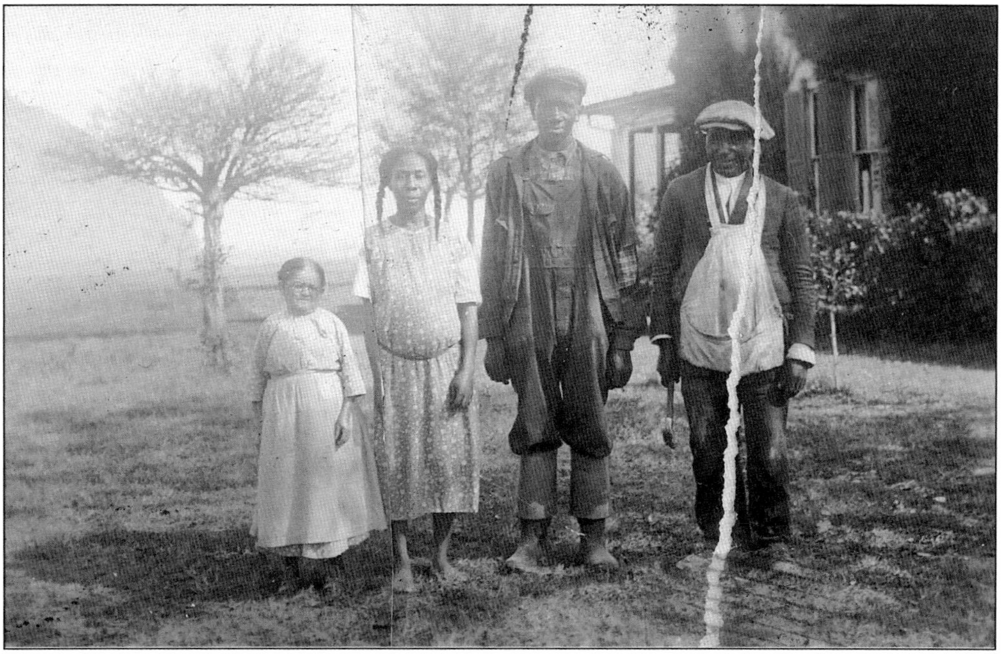

Mary Stegar, Lucy Hackett, Clarence Dixon, and Benny Dixon pose for this photograph at Cabin Point. (Courtesy of the Arnest family.)

Rebecca Carey Johnson is seen here holding her great-niece, Reginia Lumpkin. Mrs. Johnson was famous for her Dandelion Blossom Wine. The recipe reads as follows:

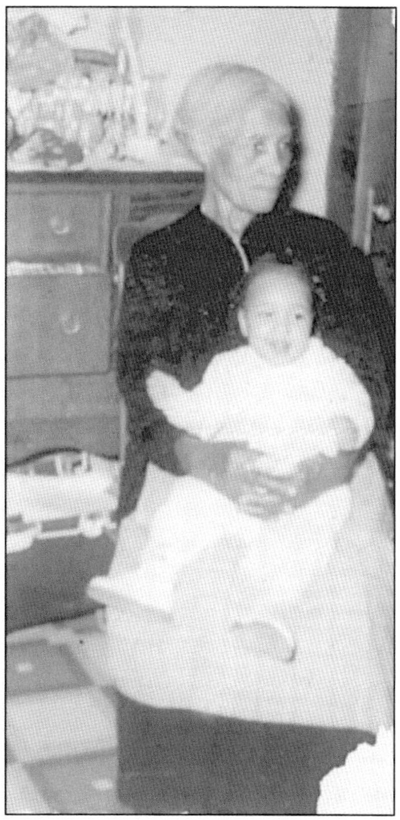

Ingredients

1 gallon open dandelion blossoms
5 quarts boiling water
3.5 pounds of sugar

Directions

1. Pick dandelion blossoms in an open field (best if picked before noon);
2. Remove any bugs from blossoms;
3. Pour boiling water over the blossoms in a 5-gallon stone crock;
4. Cover with clean, white napkin and let stand for three days (put in a place where it is not too cold, for it needs warmth to ferment);
5. Strain water through a piece of cheese cloth;
6. Add sugar and stir and cover again for three weeks;
7. Strain into 1-quart bottles and tie a clean cloth over the mouth of each bottle and leave in the same cool place for four months;
8. Strain into clean bottles and cork;
9. Store in a cool, dry place until needed.

(Courtesy of Bessie Green Brown.)

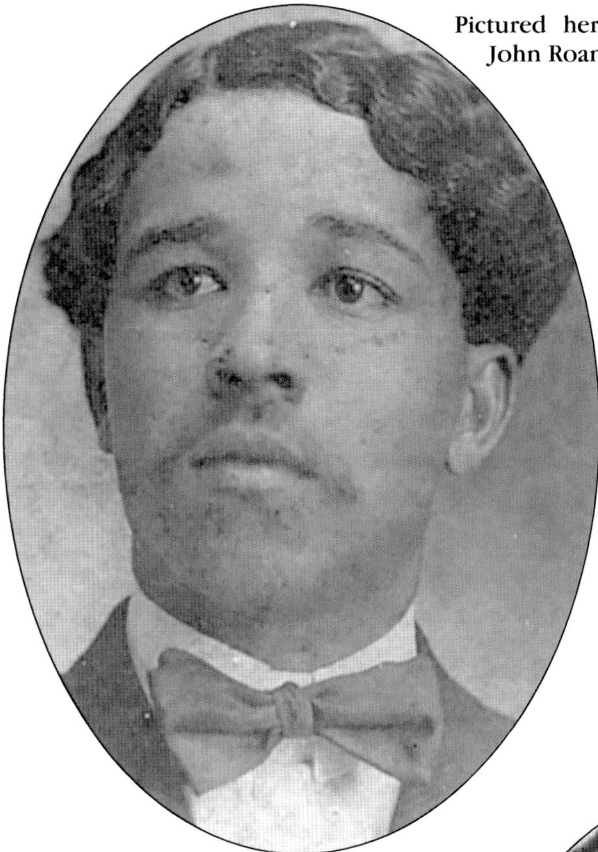

Pictured here is Richard Griggs, an uncle of John Roane.

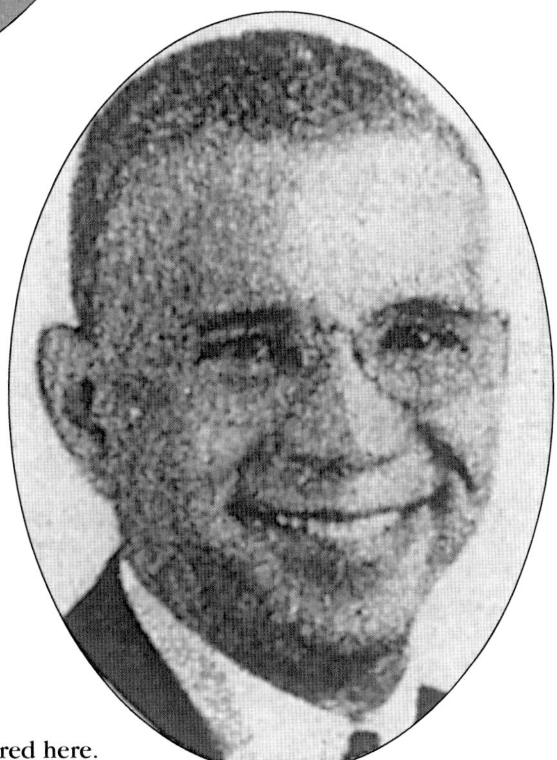

Reverend Victor Sylvester Griggs is pictured here.

Jack Lowe was a farmer in Westmoreland County. (Courtesy of Calvin Jenkins.)

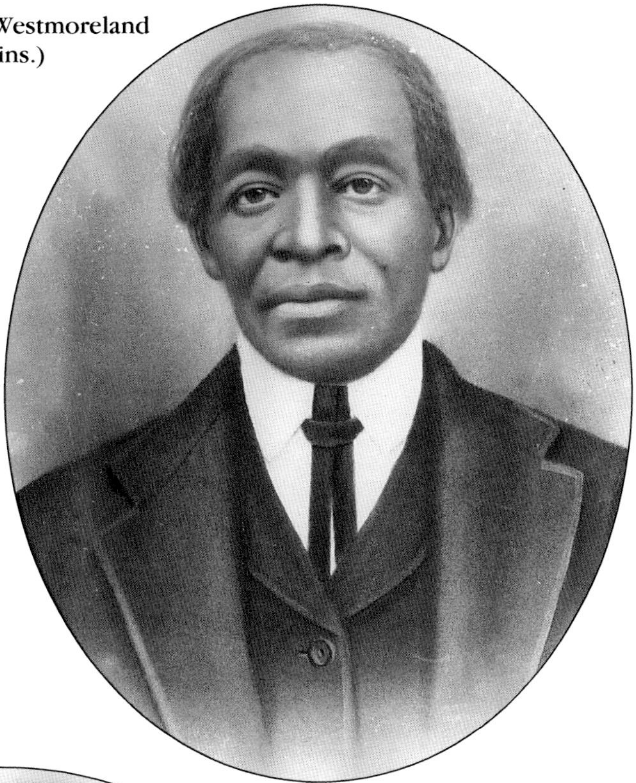

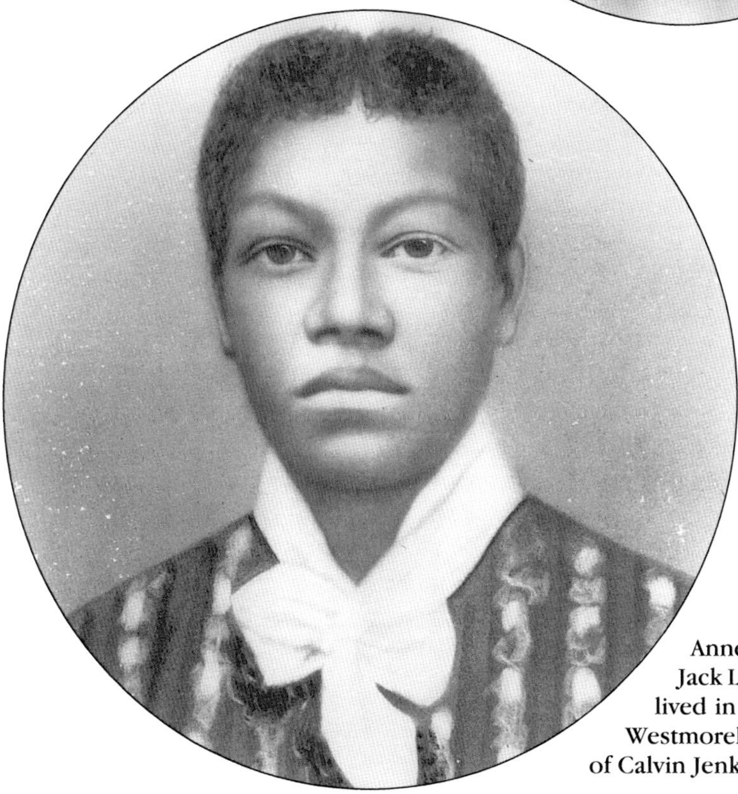

Anne Lowe was the wife of Jack Lowe. She and her family lived in the Tucker Hill area of Westmoreland County. (Courtesy of Calvin Jenkins.)

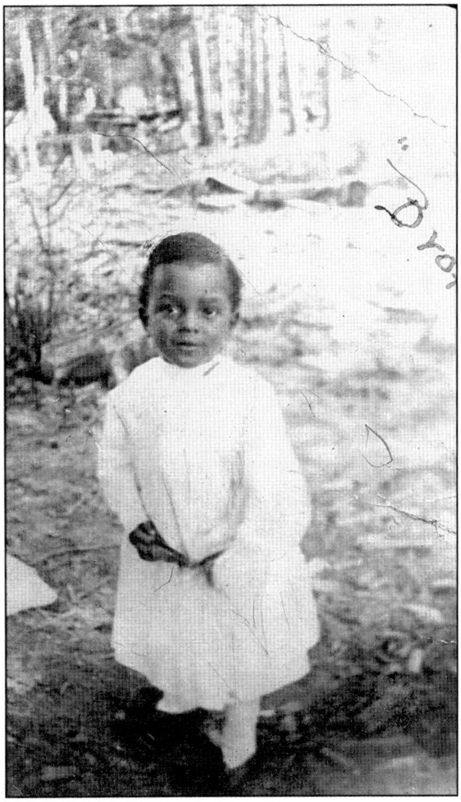

Pictured here is Levi Lowe as a young child.

This photograph shows Blanche Courtney Lowe and Daniel Lowe.

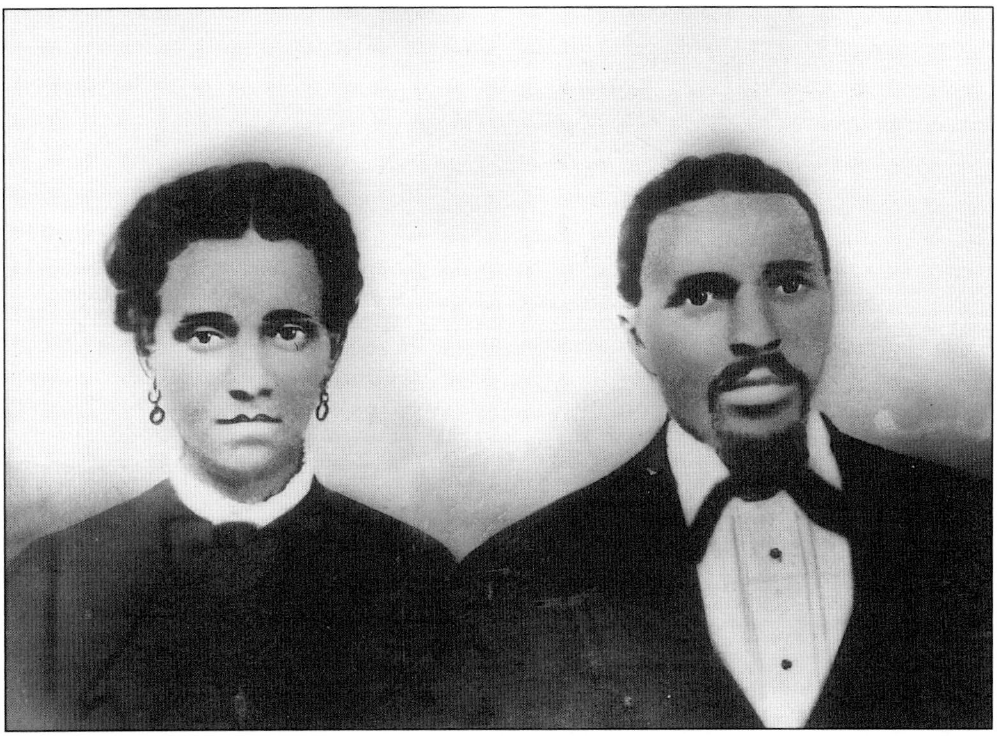

Martha Lowe Jenkins Roane was a community leader, tireless church worker, and a dedicated schoolteacher. The bell tower at Zion Baptist Church in Tucker Hill was given in her honor.

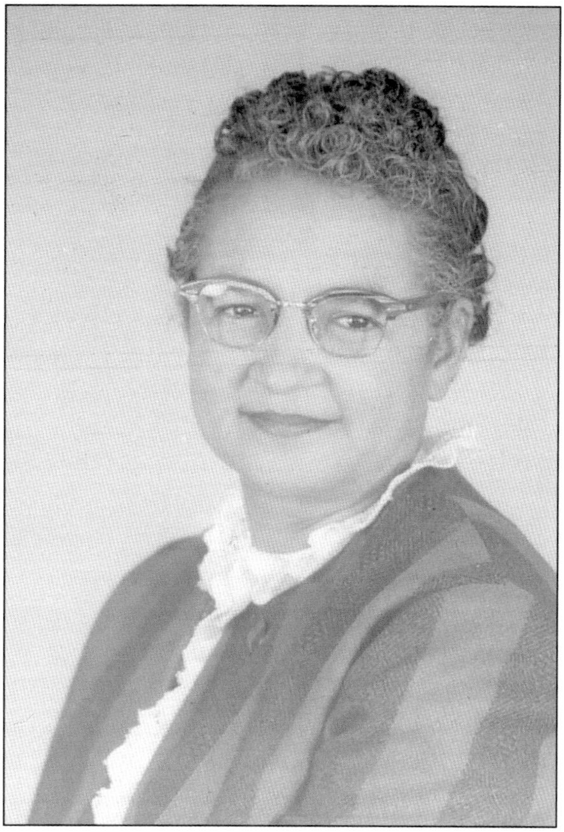

Reverend Henry Lee is seen here at the homeplace of his grandfather, Robert E. Lee, a black man who was a farmer and a member of Pope's Creek Episcopal Church. Robert Lee was born at Hazel Hill in Westmoreland County, and his father was a white man named Miller.

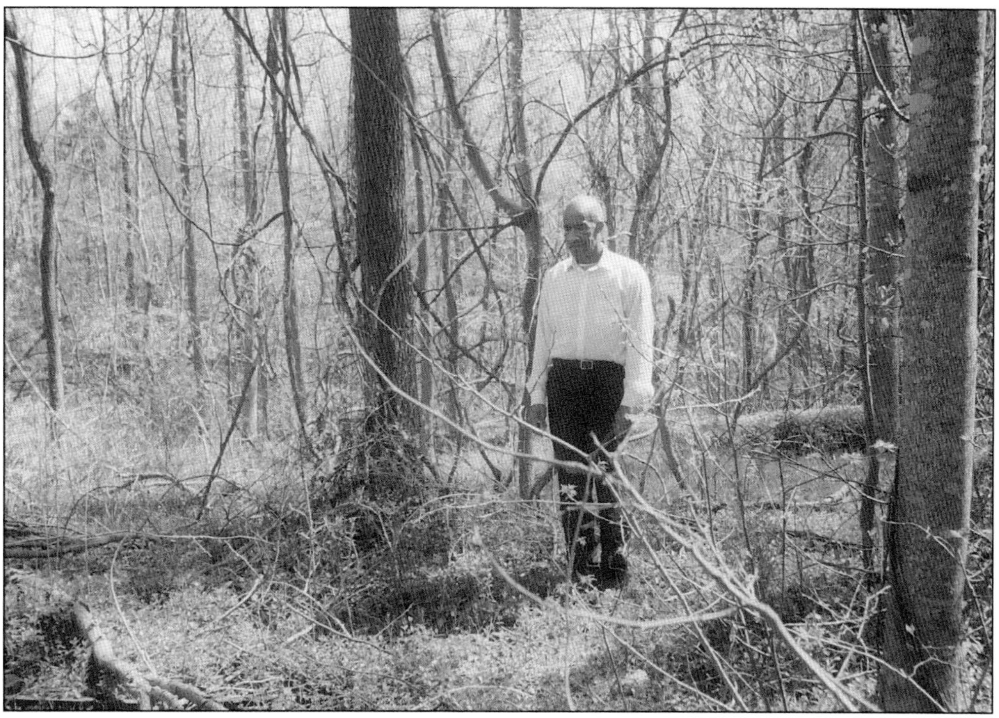

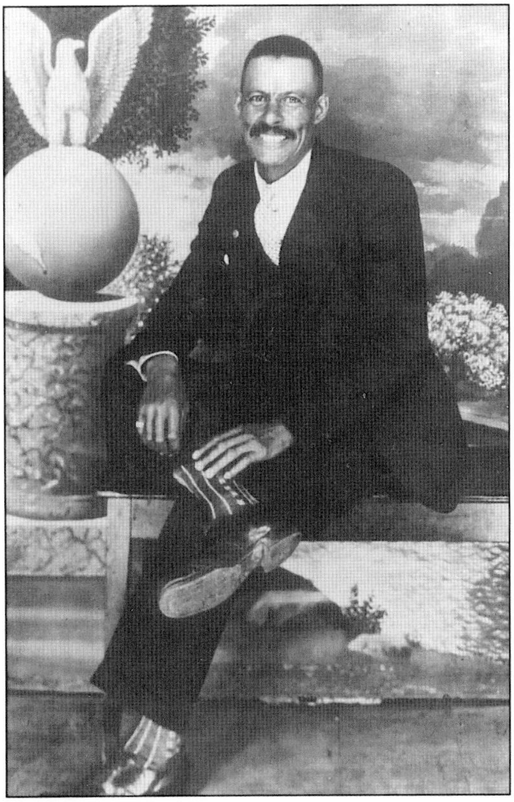

Born to Robert E. Lee and Mageline Lee in 1899, Reverend Johnson Benjamin Lee was a highly respected preacher. He married Mattie L. Hunter. Lee served as a pastor for his home church, Shiloh Jerusalem, in Oldhams; for Siloam Church, in Montross; and for the First Baptist Church, in Loretta. (Courtesy of Reverend Henry Lee.)

Adele Page Roane is seen her looking at the ruins of her childhood home on the Allen property down at White Point.

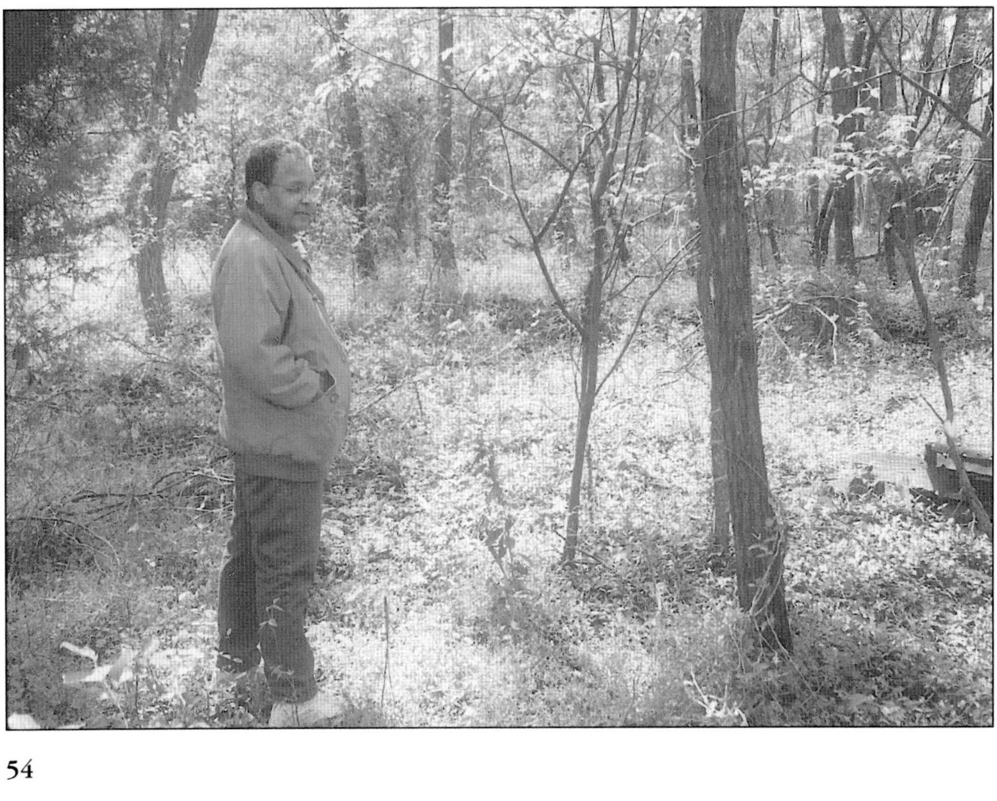

Helen Gordon Page Jackson loved life in the rural community of Westmoreland County. Trips away from this rural paradise, even after her children were grown, were difficult.

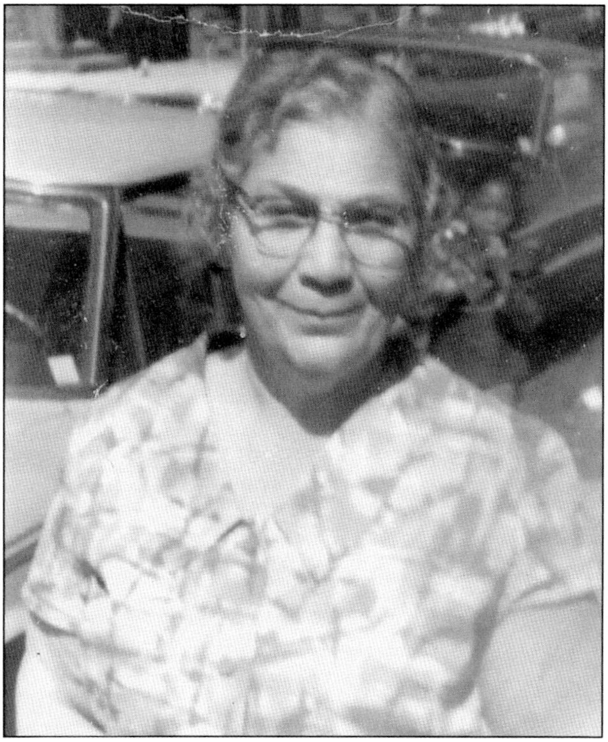

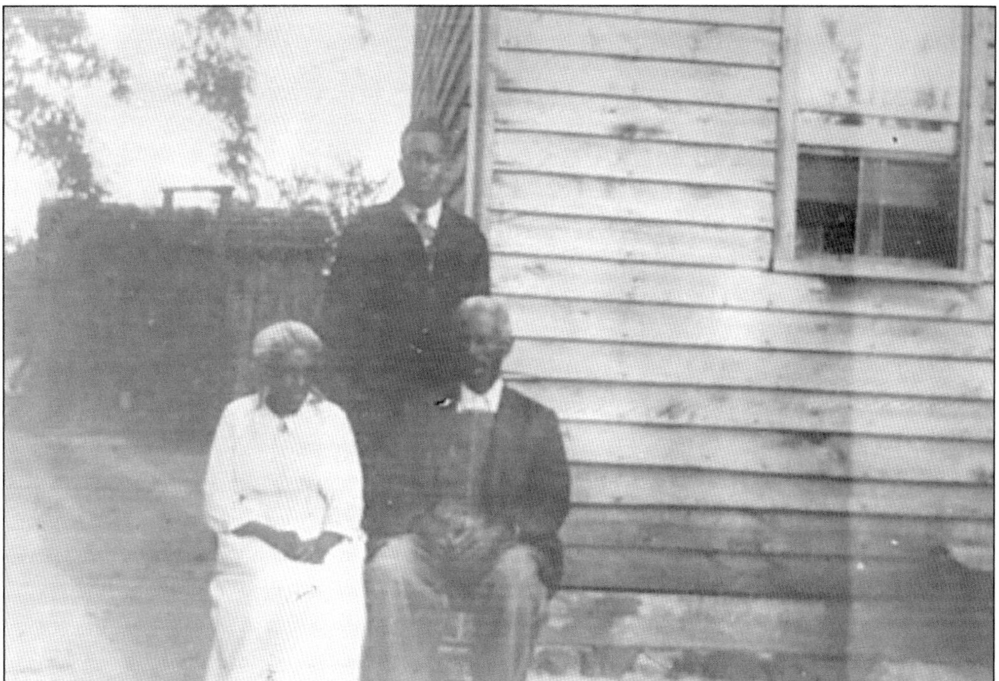

Cecelia Hawkins Fauntleroy poses with her husband, Sampson Fauntleroy, and an unidentified man in front of their log home in Kinsale.

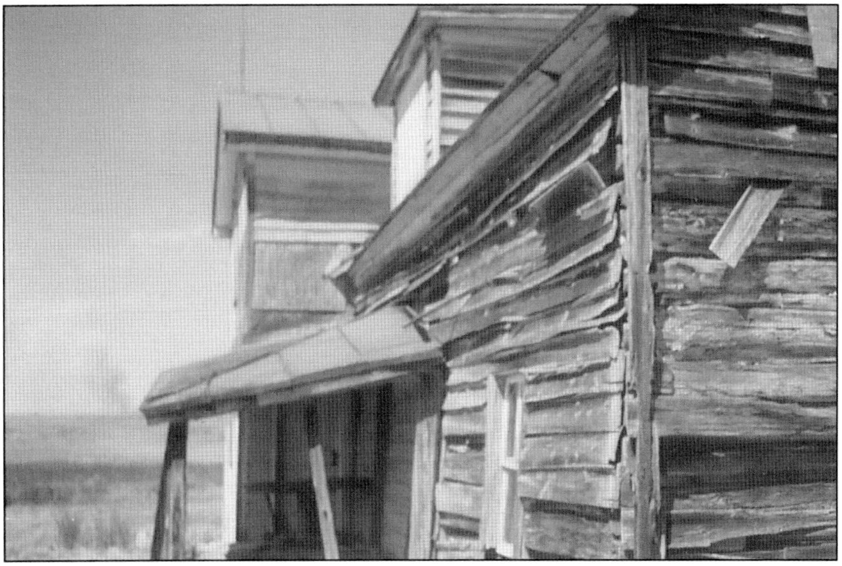

This view shows the Fauntleroy log home in Kinsale.

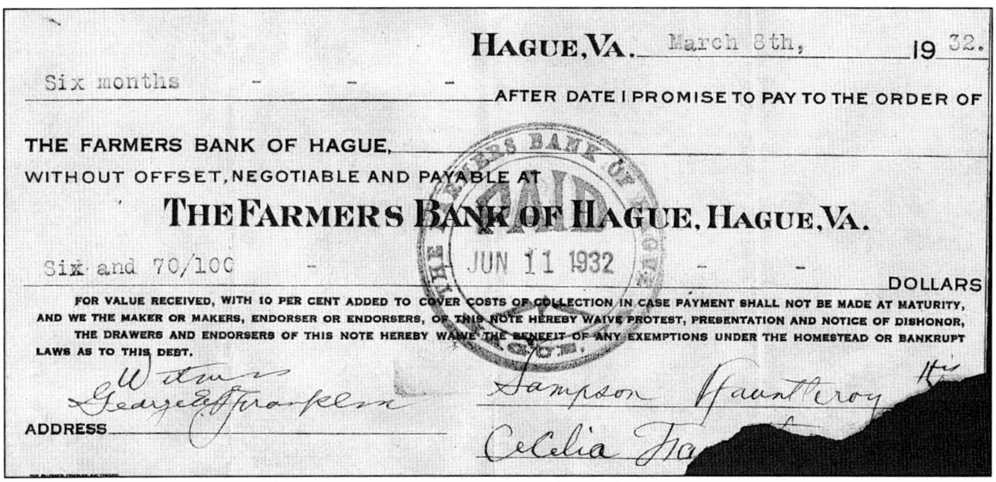

HAGUE, VA. March 8th, 1932.

Six months - - - AFTER DATE I PROMISE TO PAY TO THE ORDER OF

THE FARMERS BANK OF HAGUE,

WITHOUT OFFSET, NEGOTIABLE AND PAYABLE AT

THE FARMERS BANK OF HAGUE, HAGUE, VA.

Six and 70/100 - - - DOLLARS

FOR VALUE RECEIVED, WITH 10 PER CENT ADDED TO COVER COSTS OF COLLECTION IN CASE PAYMENT SHALL NOT BE MADE AT MATURITY, AND WE THE MAKER OR MAKERS, ENDORSER OR ENDORSERS, OF THIS NOTE HEREBY WAIVE PROTEST, PRESENTATION AND NOTICE OF DISHONOR, THE DRAWERS AND ENDORSERS OF THIS NOTE HEREBY WAIVE THE BENEFIT OF ANY EXEMPTIONS UNDER THE HOMESTEAD OR BANKRUPT LAWS AS TO THIS DEBT.

PAID JUN 11 1932 THE FARMERS BANK OF HAGUE

Witness George E. Franklin

ADDRESS

Sampson Fauntleroy

Cecelia Fa

Sampson and Cecelia were hard-working people, and when they borrowed money from the bank, they repaid their obligations.

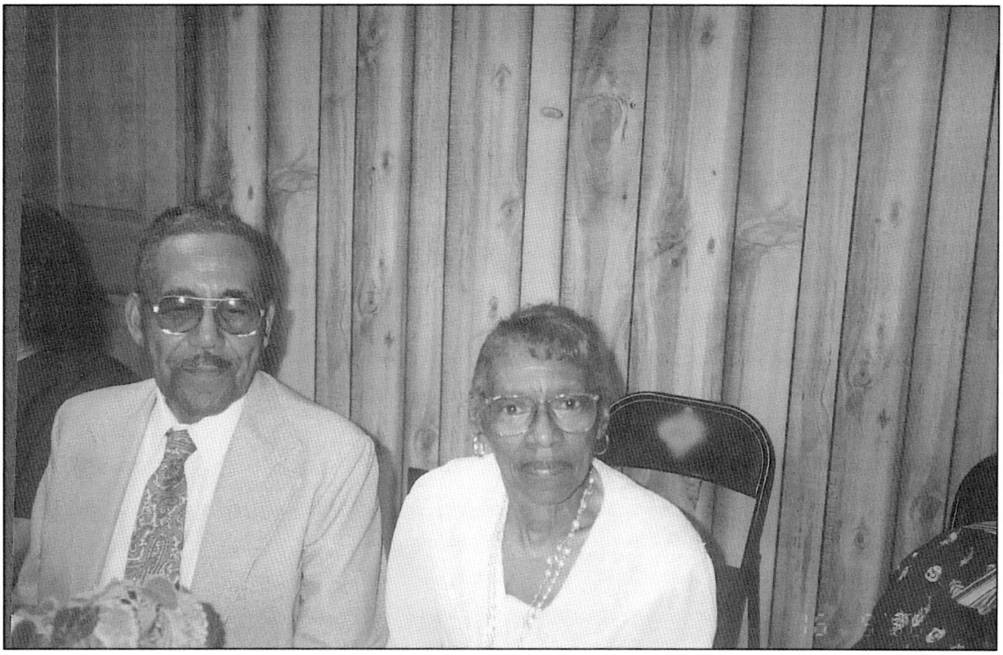

Charles Israel Jones and wife, Evelyn Jones, a renowned artist in her own right, are the parents of acclaimed artist Sichester Jones.

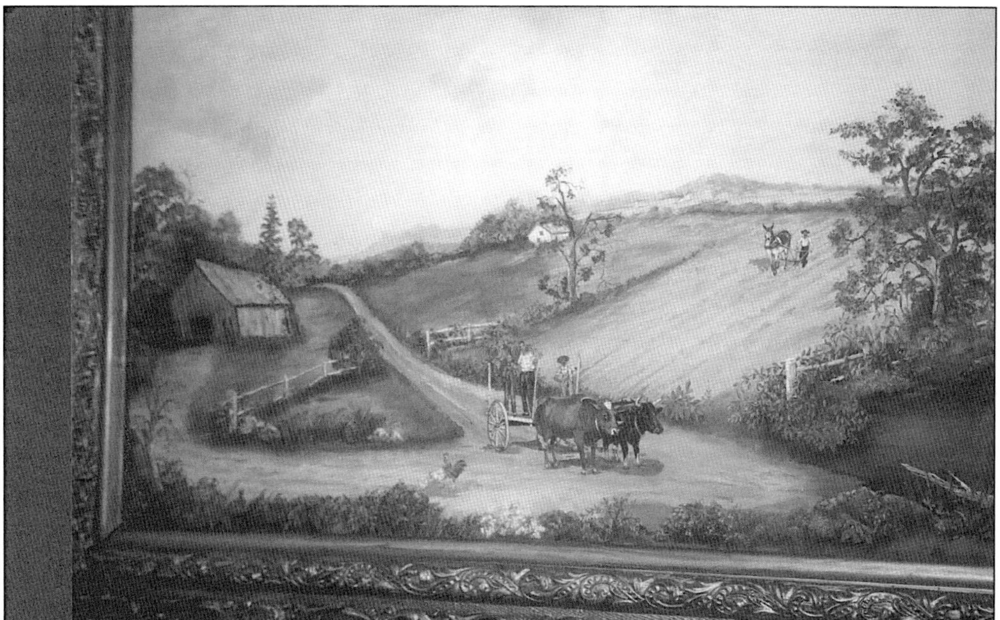

Evelyn Jones's painting of the Springfield farm shows where her husband, Israel, grew up in Westmoreland County.

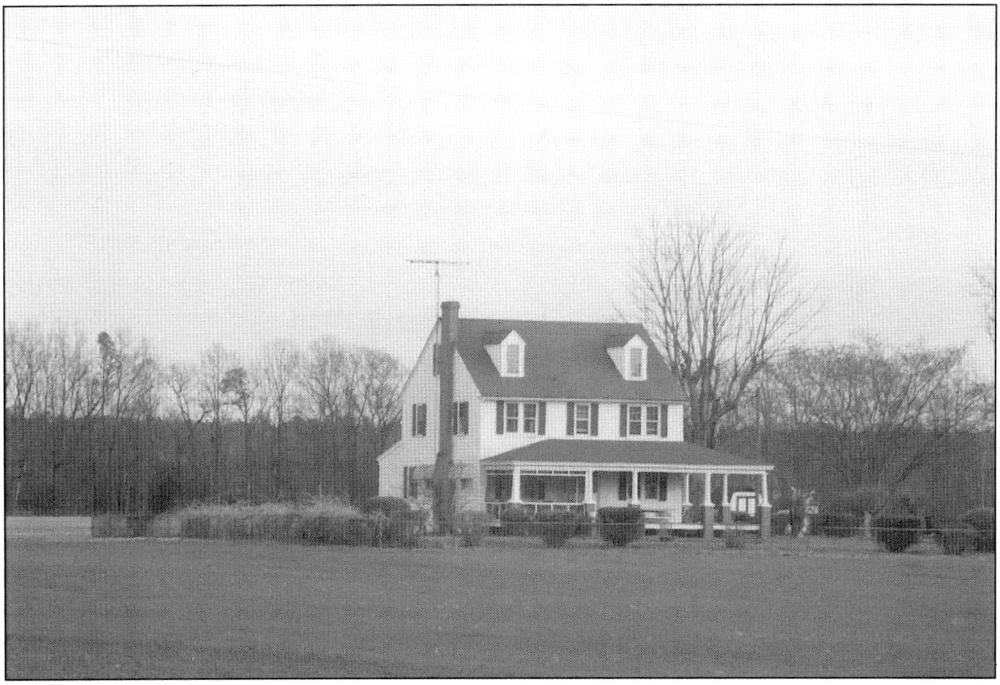

This is the picturesque homeplace of Alexander and the late Mary T. Smith. Mr. Smith went to Philadelphia as a young man, made some money, and came back home to build his home, to marry, and to raise a family.

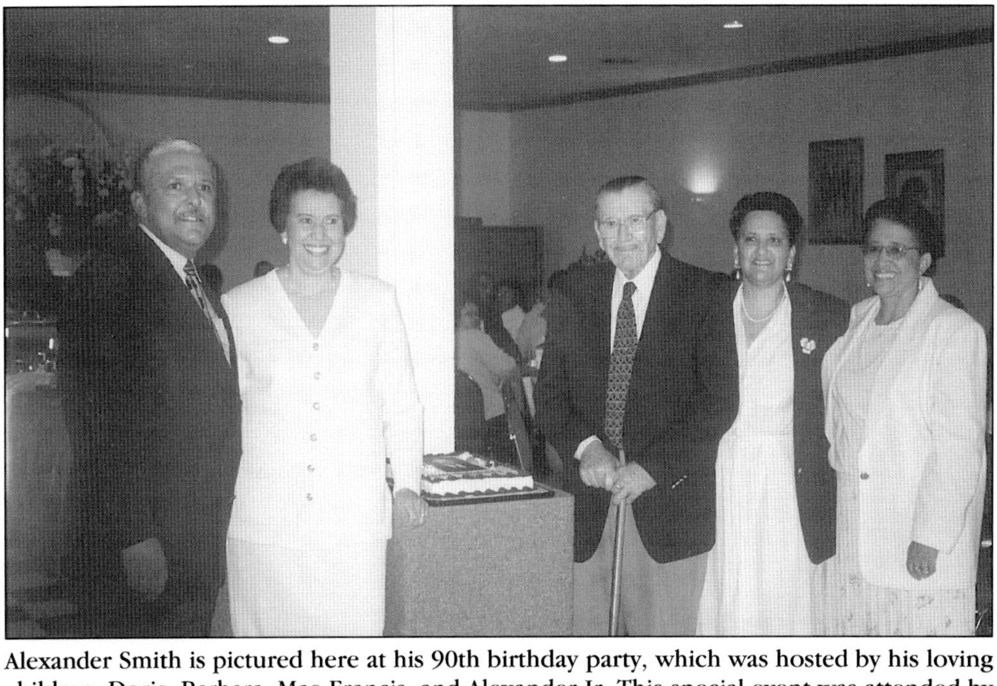

Alexander Smith is pictured here at his 90th birthday party, which was hosted by his loving children: Doris, Barbara, Mae Francis, and Alexander Jr. This special event was attended by family members from around the country.

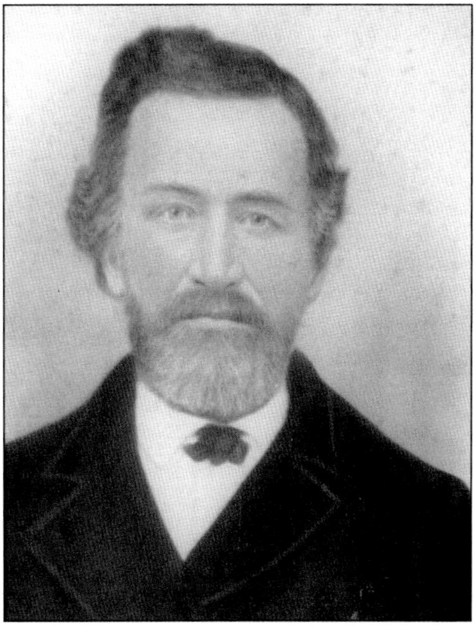

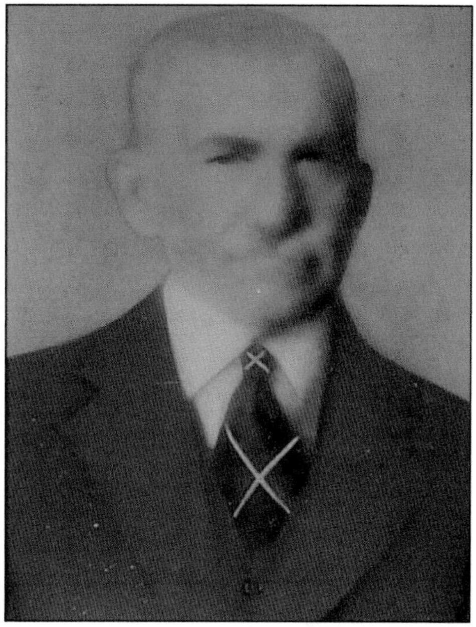

Left: Rodham McCoy fought in the Revolutionary War and has had many descendants who have also served the nation in times of need. ***Right:*** John H. Roane was a free man of color during the era of slavery. A prominent citizen in the Westmoreland community, he worked as a business man and a farmer.

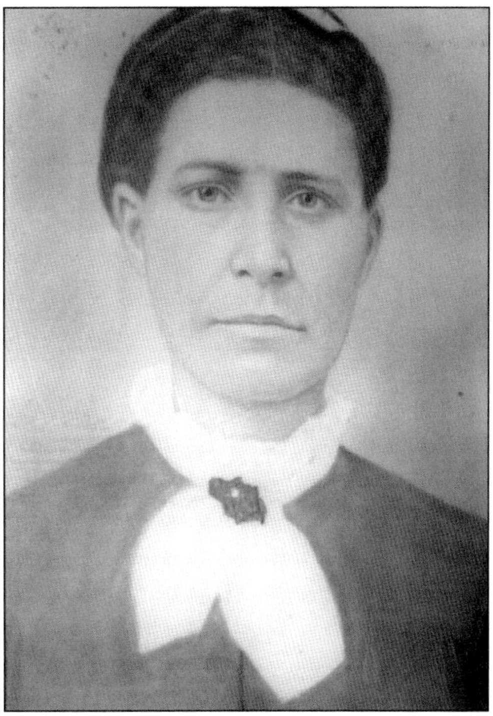

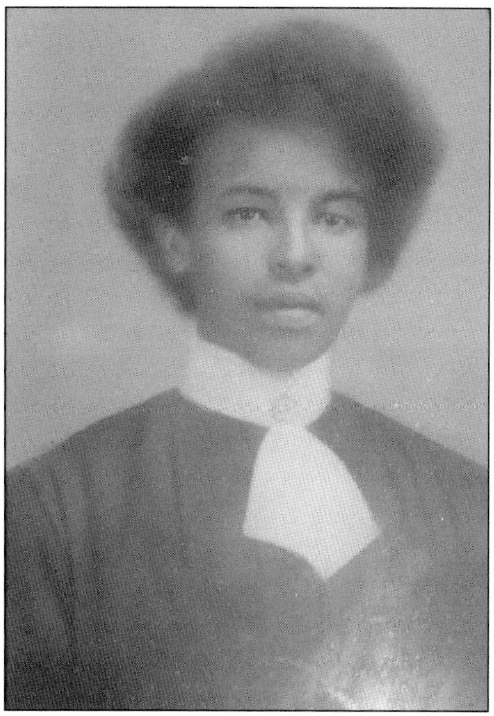

Left: An early McCoy woman, she was an American Indian who married Rodham McCoy. *Right:* Virginia E. Griggs Roane was a descendant of the McCoy family.

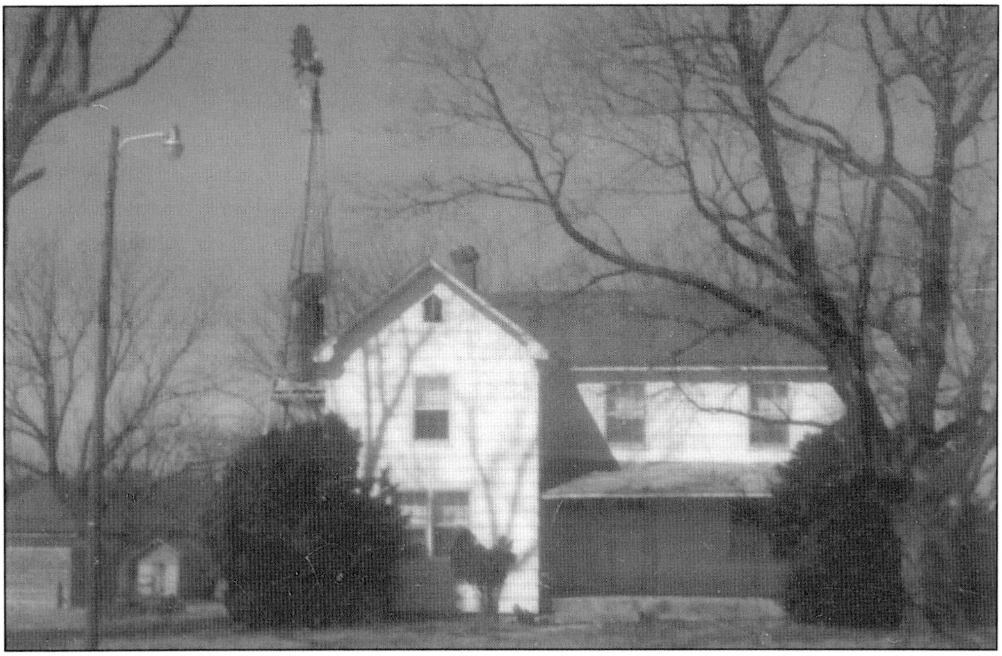

The John H. Roane homeplace reflects the wealth of the Roane family, for it had indoor plumbing and electricity generated by the property's windmill long before other homes in the area acquired the same amenities.

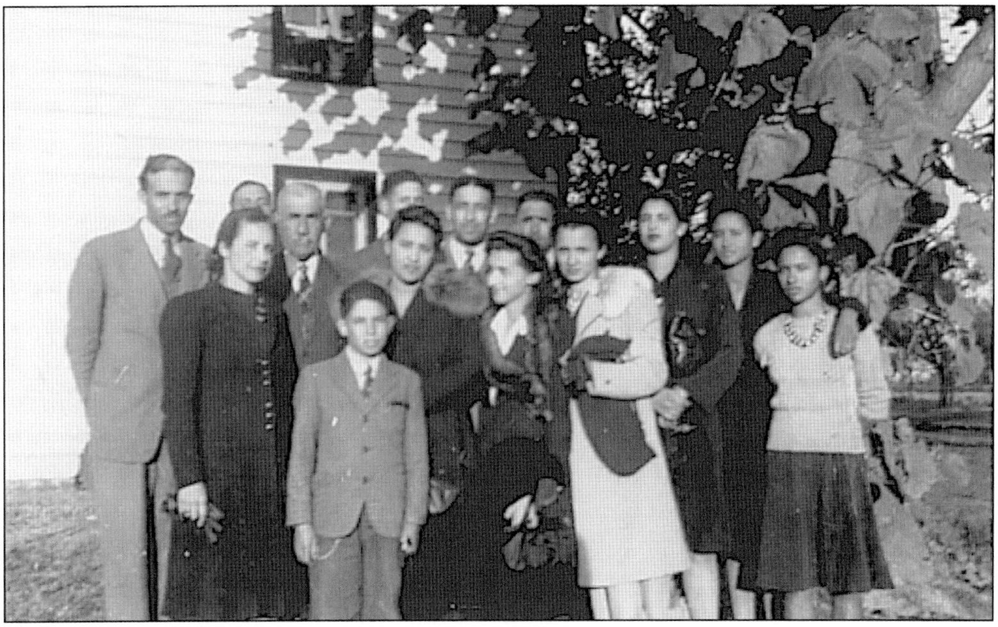

This is a Roane family photograph taken on the day of Virginia Roane's funeral. There were 15 children: Levernia Roane Savage, Joseph Roane, Griggs Roane, Ruby Roane Thompson Collins, Elwood Roane, Romanine Roane Synder Ellis, Gatewood Roane, Earl Roane, Mildred Roane Benton, Derenda Roane Dixon, Lola Roane Gordon, Christine Roane Slayton, Alfonso Roane, Florine Roane, and John H. Roane Jr.

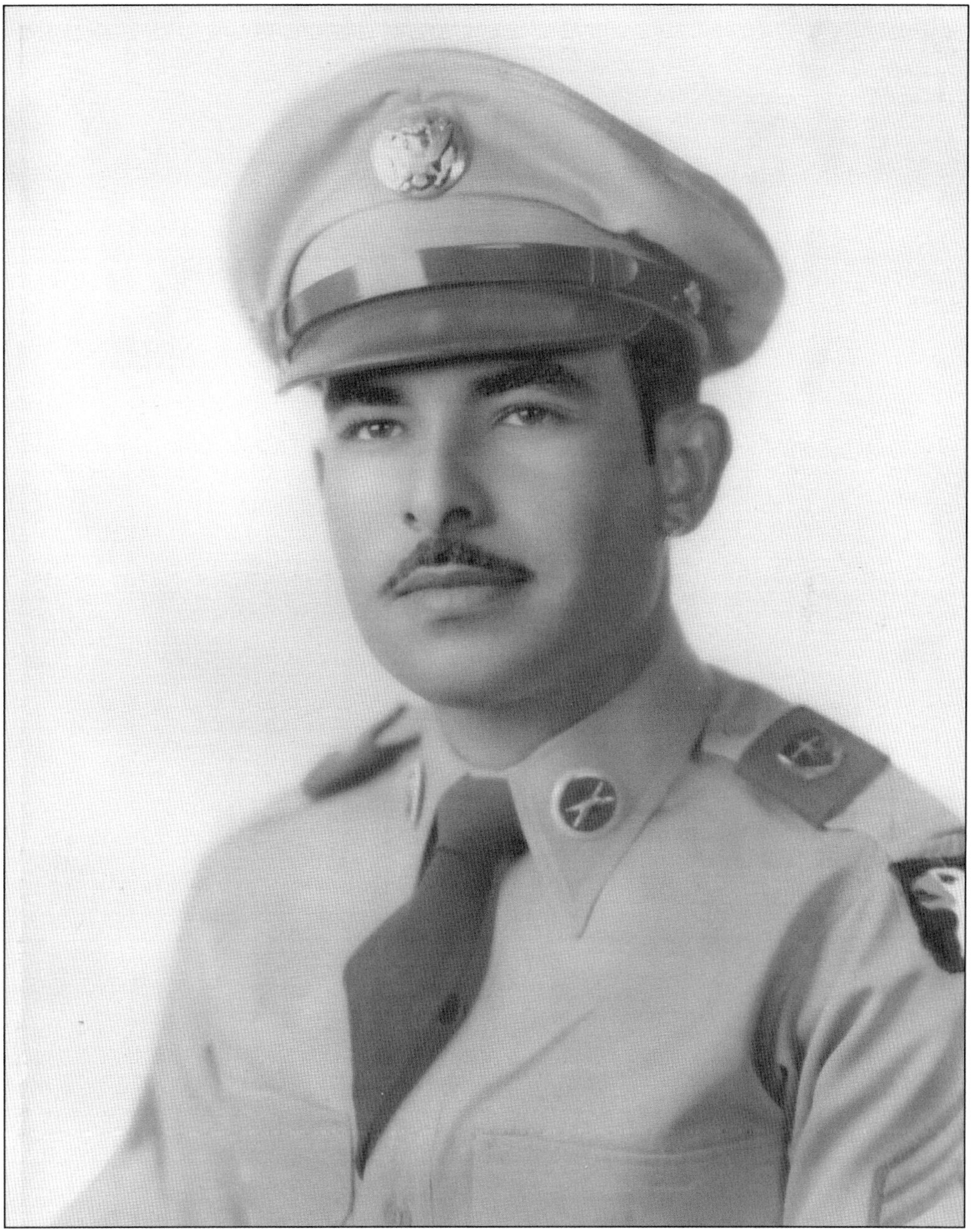

During the Korean conflict, John Roane Jr. continued the family tradition of service to the country, following in the footsteps of his McCoy ancestors who fought in the Revolutionary War.

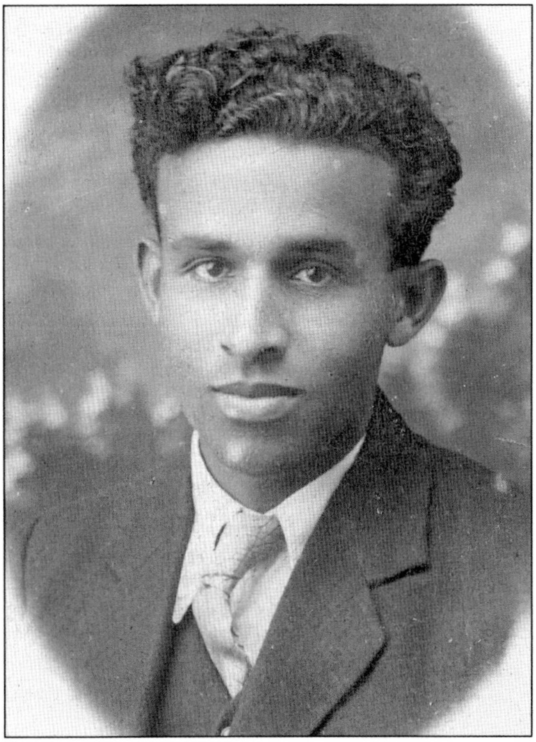

Son of John and Virginia Griggs Roane, Joseph Roane would come home from college and work for his father. (Courtesy of Yosif Roane.)

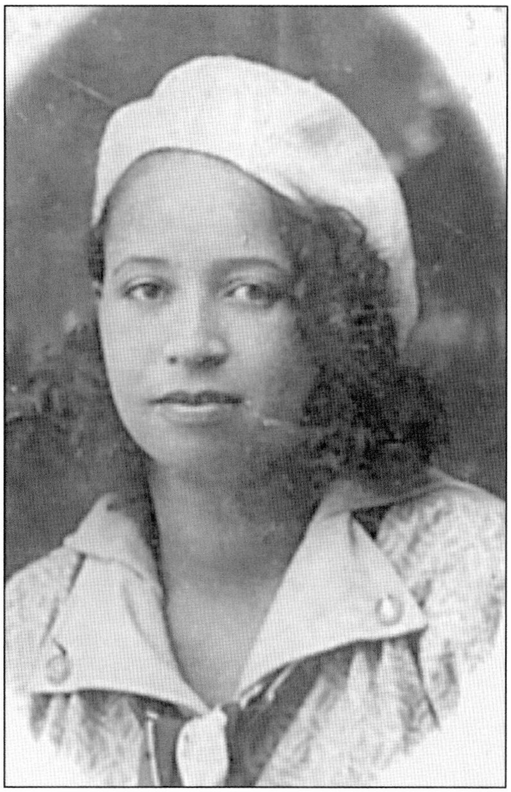

Sadie Vivian Russell, wife of Joseph Roane, bore her son, Yosif, while the couple lived in Russia. As the story goes, the Russians had a problem understanding how this young couple who had been sent from the Westmoreland County community called Kremlin to Russia would be trying to name their child Joseph, so they named him Yosif, after the Russian leader of the time.

Yosif Roane is seen here as a young child in Russia, *c.* 1935. Today, he lives in Westmoreland County and is a civic leader working and giving much time to the Optimist Club and the Westmoreland County Rescue Squad. Following in the Roane family tradition, he has also been a successful businessman.

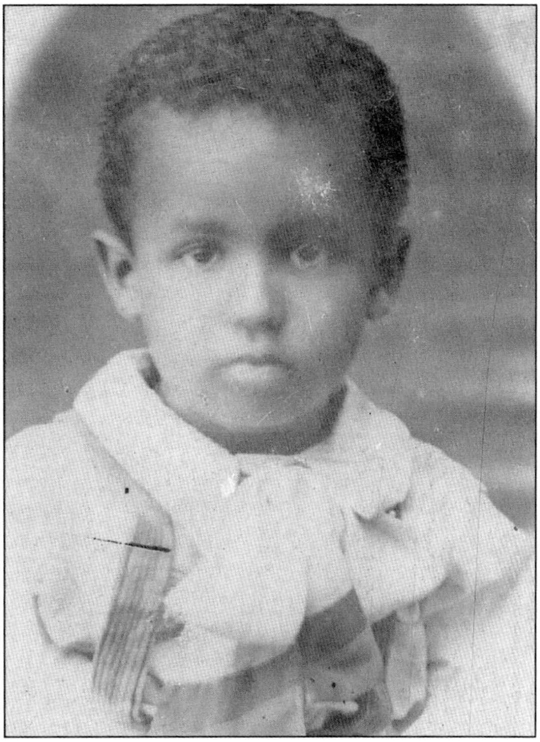

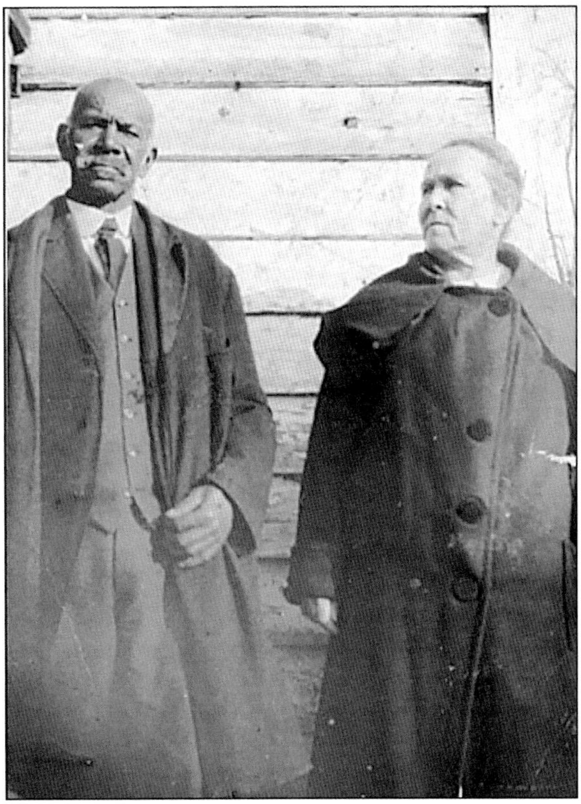

Richard Johnson served as a "Buffalo soldier," and his wife, Judith McCoy Johnson, was a descendant of Rhodom McCoy.

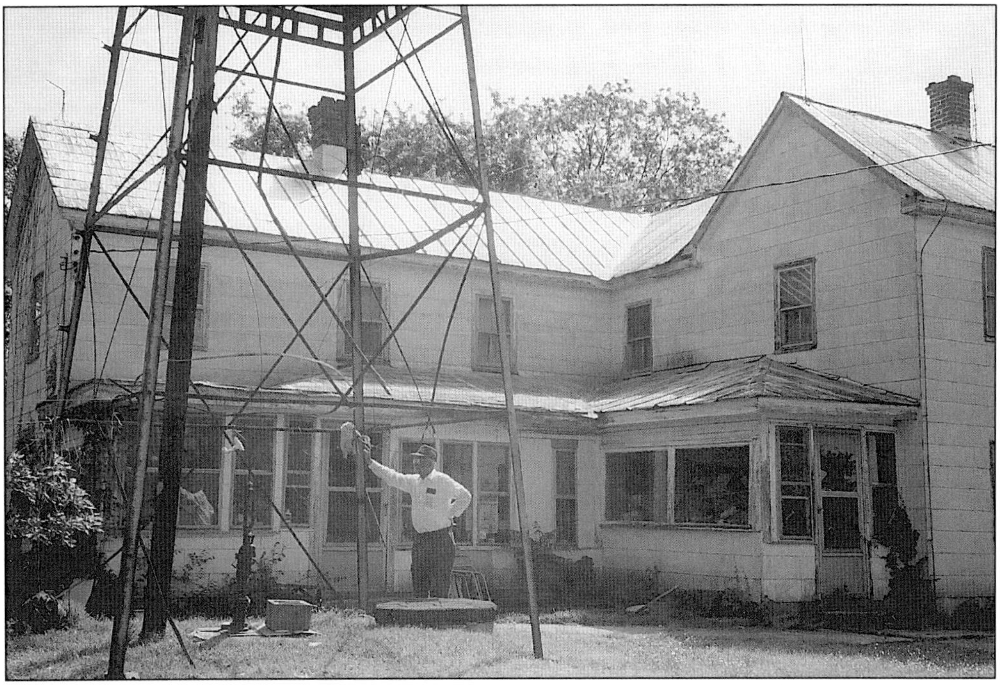

Joseph Graham is seen here behind what had been Oliver Clayton's family home, which the Claytons later sold to the Weldon family. Today, the house is occupied by Mr. Weldon's granddaughter, Lola Graham, and her husband, Joseph.

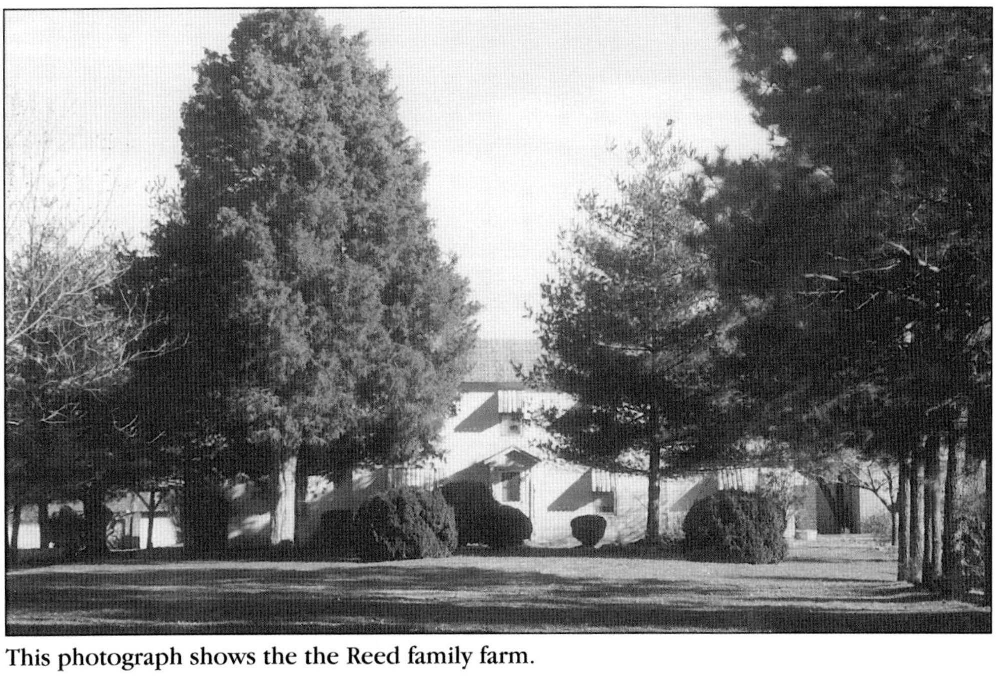

This photograph shows the the Reed family farm.

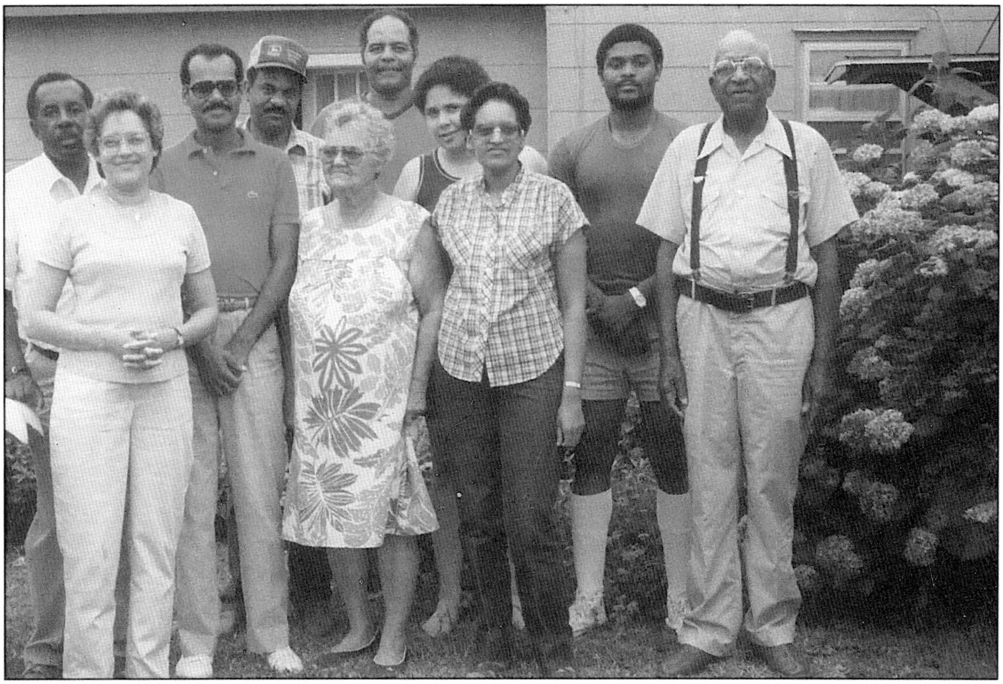

Joseph and Margaret Reed are pictured here with their family.

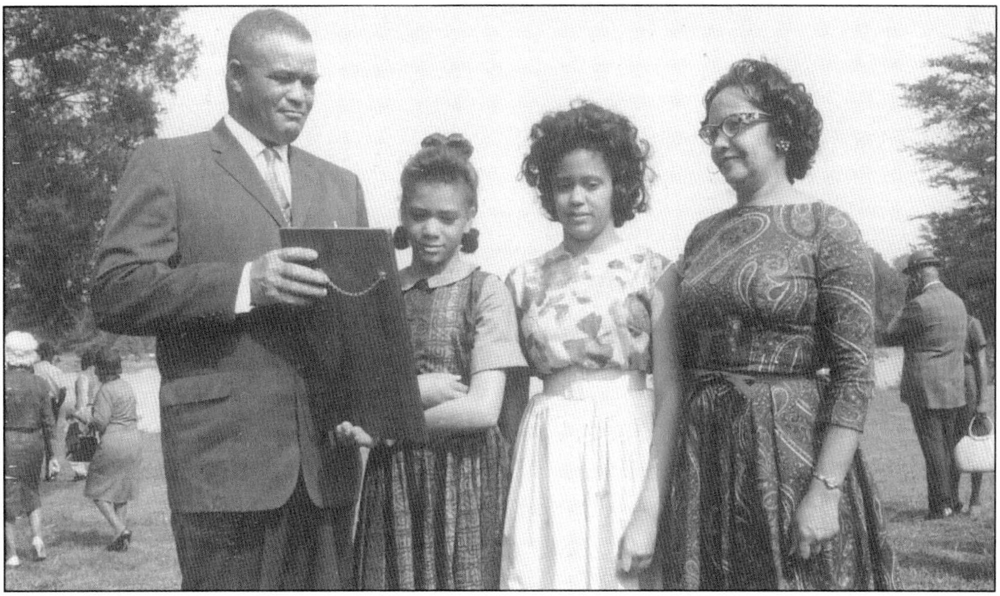

Pictured, from left to right, are Jacob Ashton, daughters Brenda and Jacqueline, and Mrs. Ashton from Erica at an event honoring their family. According to the *Richmond Times Dispatch* in 1963, Jacob Ashton, a former taxi driver in Washington, D.C. who came to Westmoreland County, was a leading commercial poultryman, with 11,500 laying hens in cages, and all of his crops above yields for the state average. His daughter Brenda was the president of the local 4-H Club and his daughter Jacqueline had won second place in the district sewing contest in 1962. (Courtesy of Mary Dixon Jones.)

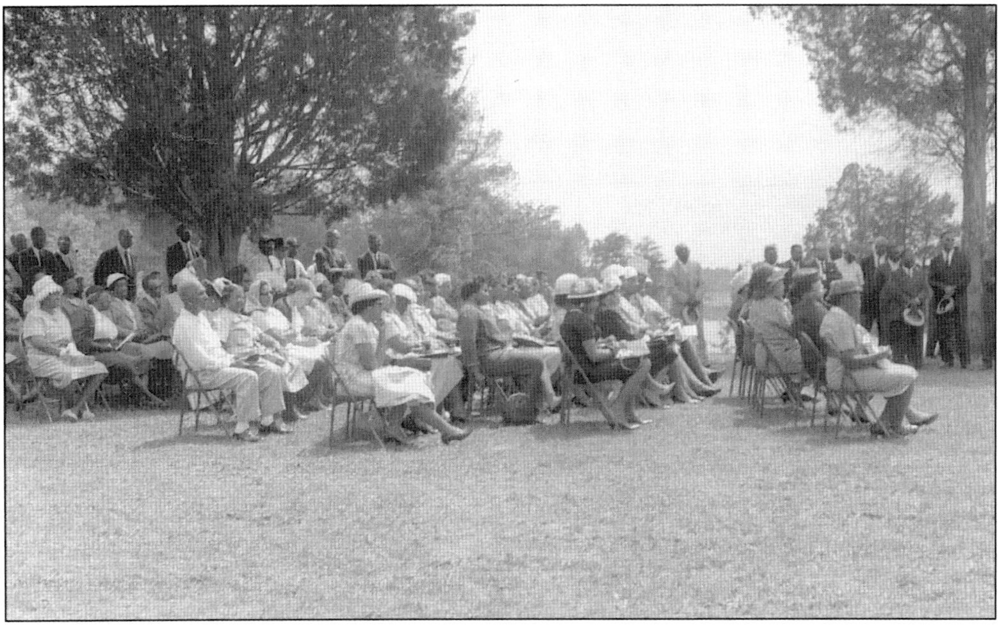

Jacob Ashton, at the awards program, shared how his first ventures of raising sheep and hogs failed because of disease. By 1967, Ashton went on to be a member of the Virginia State Commission for the Industry of Agricultural. On February 20, 1967, President Lyndon Johnson invited Mr. Ashton and other farm leaders to a luncheon at the White House.

"OUTSTANDING FARM FAMILIES"

The award program is designed to give recognition to one farm family annually. Families receiving the award-plaque—have made considerable progress in areas of soil and water conservation, crop, livestock, and poultry production, sound business methods for the farm and home, good family relations, and community and county leadership.

The Harvey M. Thomas Family 1953
Caroline County

The Theodore B. McClenny Family 1954
Southampton County

The Arthur R. Glover Family 1955
Isle of Wight County

The John H. Maclin, Sr., Family 1956
Brunswick County

The Frank E. Owens Family 1957
Nansemond County

The James Tucker Family 1958
Greensville County

The A. D. Curley Family 1959
Sussex County

The McKenzie Talley Family 1960
Mecklenburg County

The P. S. Brown Family 1961
New Kent County

The C. R. Vaughan Family 1962
Brunswick County

The Jacob Ashton Family 1963
Westmoreland County

"We judge ourselves by what we feel capable of doing, while others judge us by what we have already done."

—Longfellow

PROGRAM

MRS. SADIE R. ROANE, Local Home Agent
Westmoreland County, Presiding

NATIONAL ANTHEM .... School Band

THE INVOCATION

WELCOME .... Mrs. Marie Ashton

MUSICAL SELECTION .... School Band

HISTORY AND OPERATION OF THE ASHTON FARM .... Mr. and Mrs. Jacob Ashton

REMARKS .... Mr. Denver Bragg
Associate Extension Poultry Specialist
Virginia Polytechnic Institute
Mr. S. J. Dawson
County Agent

MUSICAL SELECTION .... School Band

ADDRESS .... Mr. M. T. Carter
Acting Director of the
School of Agriculture
Virginia State College

PRESENTATION OF AWARD .... Mrs. Bernice Vaughan
President of
State Advisory Board

MUSICAL SELECTION .... School Band

THE BENEDICTION

Pictured here, Leslie Fauntleroy Wilson and Levinia Fulcher Wilson share a tender moment before a photographer's lens.

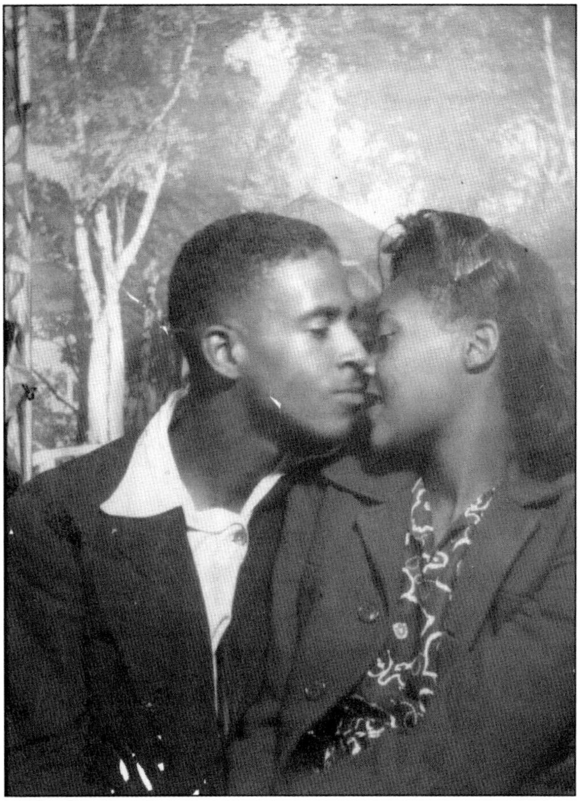

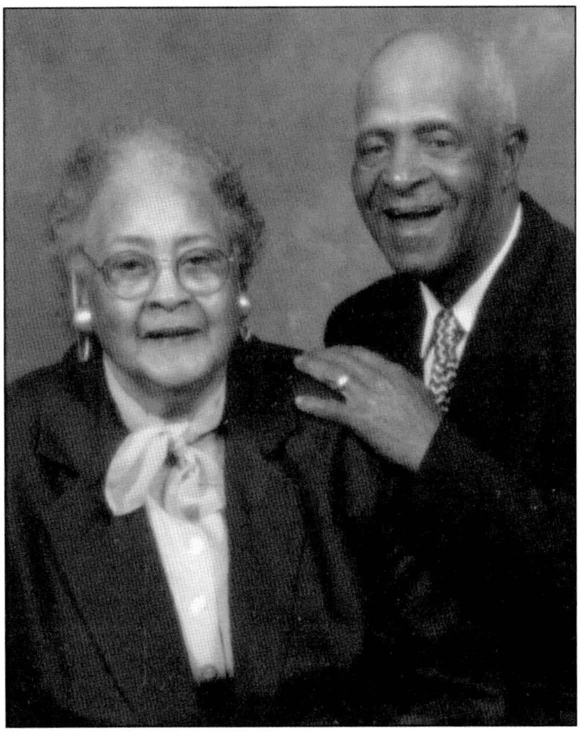

After more than 50 years of marriage, Leslie and Levinia Wilson have stayed true to their vows and have enjoyed many years of wedded bliss.

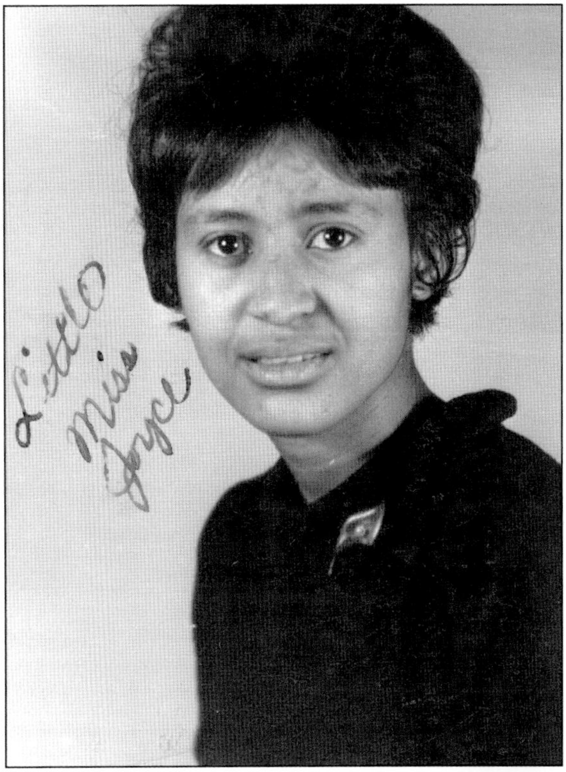

Known as "Little Miss Joyce," Joyce Wilson Jones upholds the family tradition of reaching out to help others and serving as a pillar in the family and the community.

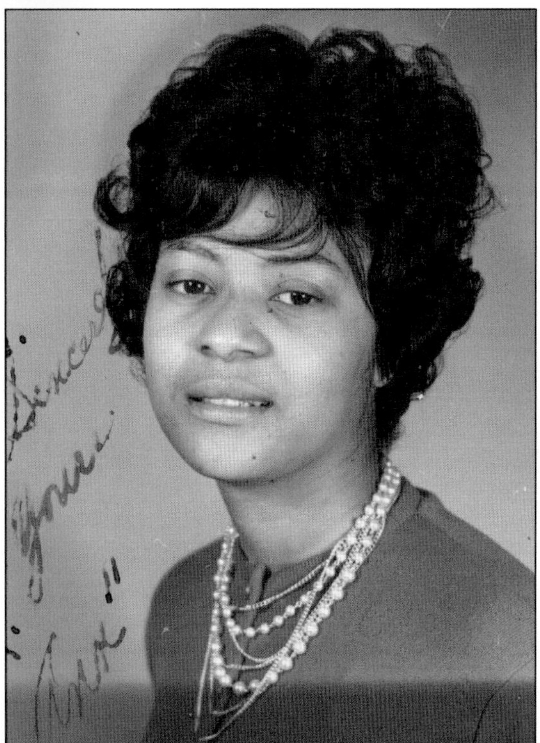

This portrait photograph shows Ann Wilson.

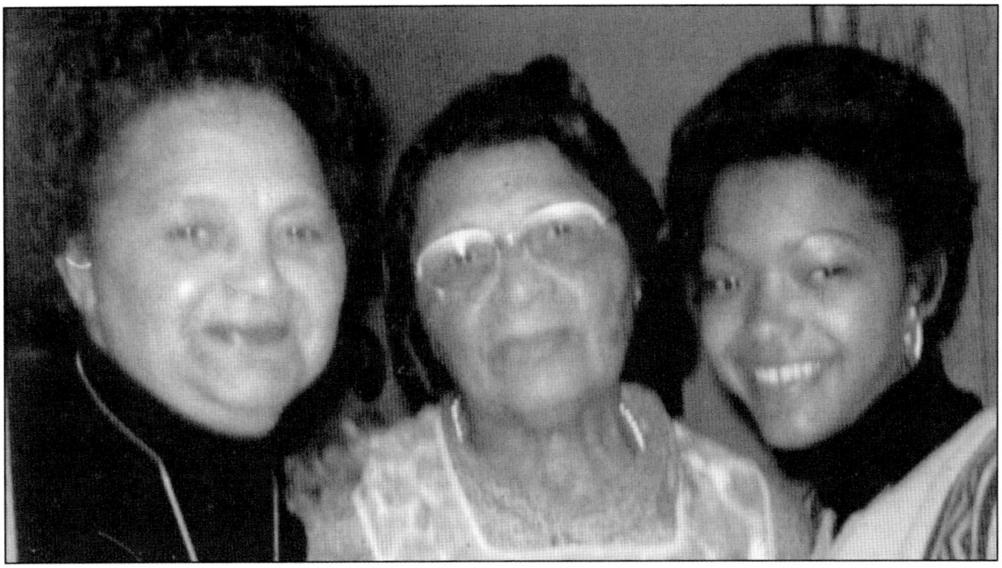

Three generations of family appear here: (from left to right) Bessie Green Lumpkin Brown, Hannah Curry Green, and Reginia Lumpkin (mother, grandmother, and daughter, respectively). Many traditions have been passed down, such as the one that requires a man to be the first to enter one's home on New Year's Day, for this ensures good luck for the rest of the year. Some men believed that it was their duty to visit many homes on New Year's Day, especially those headed by females. It was only after a male had entered and gone back out and reentered could others visit on New Year's Day.

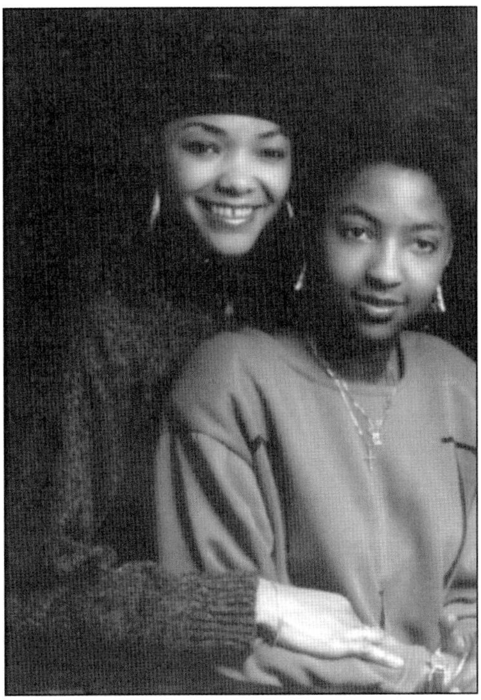

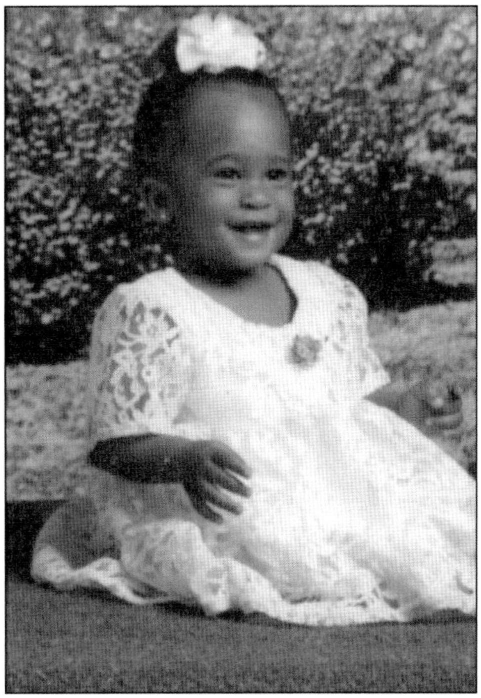

Left: Yvonne Gale (right), the daughter of Reginia Lumpkin, appears here. ***Right:*** Yasmin Gale, the daughter of Yvonne Gale, poses for this memorable studio portrait.

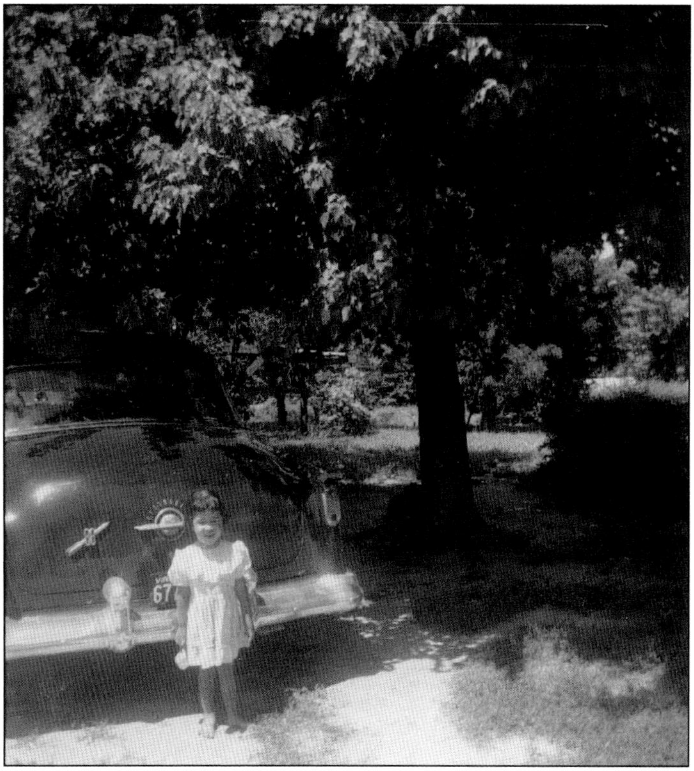

Virginia Roane is pictured here near the family's vintage automobile of the time.

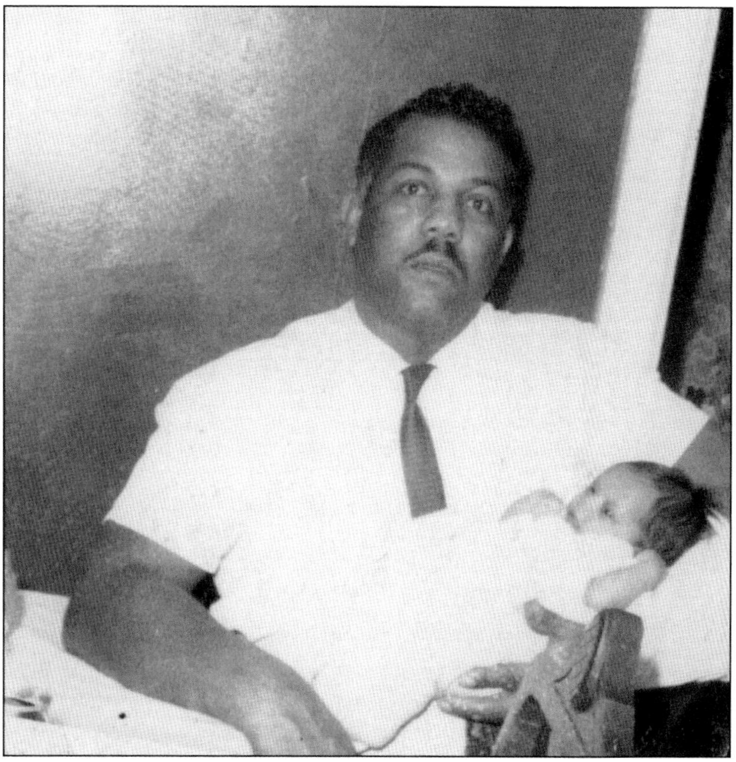

Shirley Page is seen here holding his nephew, Terry Page. The entire family and the community participate in the caring and nurturing of its children.

Even as a young boy, Sichester Jones showed artistic talent for painting like his mother, Evelyn Jones.

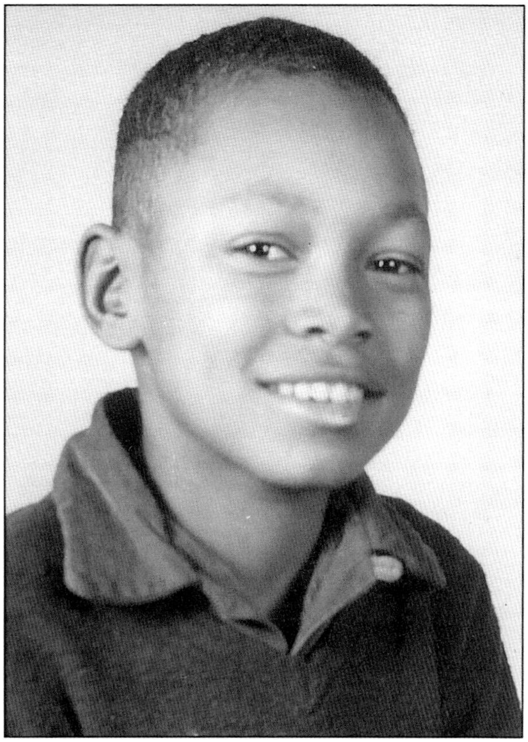

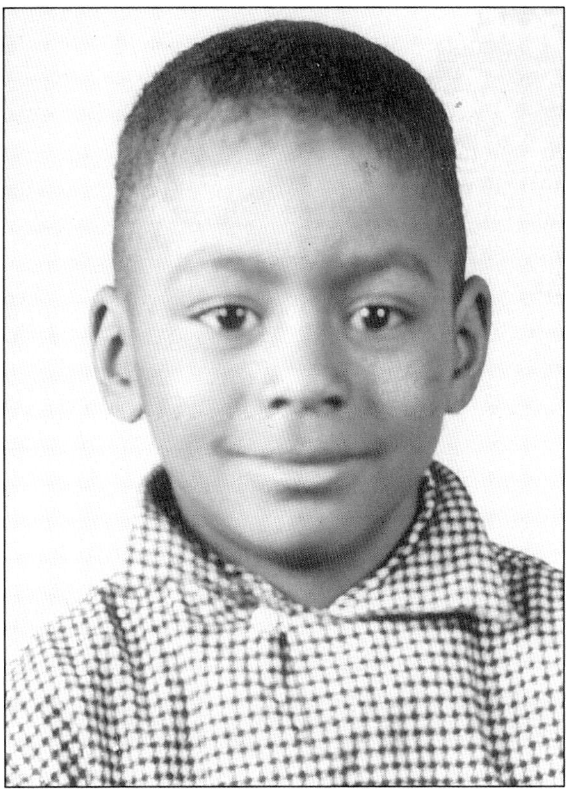

This portrait shows a young Paul Jones. Both Paul and his brother, Sichester, are the sons of Israel and Evelyn Jones.

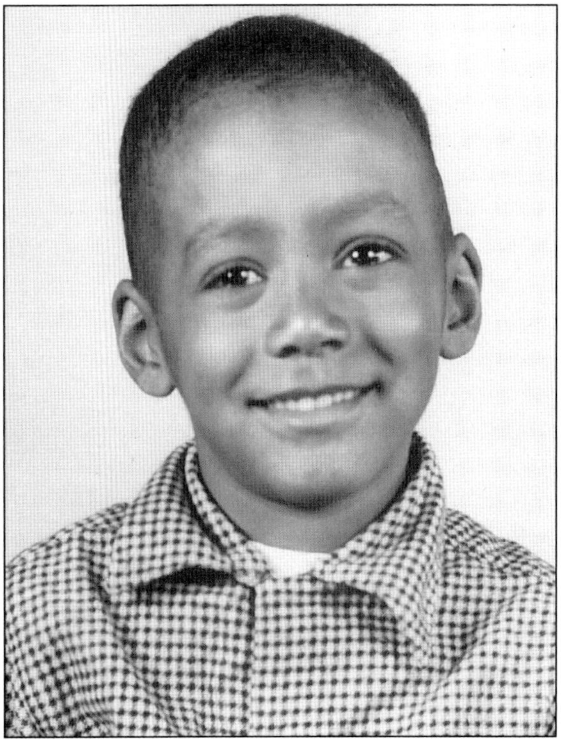

A young Gayland Jones poses for this studio portrait.

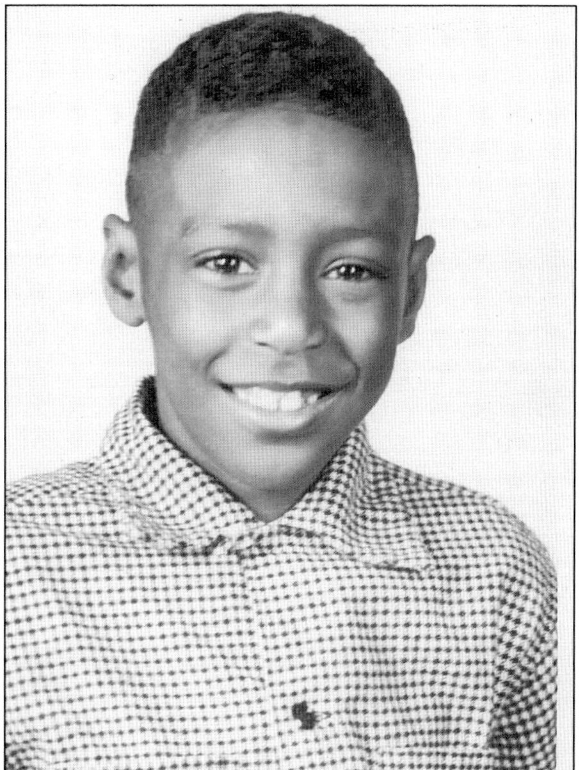

A young Roland Jones smiles for this photograph.

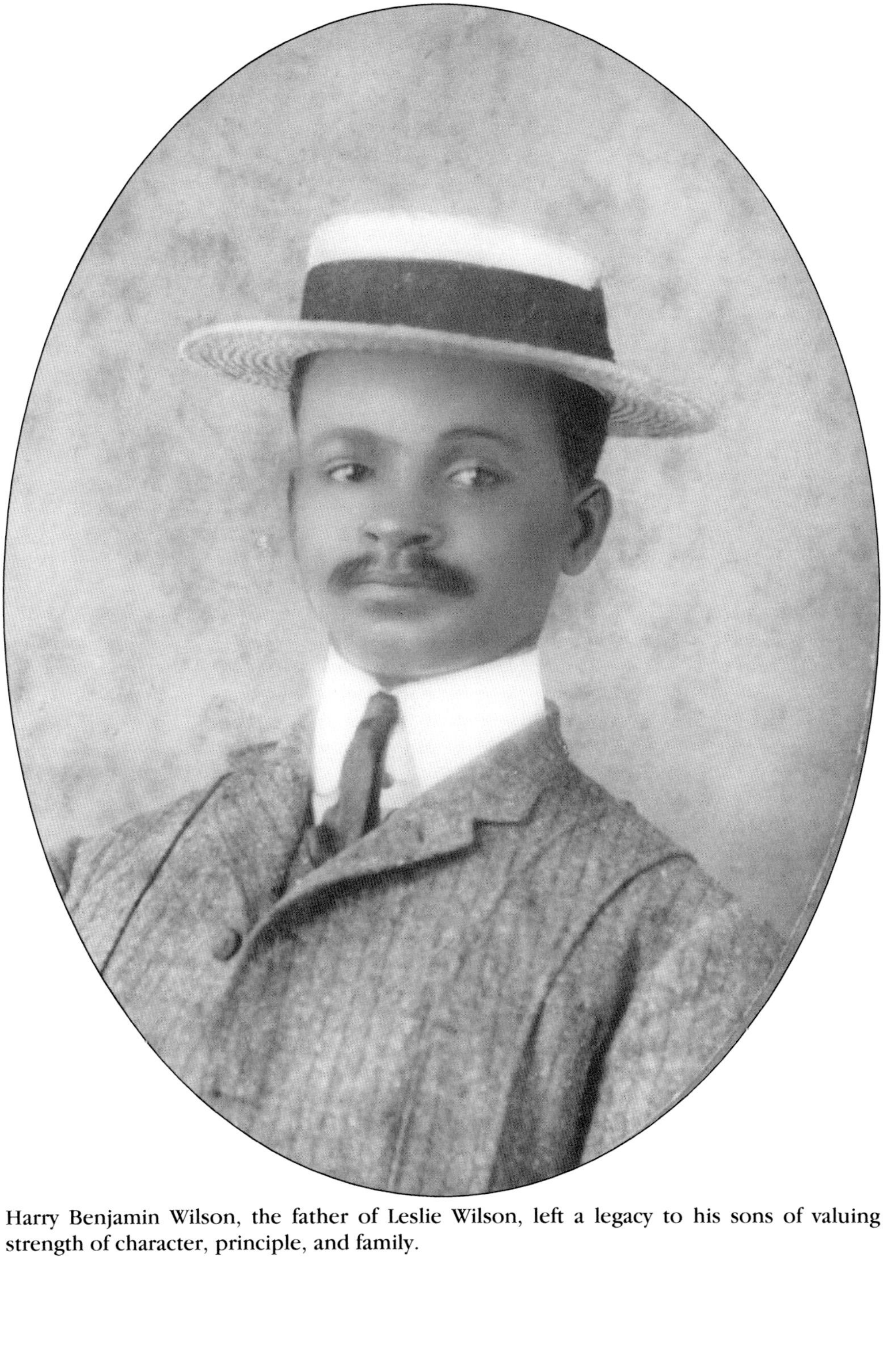

Harry Benjamin Wilson, the father of Leslie Wilson, left a legacy to his sons of valuing strength of character, principle, and family.

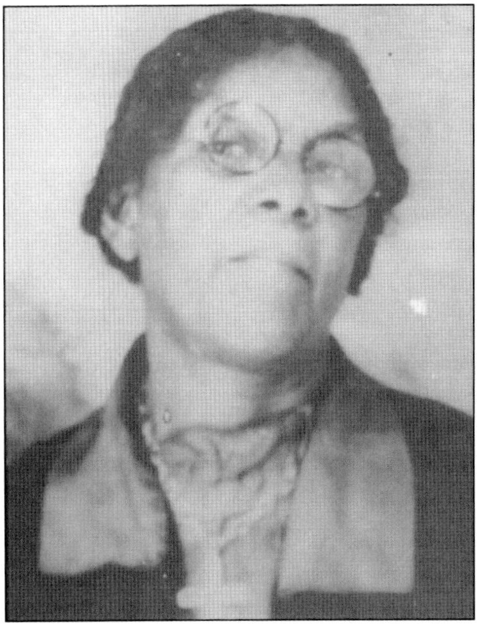

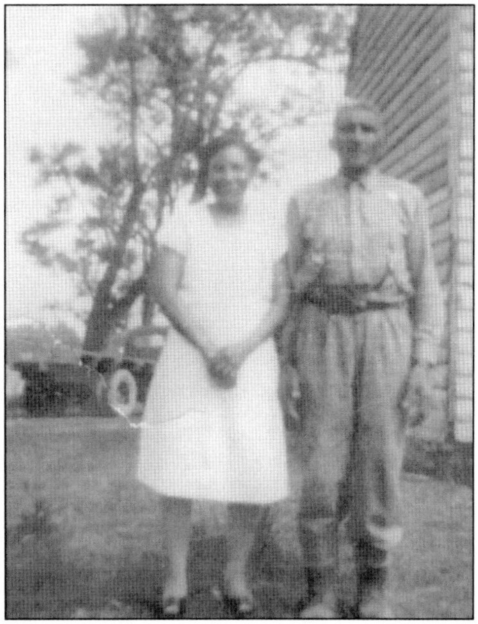

Left: Ann Amelia Miller, of Tucker Hill, married George Thomas, the son of Martha and Acery Thomas. She had ten children: six girls and four boys. In her eighties, she passed away while sitting on her favorite pew in the Zion Baptist Church while attending a funeral service on May 13, 1958. ***Right***: The son of Richard Benjamin Plummer and Eliza Jane Plummer, Moses Plummer married Martha Anne Thomas, the daughter of Ann and George Thomas. Her ten children went on to become farmers and sharecroppers. The family moved in 1924 to work for the Frank P. Delano family on Locust Hall in Oldhams.

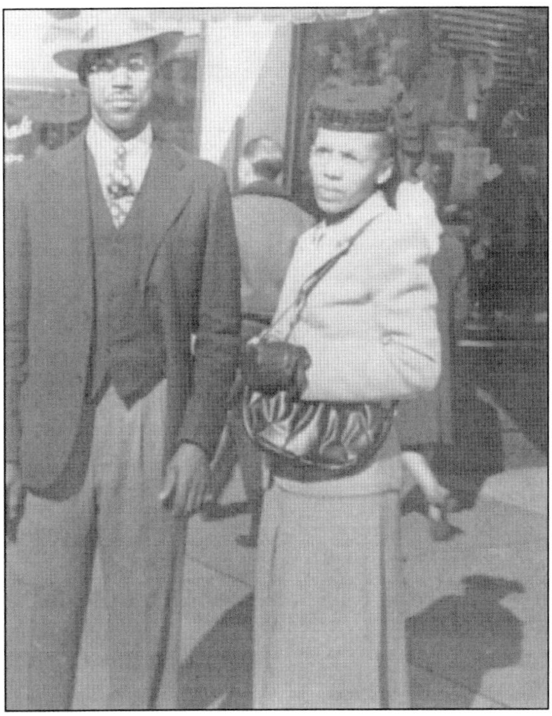

Martha Ann Plummer Carey, daughter of Moses and Martha Plummer, appears here with her husband, James Carey.

Three

MAKING A DIFFERENCE

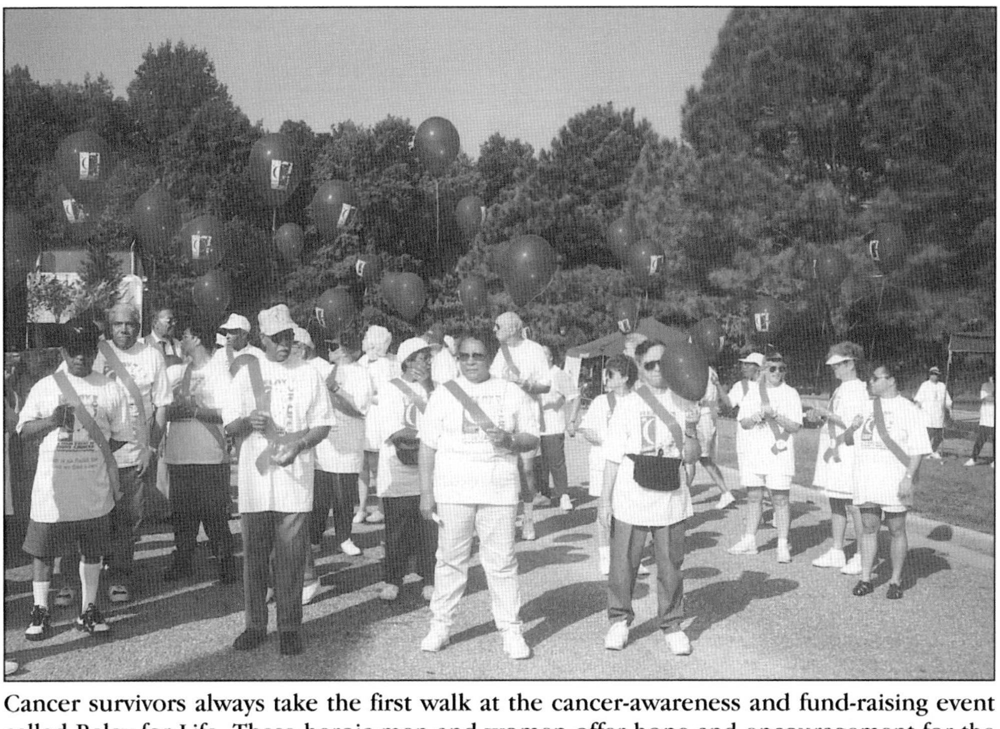

Cancer survivors always take the first walk at the cancer-awareness and fund-raising event called Relay for Life. These heroic men and women offer hope and encouragement for the many others suffering from cancer.

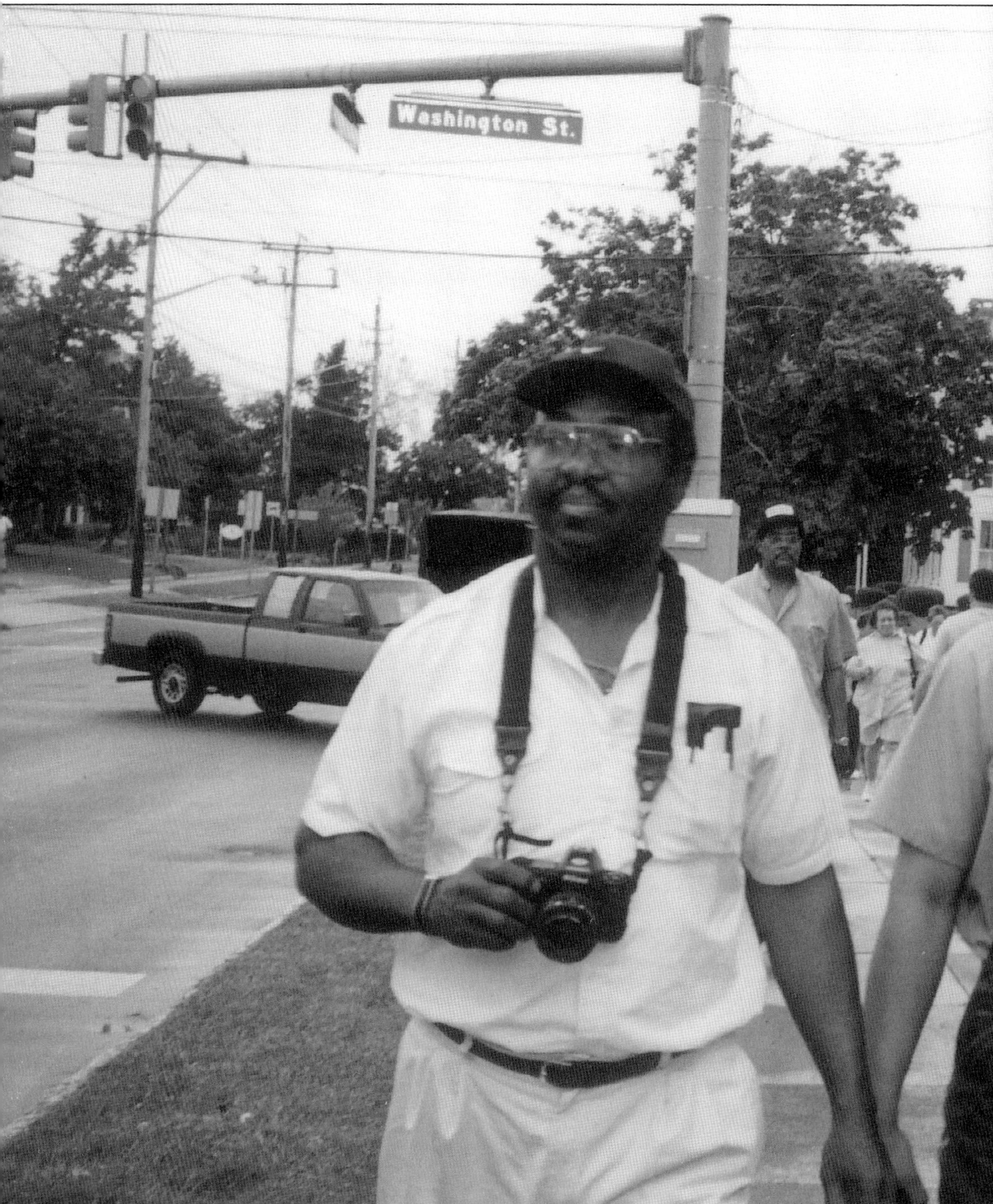

Appearing here, from left to right, are Malachi Burton, P.J. Hainey, and John Boyd. In a struggle to fight discrimination by the USDA for denying black farmers loans and the loss of many black-owned farms, concerned citizens rallied in support to keep more black farmers from losing their land. A lawsuit was filed against the USDA, and they admitted wrongdoing

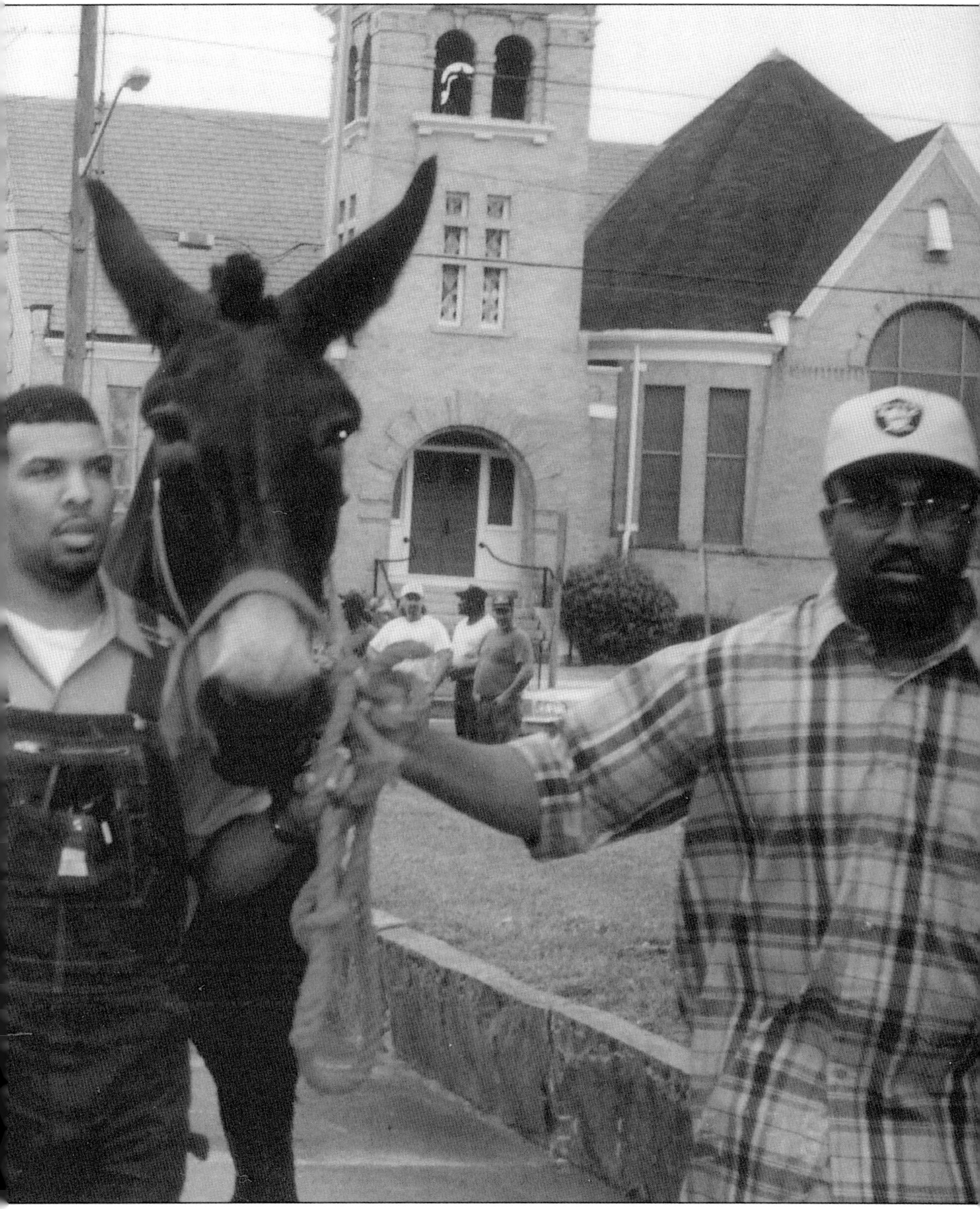

and discrimination against minorities. Pictured here, Struggle, a mule from Kinsale, traveled many places, such as the White House, U.S. Capitol, and the Department of Justice, as well as to courthouses in the tri-state area, promoting awareness in other communities for the prevention of further loss—estimated to be 1,000 acres of black-owned farmlands a day!

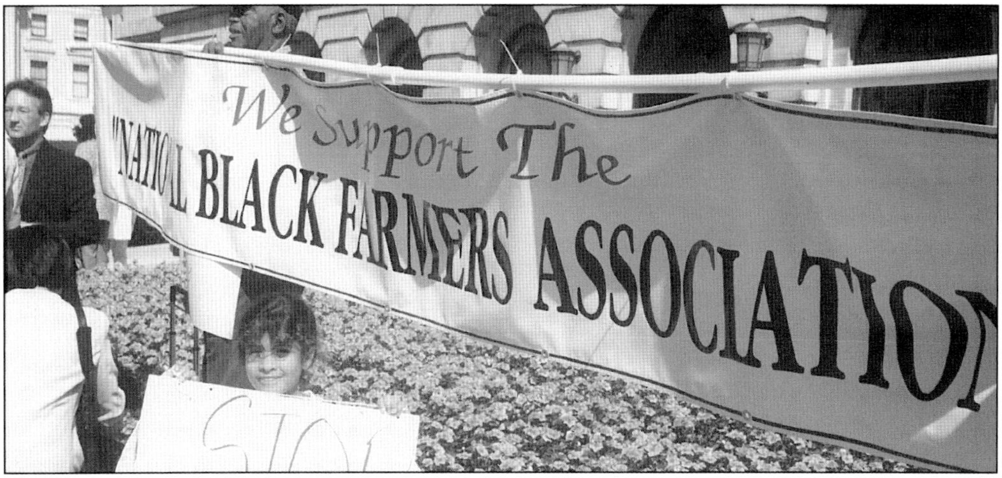

Alexis Melendez is standing tall in support of black farmers in this photograph.

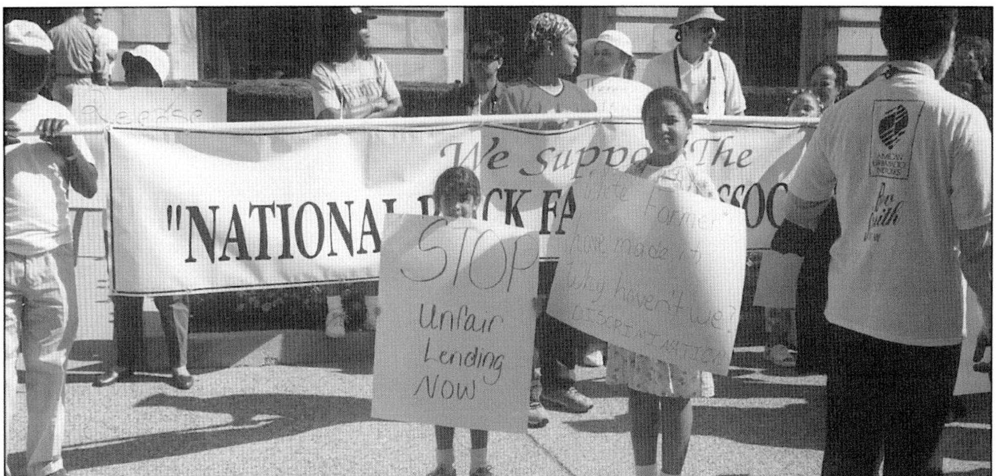

With signs to reflect what has been unfair treatment by the United States Department of Agriculture, young demonstrators, Alexis Melendez and Raven Harris, raise awareness to the plight of black farmers.

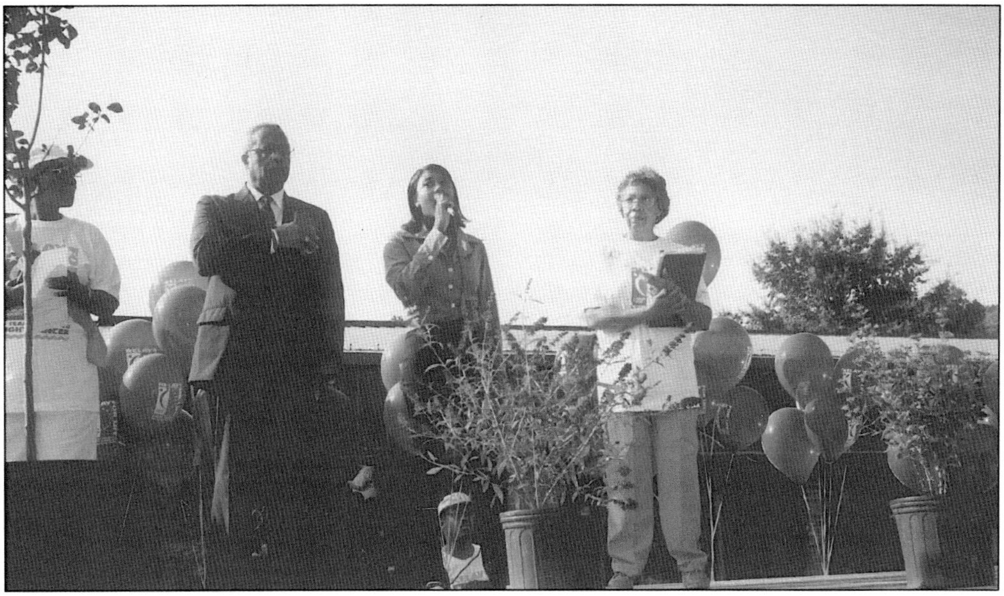

American Cancer Society's Westmoreland County chapter was chaired for many years by Hazel Edna Newton Smith Crabbe. She continues to provide money for cancer research and testing and treatment for many throughout the community.

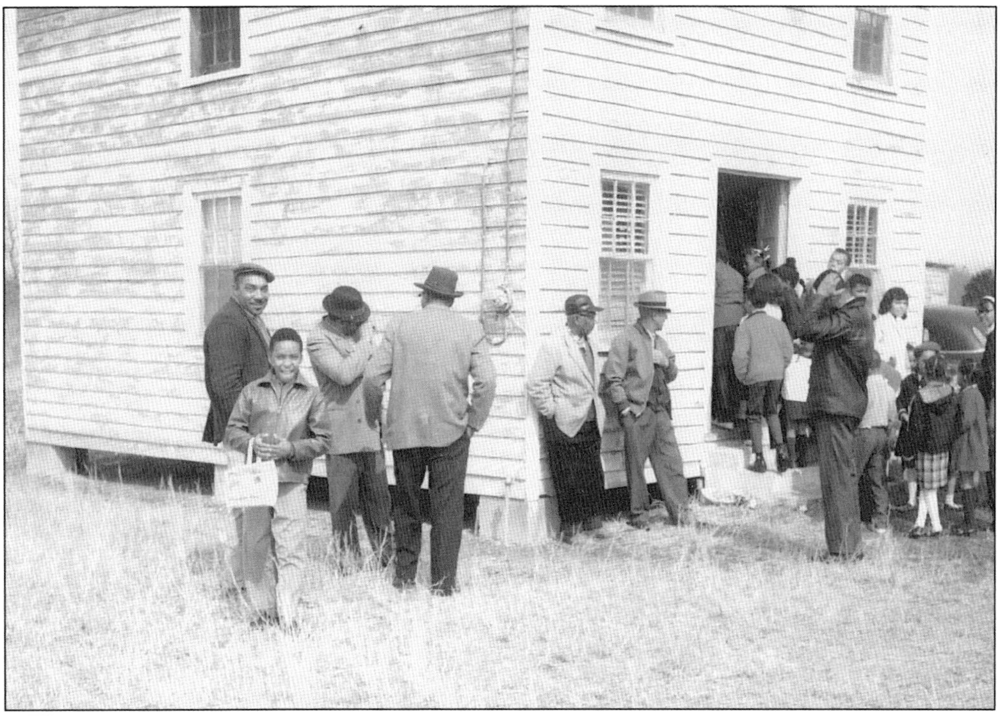

The Masonic Hall in Mount Holly provided a gathering place throughout the year and an Easter egg hunt for the children of the area, as seen here. Many other lodges once existed in the area, such as the Grand United Order of Oddfellows, House of Ruth, Golden Chain, Knights of Tuson, and the Eastern Star.

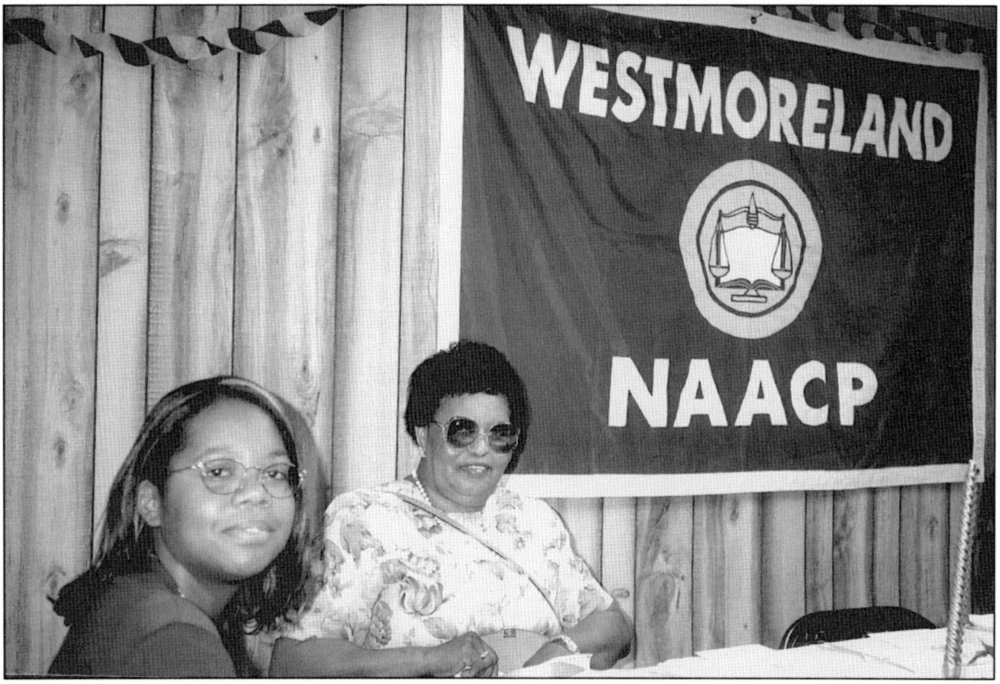

Gladys Johnson, seen here on the right, served as the president of the Westmoreland County branch of the NAACP. The branch was established by William P. Clayton, a farmer, businessman, and civic leader.

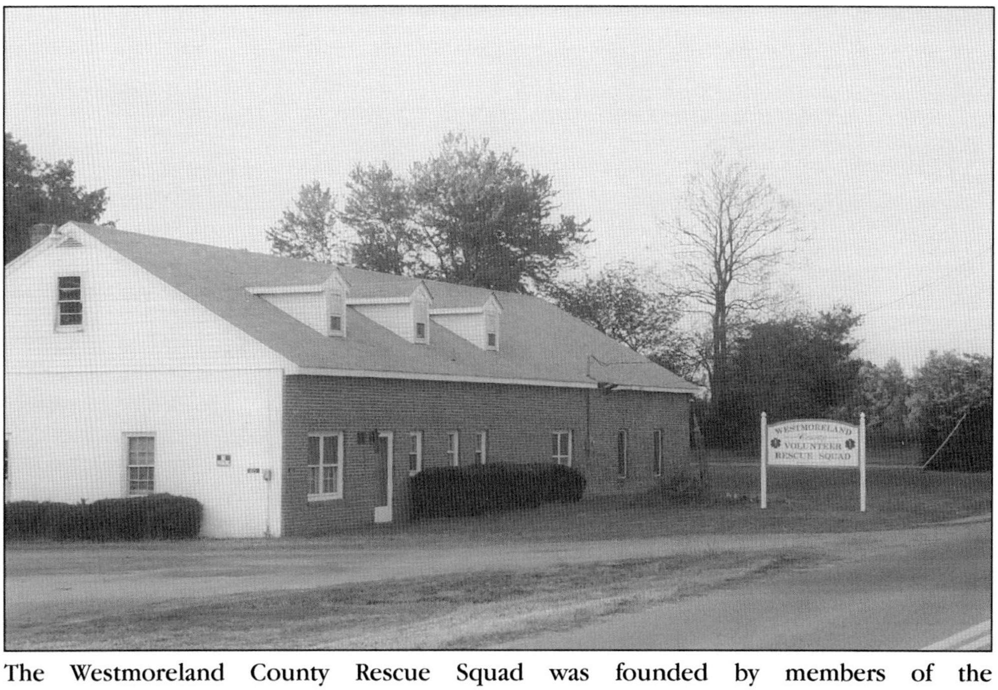

The Westmoreland County Rescue Squad was founded by members of the black community.

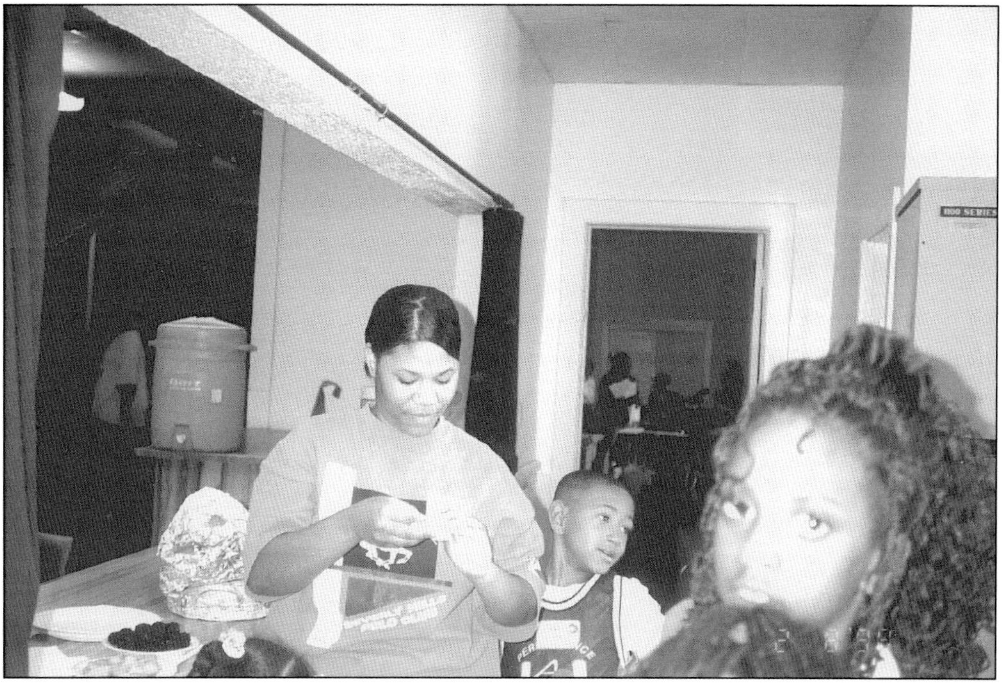

High school student Amanda Smith is shown here as a volunteer teacher's assistant at the summertime Westmoreland County Youth Camp.

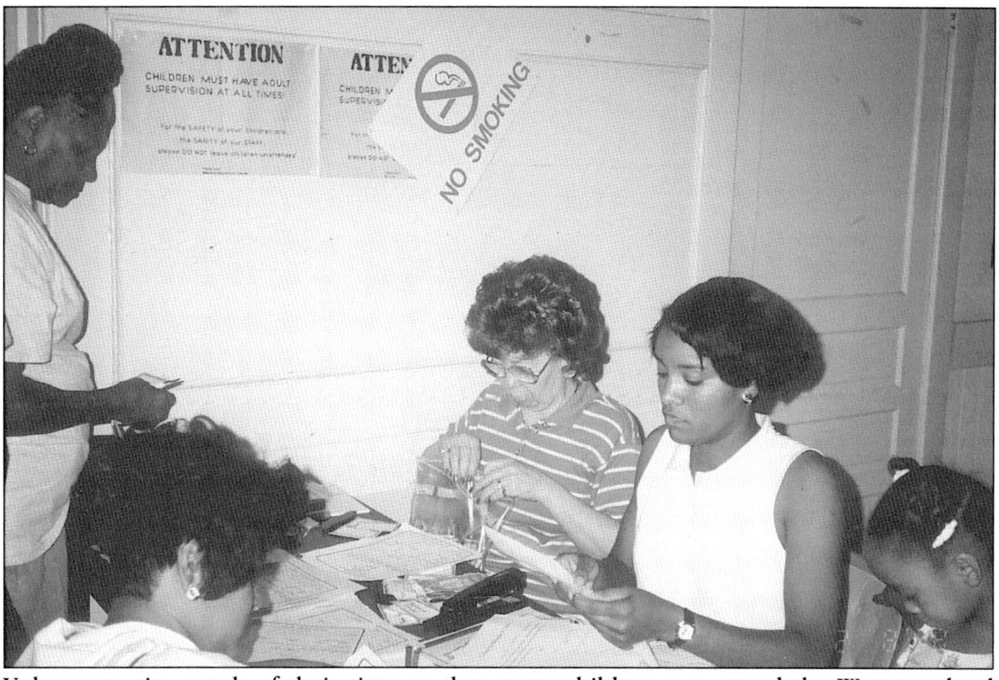

Volunteers give much of their time so that many children can attend the Westmoreland County Youth Camp. Melanie Hall and Valerie Ashton are seen here hard at work registering children for a week of learning and fun.

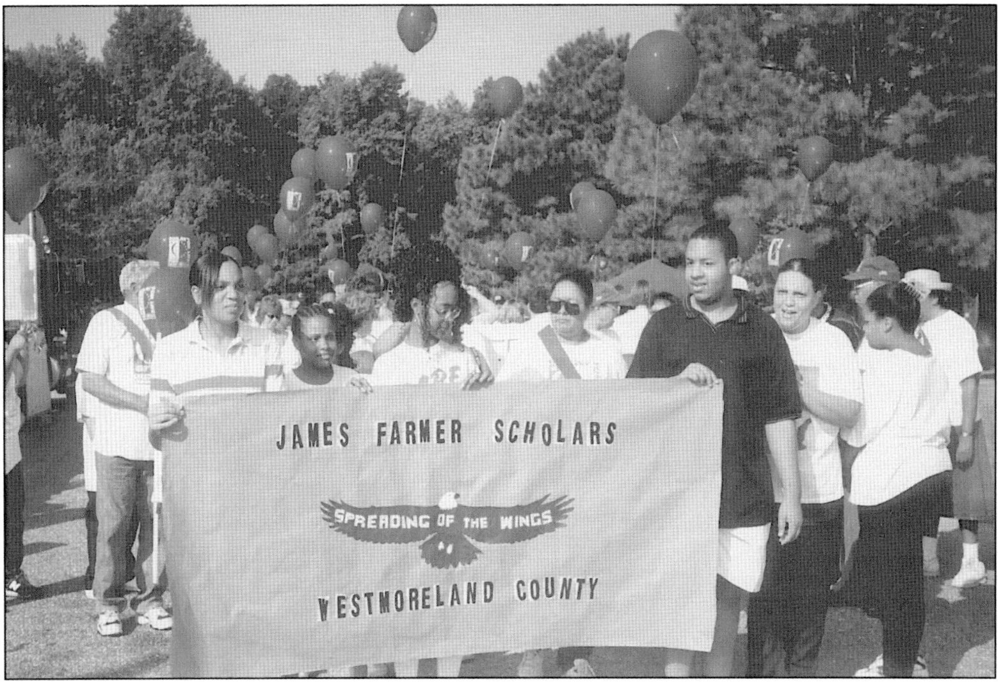

The James Farmer Scholars are the county's future leaders, for they learn the value of community involvement first hand through service. Their adult advisor is Mrs. Joan Weldon.

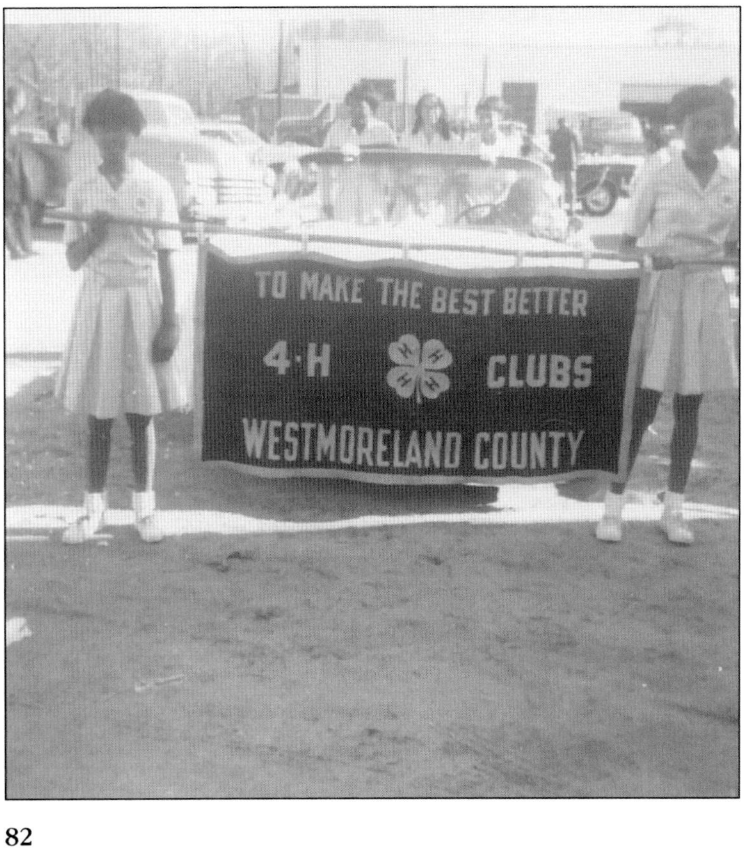

This view shows A.T. Johnson High School's 4-H Club and their display during a May Day parade. (Courtesy of Yosif Roane.)

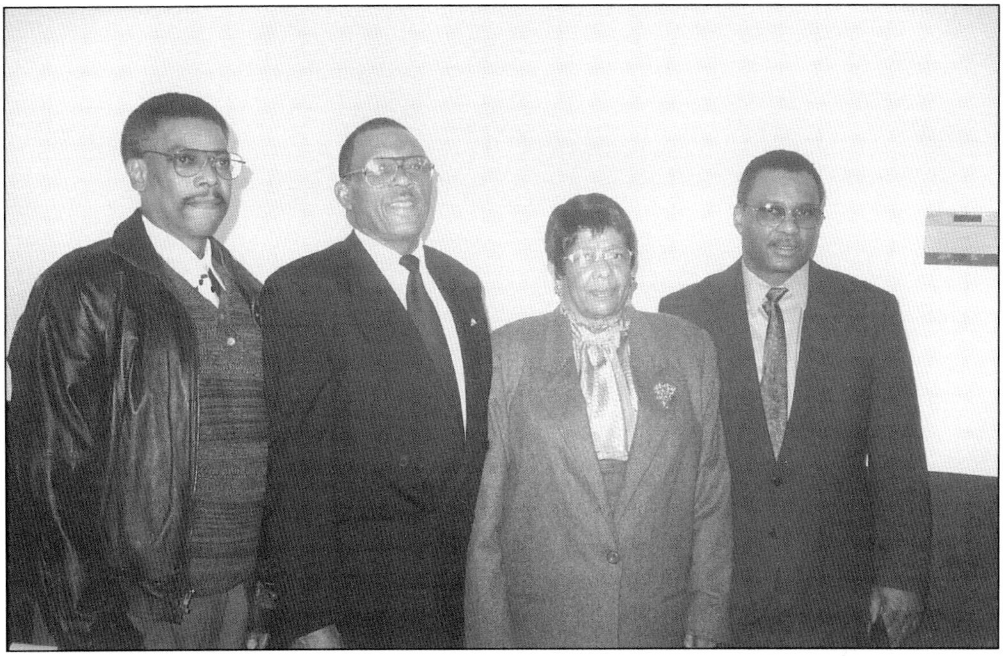

This was a day of celebration for the Smith family, as Carroll Smith was made a deacon in the Zion Baptist Church in Tucker Hill. From left to right, Norman; Carroll; wife, Pauline Miller Smith; and Carroll Smith Jr. were proud of the honor given.

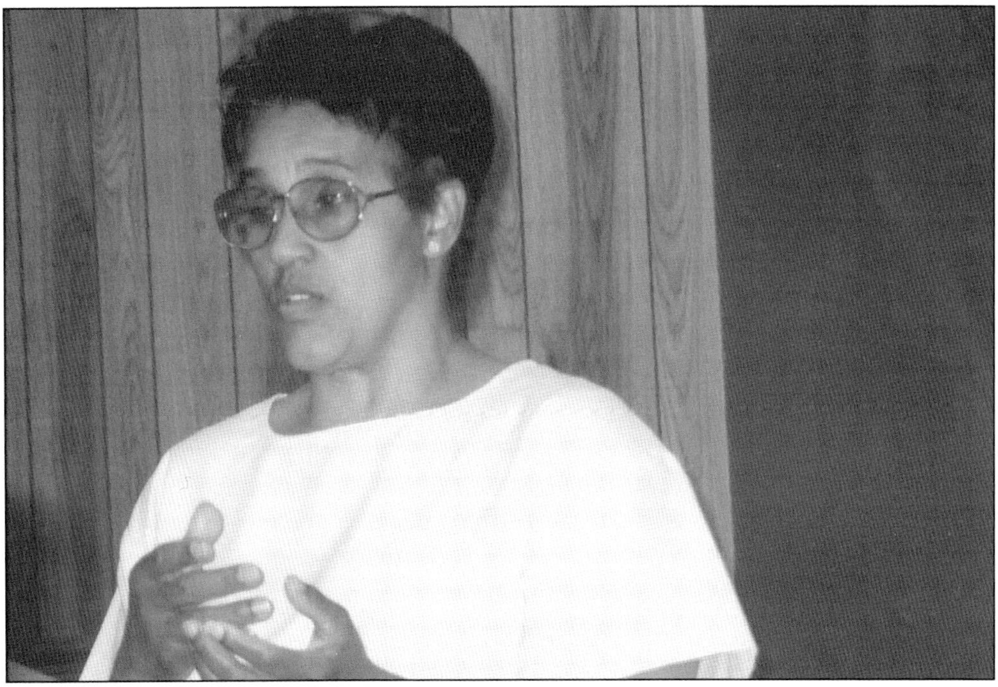

Joyce Clayton, assistant superintendent of schools in Westmoreland County, is the first black person to hold this position. She is a product of the Westmoreland County educational system.

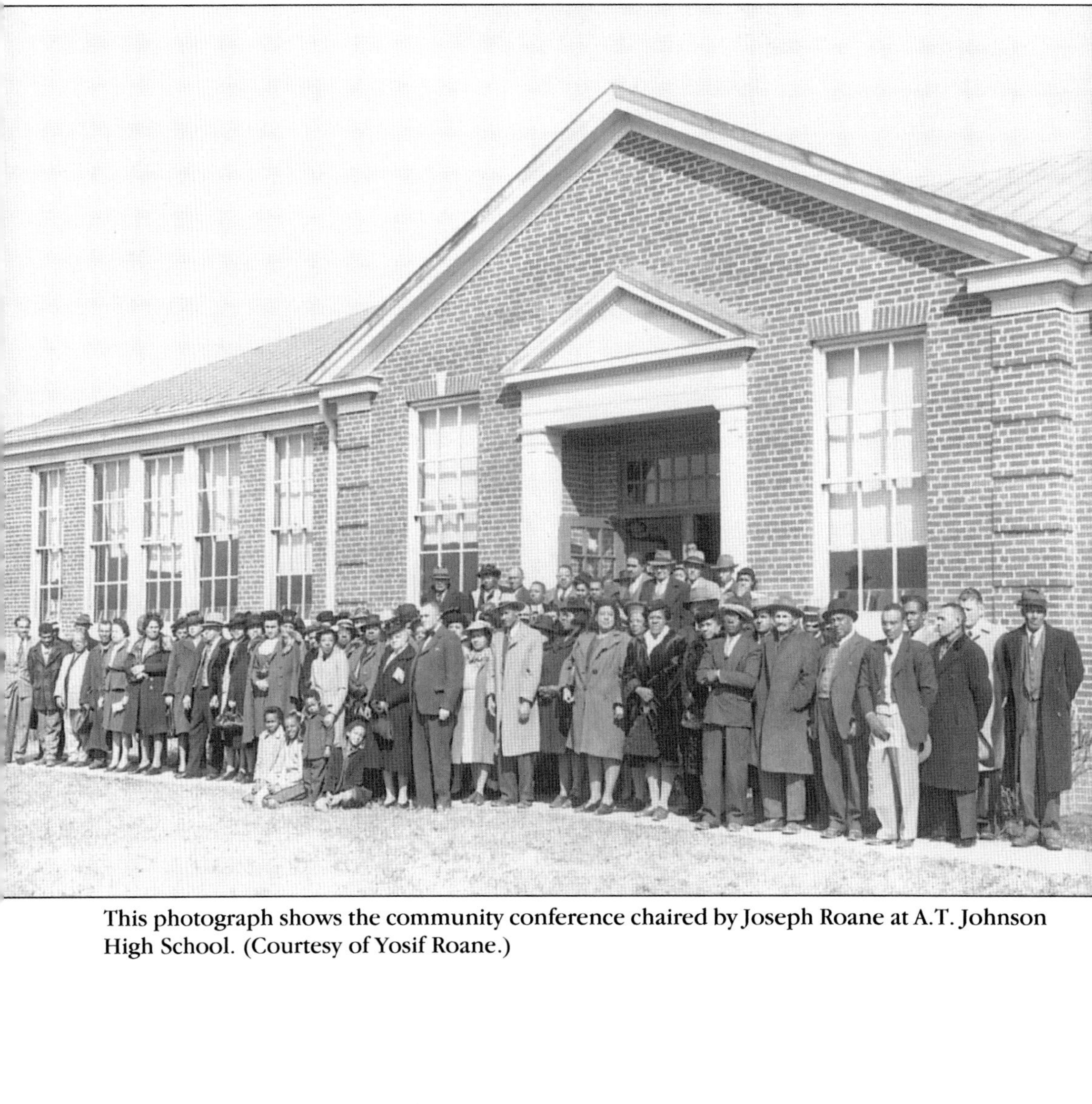

This photograph shows the community conference chaired by Joseph Roane at A.T. Johnson High School. (Courtesy of Yosif Roane.)

Four

Artists and Artisans

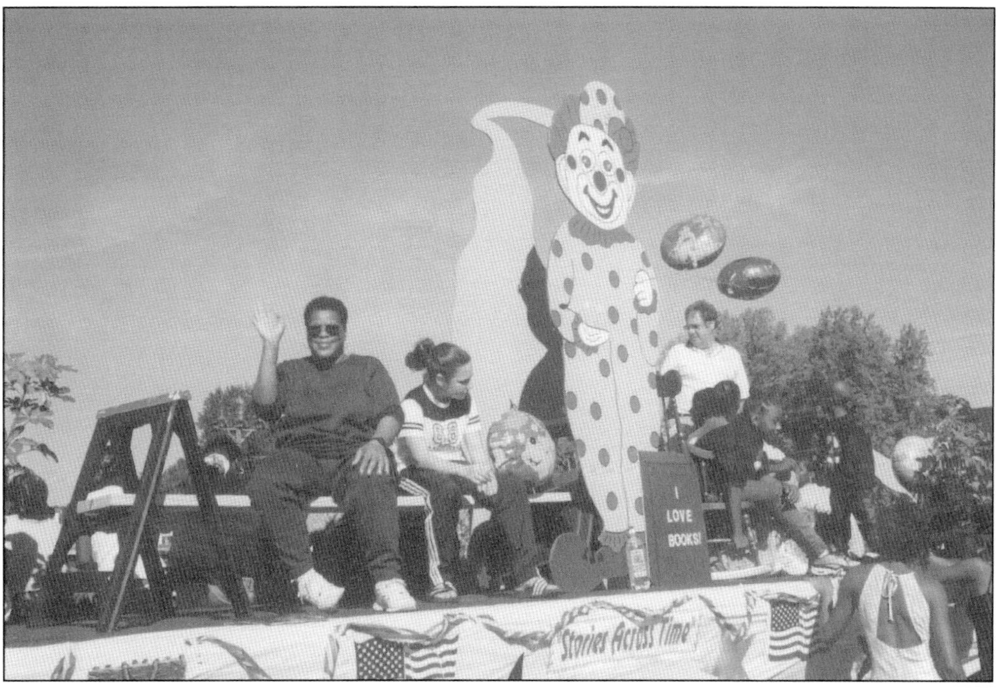

Weavers of the Word is the Westmoreland County storytelling guild. Vanessa Fisher waves to the crowd as the Weavers ride by at the Montross Fall Festival. This group is a part of the National Storytellers Association. Mrs. Daisy Howard Douglas of Sandy Point is the executive director. A yearly "Tellebration" is hosted on the same night around the world for every group in the national association.

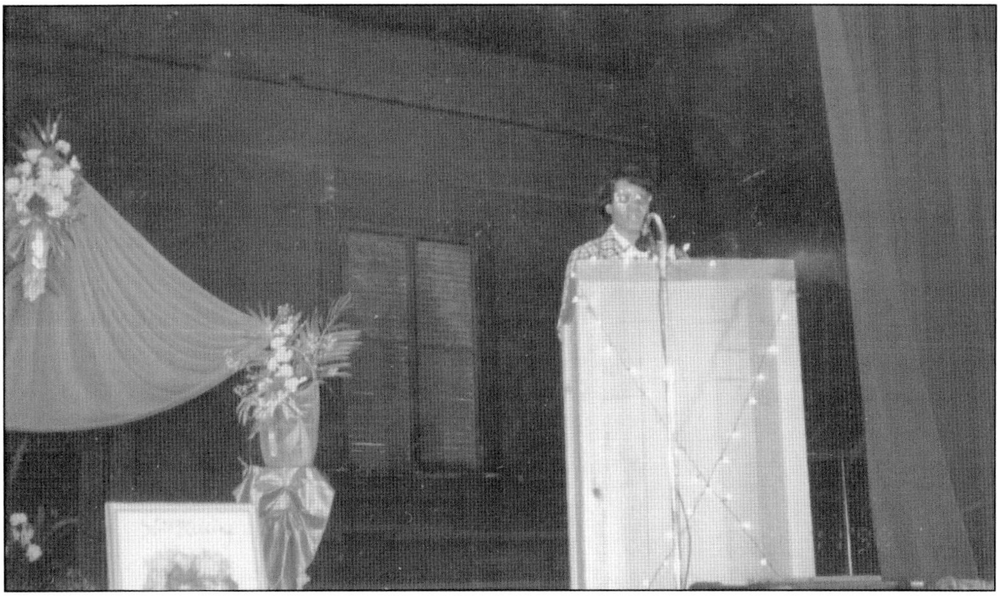

Martha Newman is a noted poet who writes original poems for many community events.

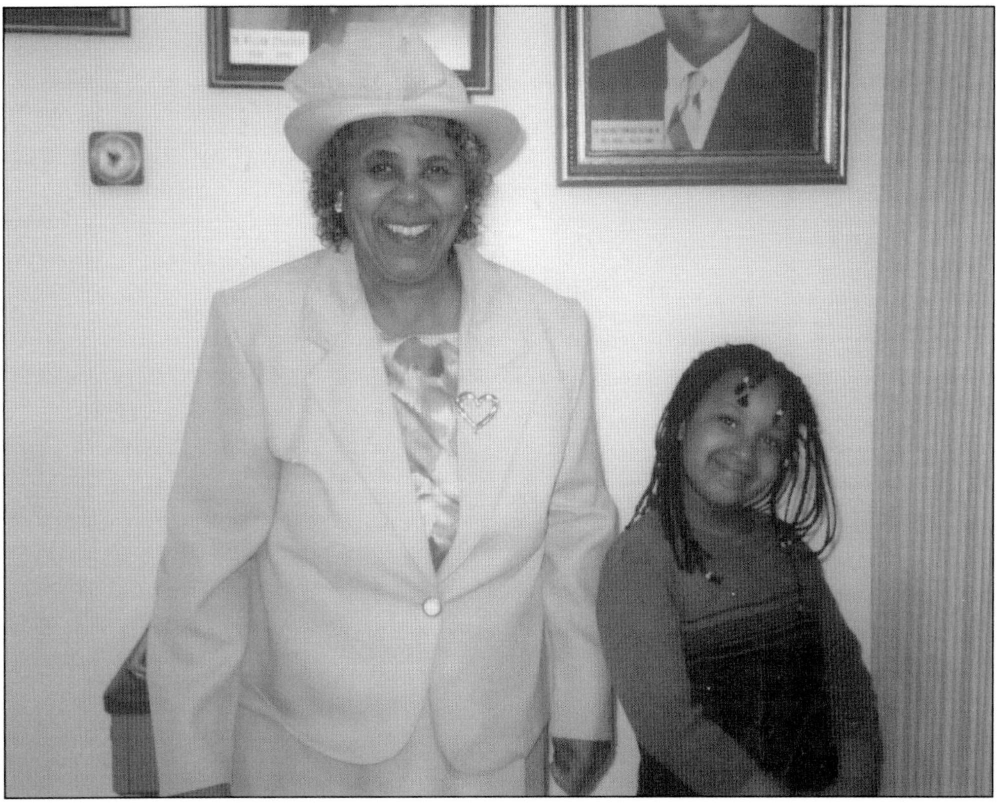

Edna Jenkins Jones recalls from memory just about every poem from her youth and writes some poetry of her own. Her great-granddaughter Katherine Stewart is gifted musically; Katherine is also the great-granddaughter of W.P. Clayton.

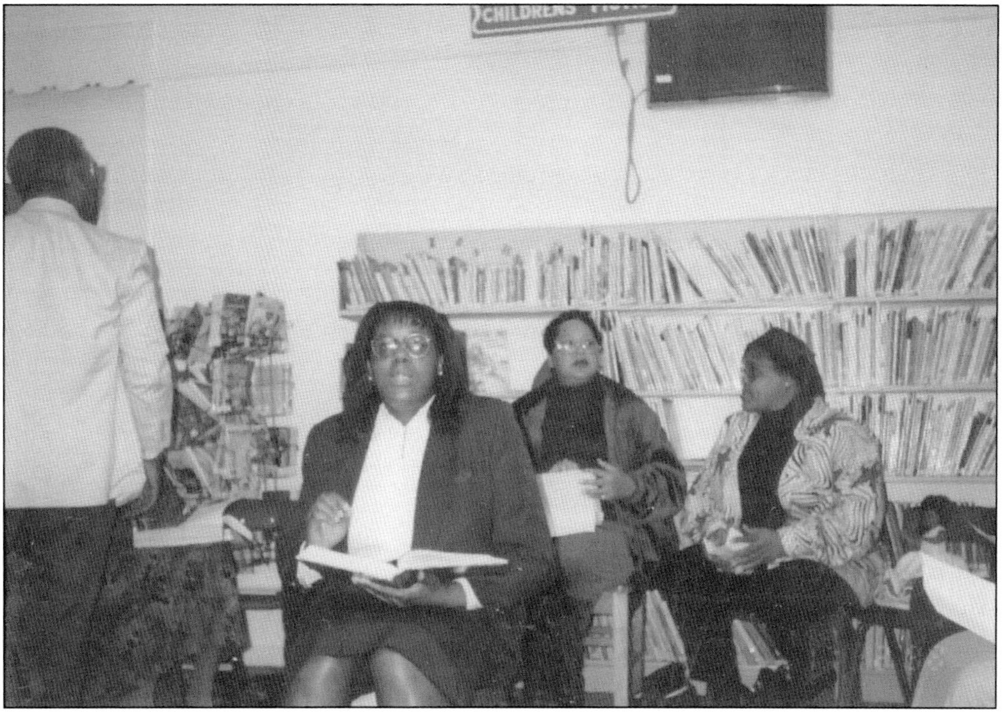

Weavers of the Word members Rita Wagstaff, Gloria Newman, and Vanessa Fisher participate in a storytelling session at the Montross Library.

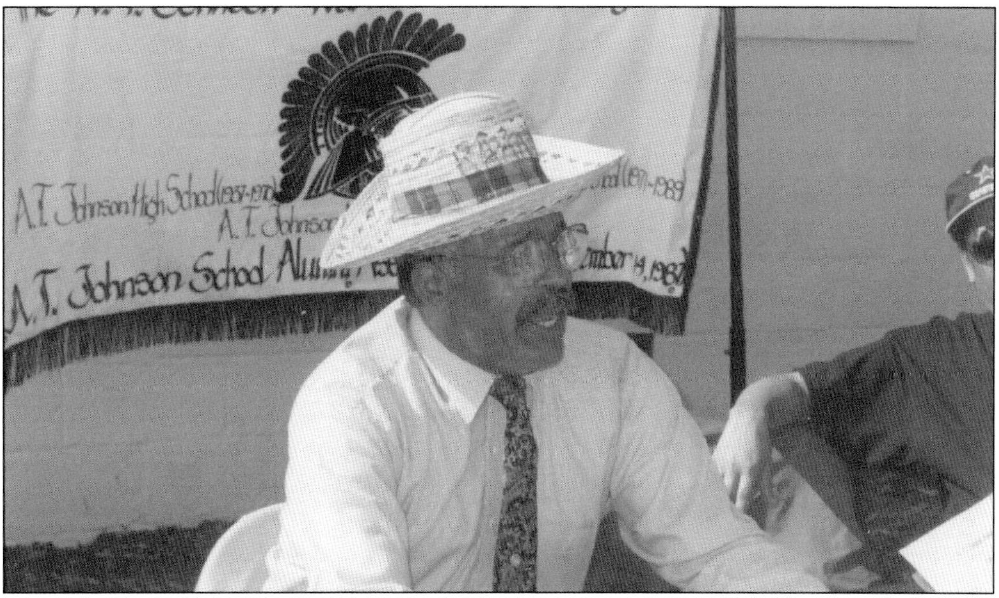

Olie O. Smith is a Westmorelander who is a product of the county's educational system. In 1958, he became the principal of Montross Elementary School, which was open when the last of the one-room and two-room "colored" schools were closed. He has gone on to become a successful businessman and author of *Find a Way or Make One*, a collection of selected writings.

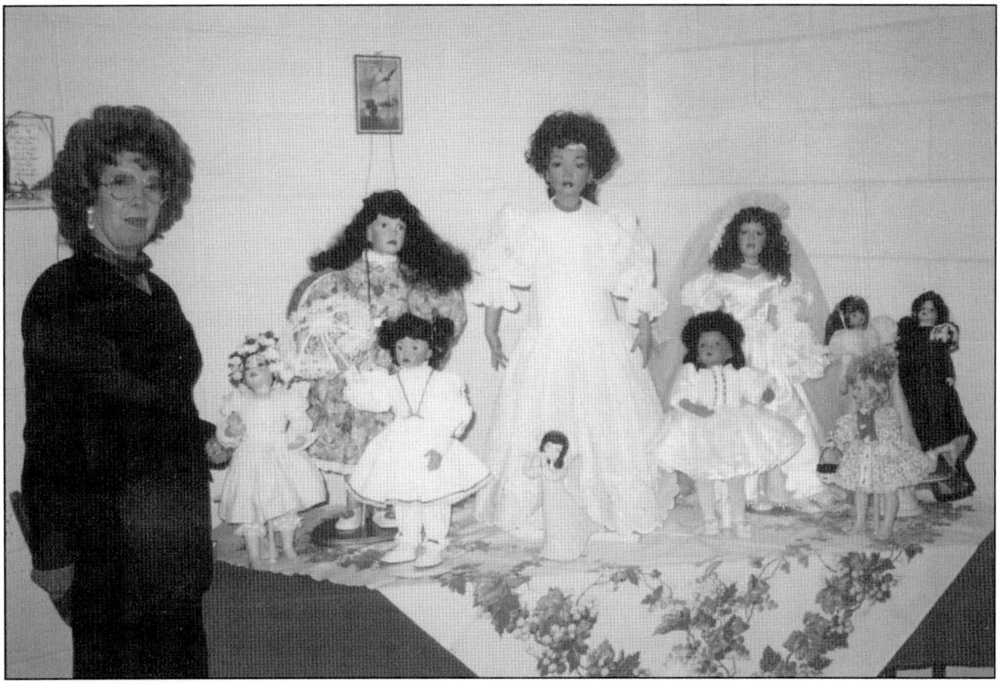

Melanie Hall, the executive director of the Jensi Ashton Art Center, designs and makes porcelain dolls.

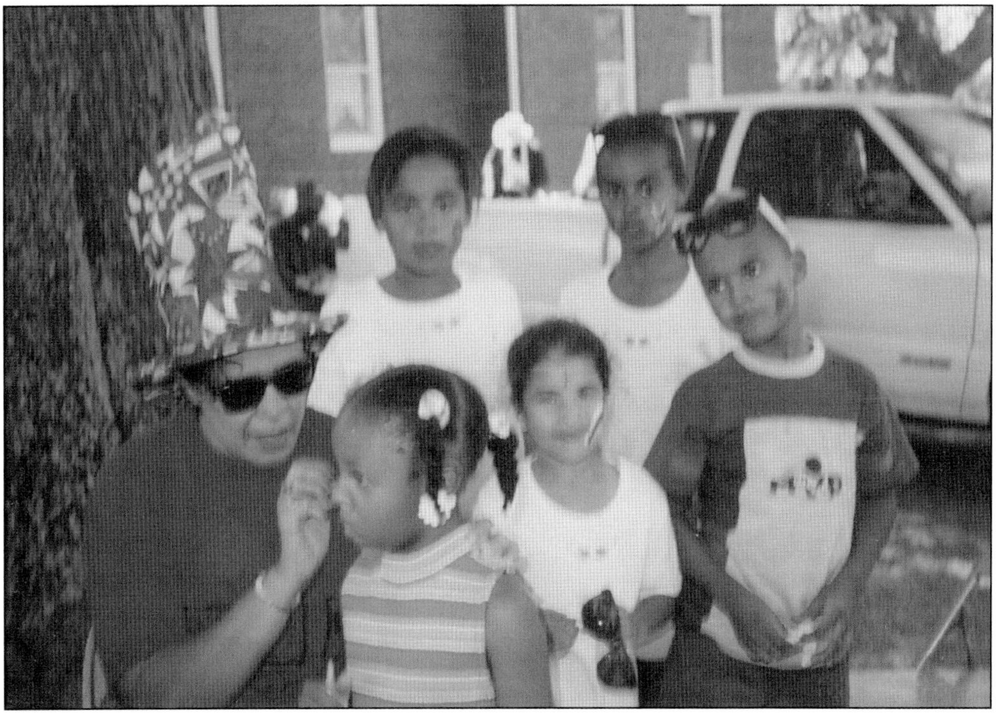

Children lined up for hours to have their faces painted by Cassandra Burton at the Zion Fun Day.

Briana Henry learns about blackberries at youth camp.

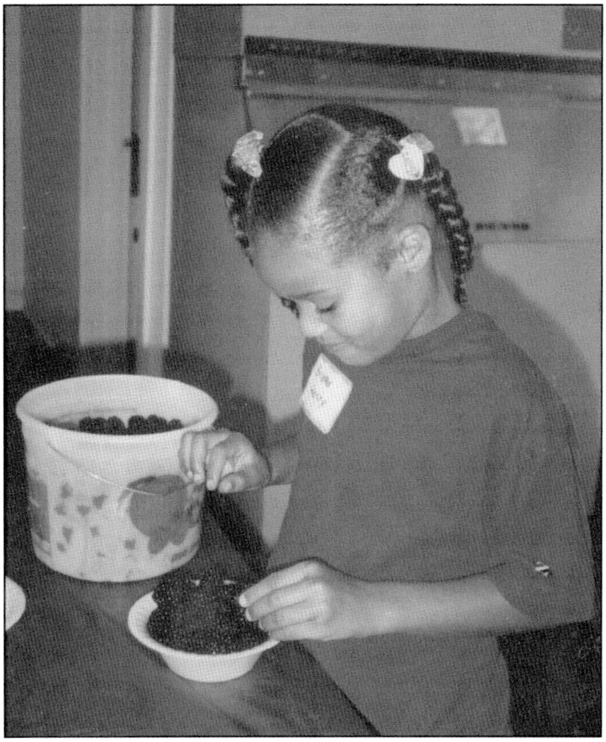

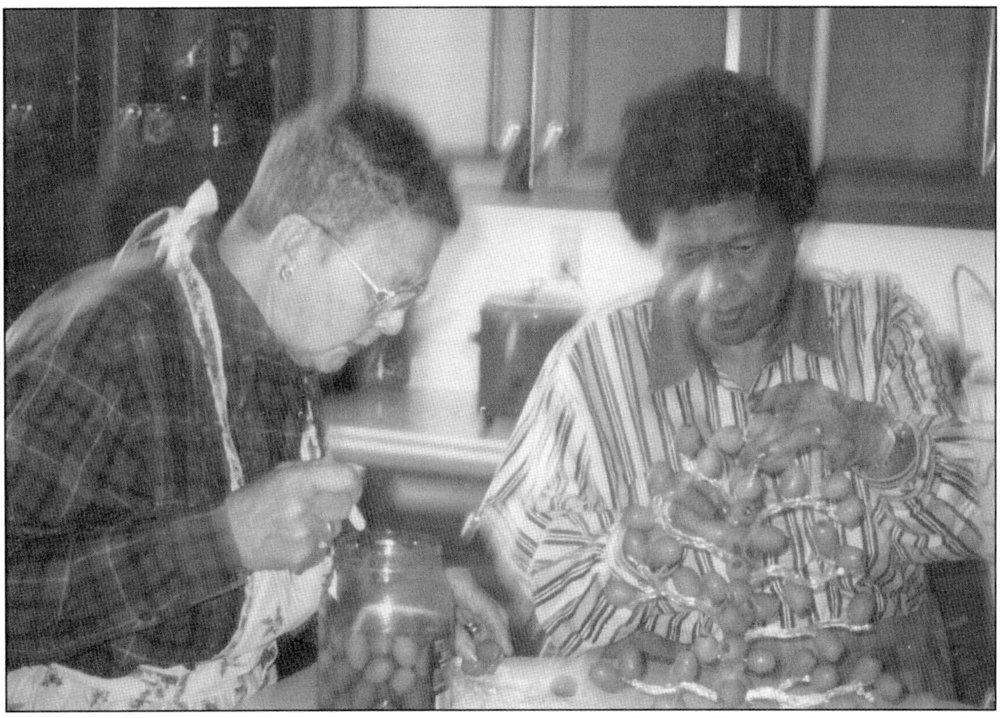

Culinary artists-at-work Bessie Brown Greene and Pauline Miller Smith create another creative food arrangement. Pauline Smith has been a Washington, D.C. caterer for years.

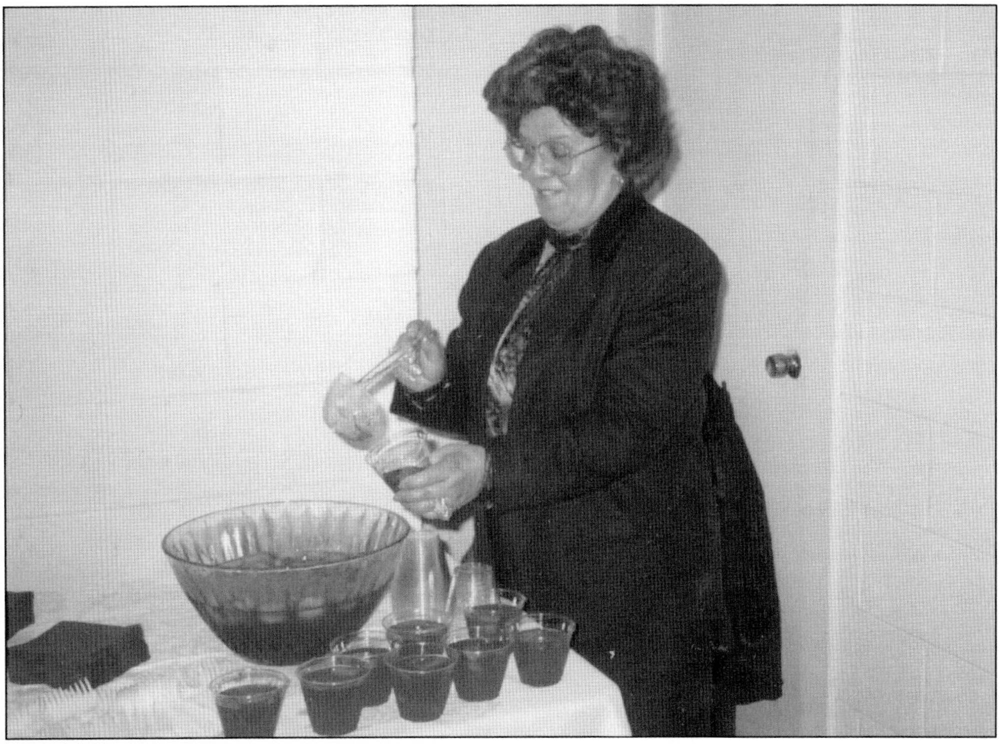

Delores Green demonstrates the art of serving.

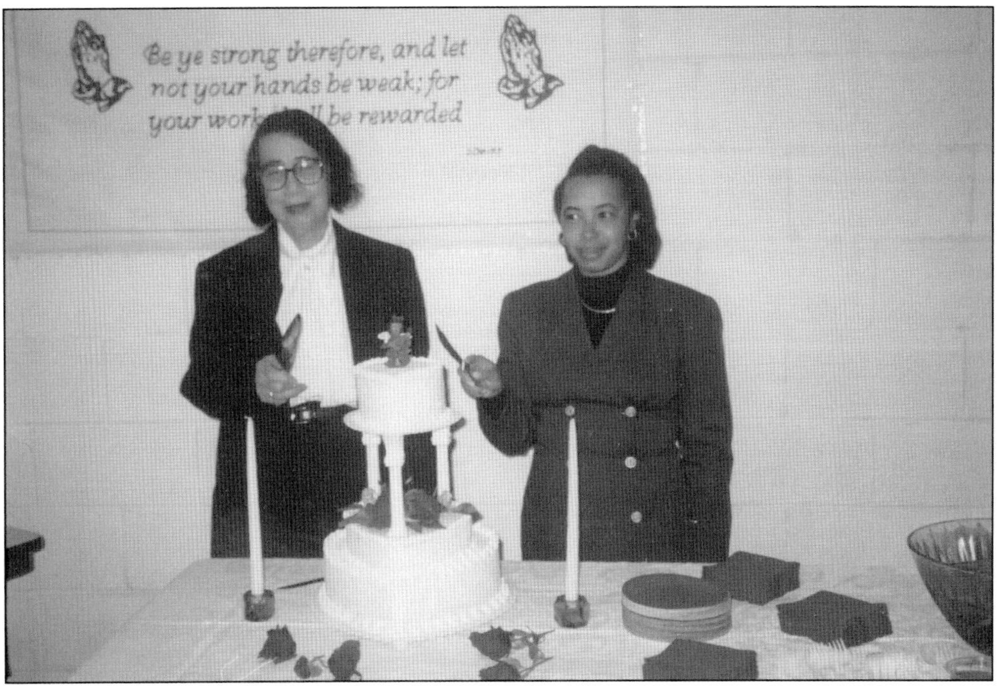

This is another beautiful culinary creation produced by cake decorator Elnora Ashton Johnson of Johnsontown Road.

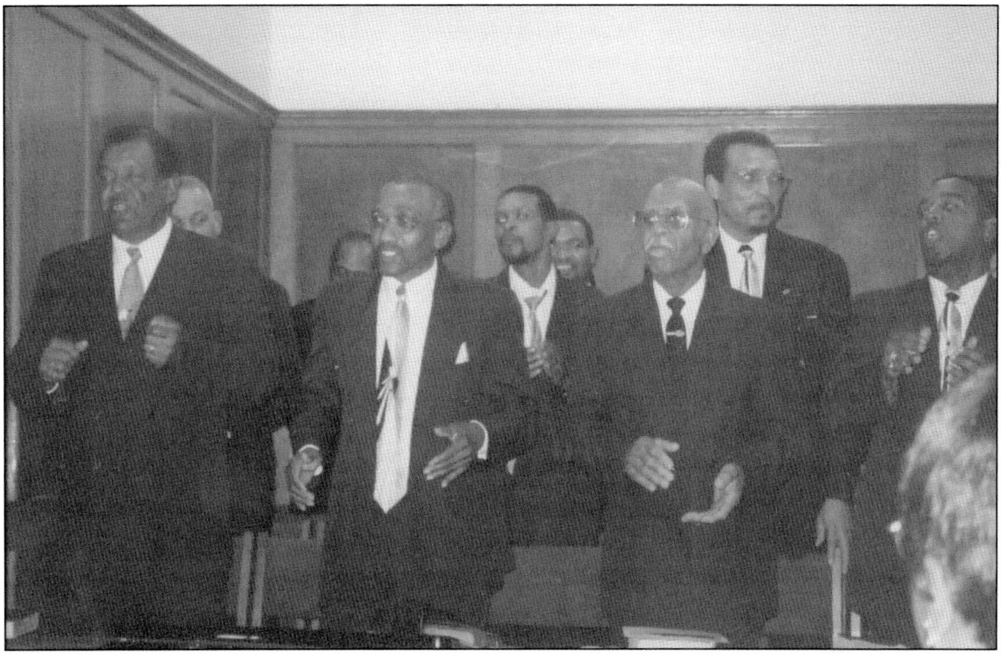

This photograph shows the men's chorus of Tucker Hill's Zion Baptist Church.

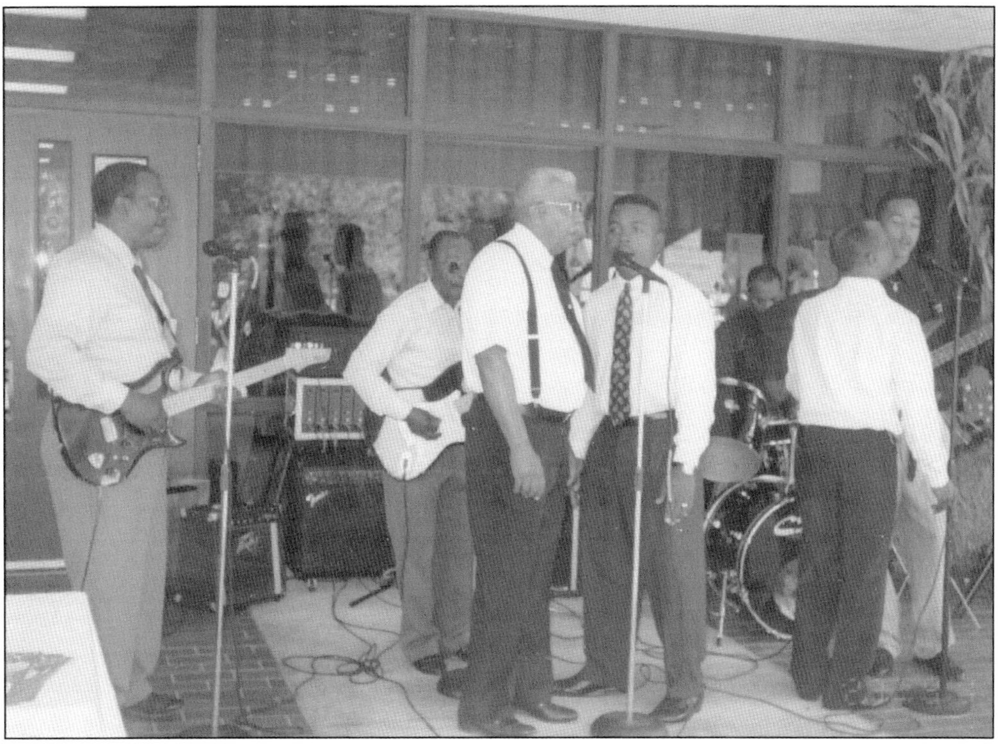

This view shows the men's chorus of Jerusalem Baptist Church. The men are identified as follows: Arthur Henry, Deacon John Tate, Norris Thompson, O'Neal Jackson, Norman Jones, and Garfield Johnson.

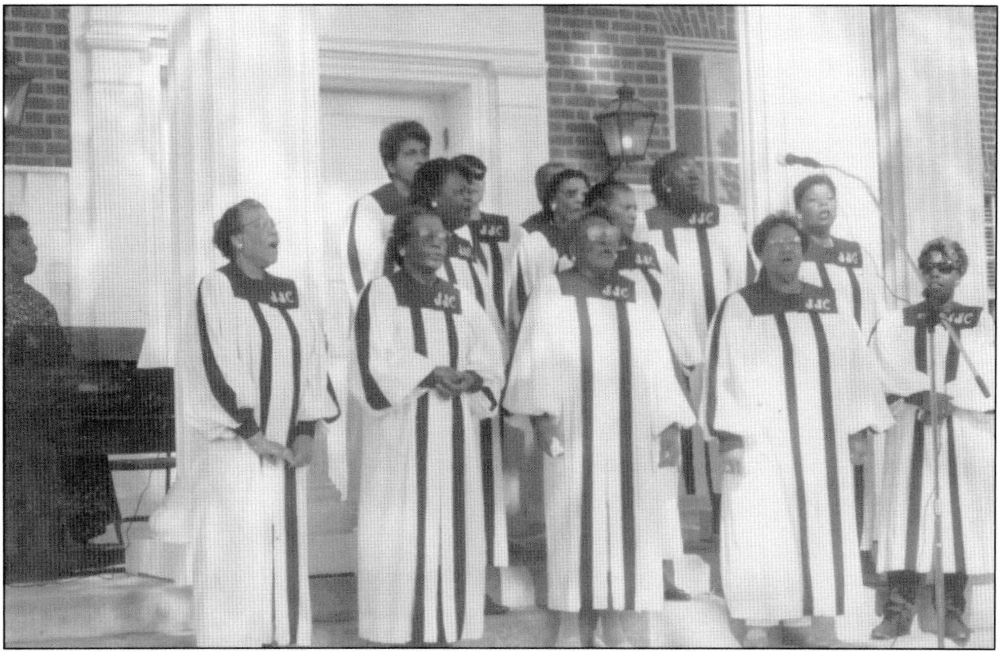

This is the Siloam Mass Choir of Montross.

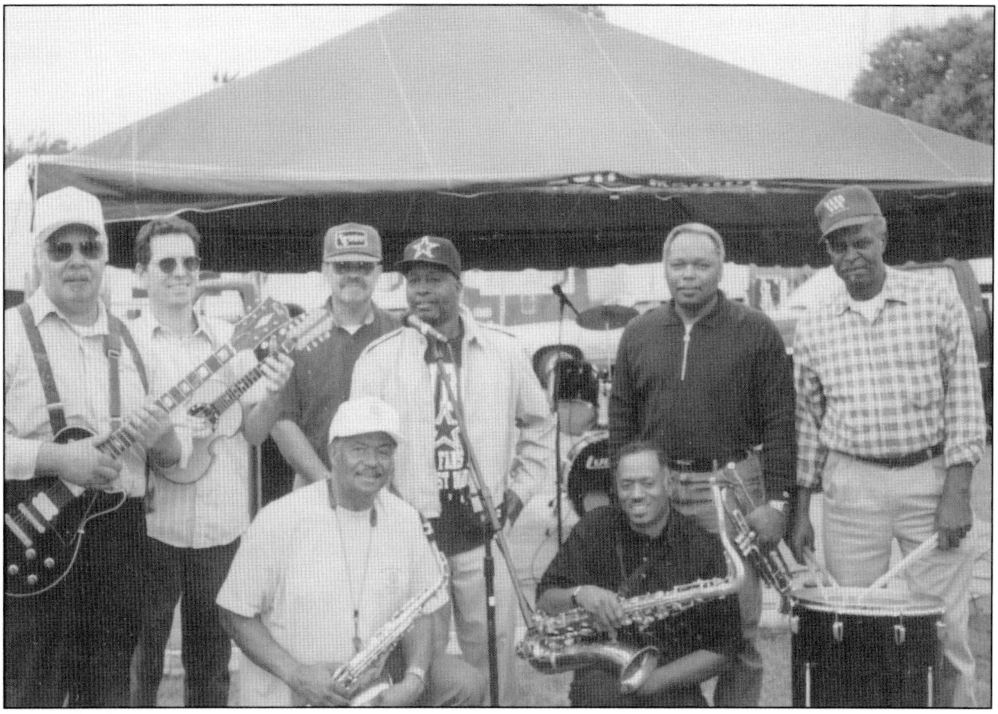

"The Blasts from the Past" is a band that plays popular tunes from the 1950s. The group, which started in their youth, is still having fun together today. They are identified as follows: William Hunter, George Hunter, Oliver Sutter, Albert Lewis, Ray Cupid, Ern Lewis, and Yosif Roane.

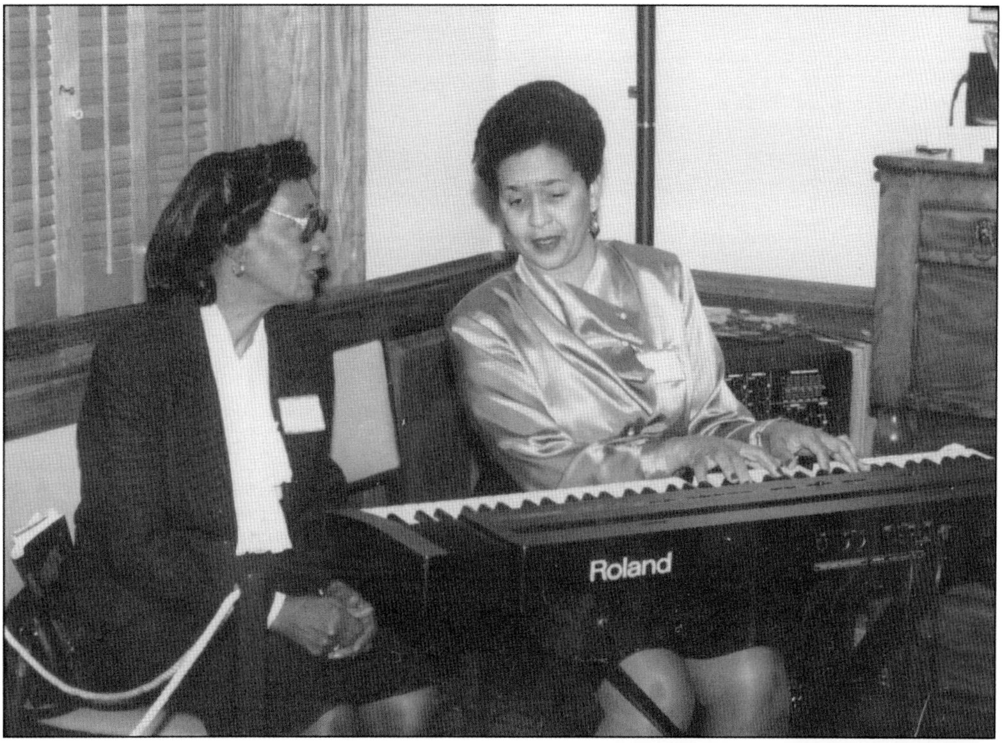

Odessa Weldon Dixon Smith, pictured here with one of her students, is an extremely talented musician.

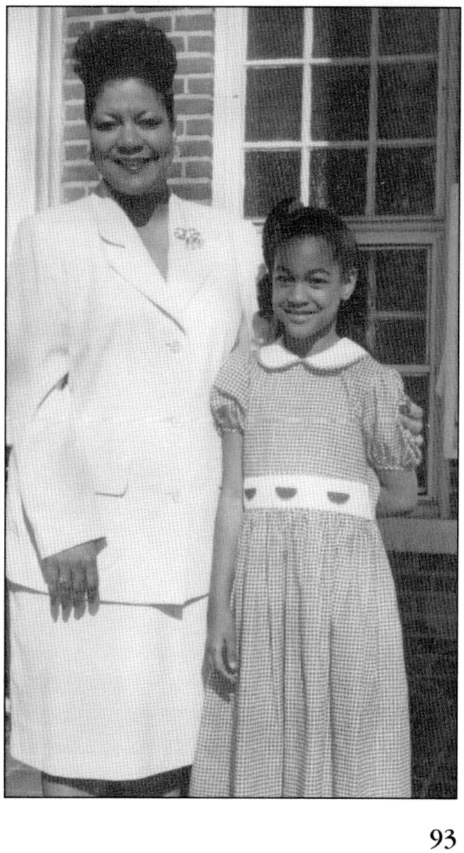

Adrianne Jones and daughter Angelica Baylor are always a delight to watch perform their extensive collection of gospel tunes.

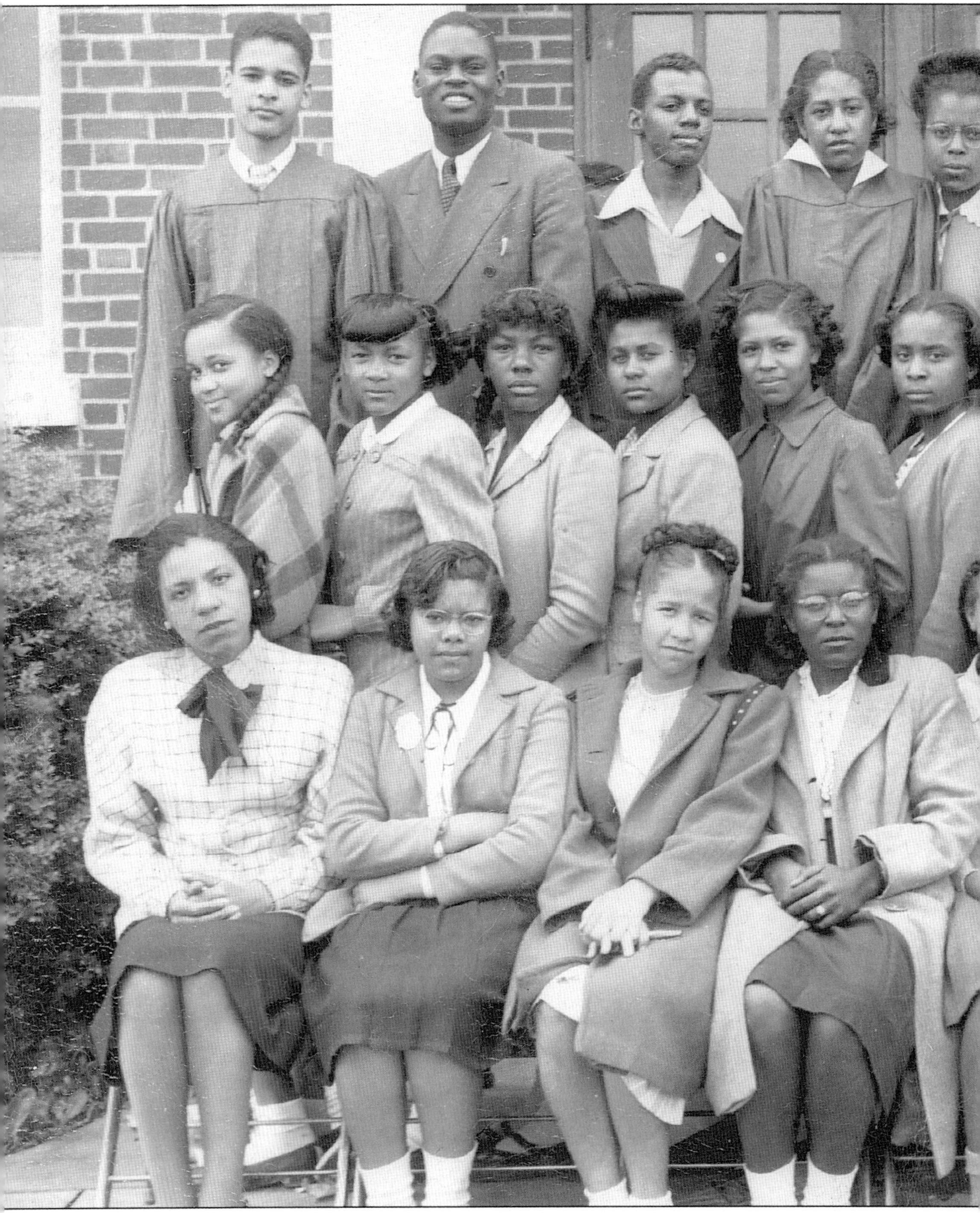

This is a portrait photograph of the A.T. Johnson High School Glee Club. Its members are identified, from left to right, as follows: (first row) Mrs. Hogan Taylor, Annibel Cary, Gladys Tate, Elizabeth Campbell, Eima Tate, Enna Tate, unidentified, Ruth Green, Jewell Taylor, and unidentified; (second row) Barbara Burrell, Lois Harrison, two unidentified girls, Elizabeth

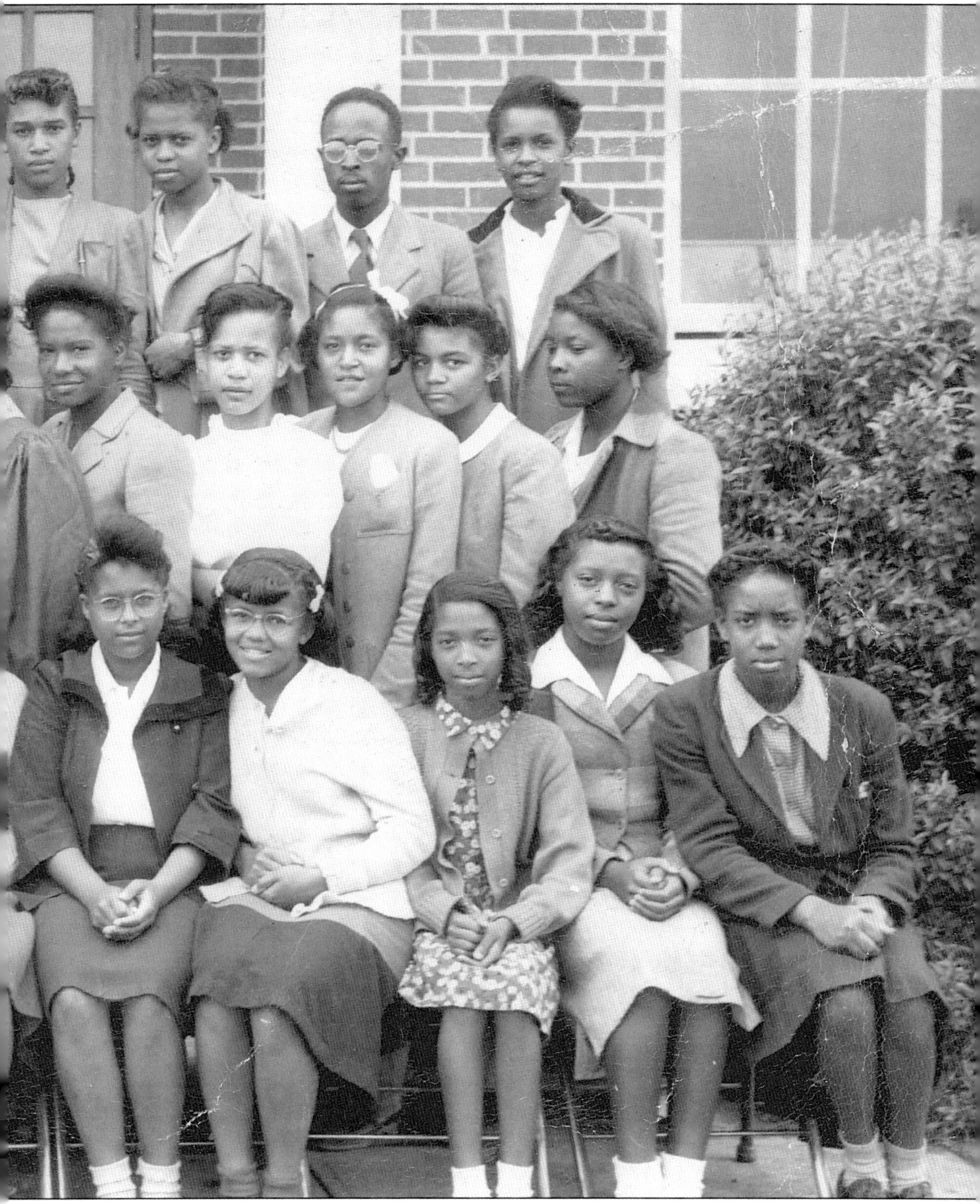

Hall, Peggy Clayton, Ethel Peterson, ? Payne, Cherry Dowling, unidentified, Irene Brown, and Plum Hall; (third row) James Roane, Ben Cupid, Clinton Richards, unidentified, Mary Tolson, Dozey Weldon, Gladys Johnson, Waverly Taylor, and Elizabeth Wilson.

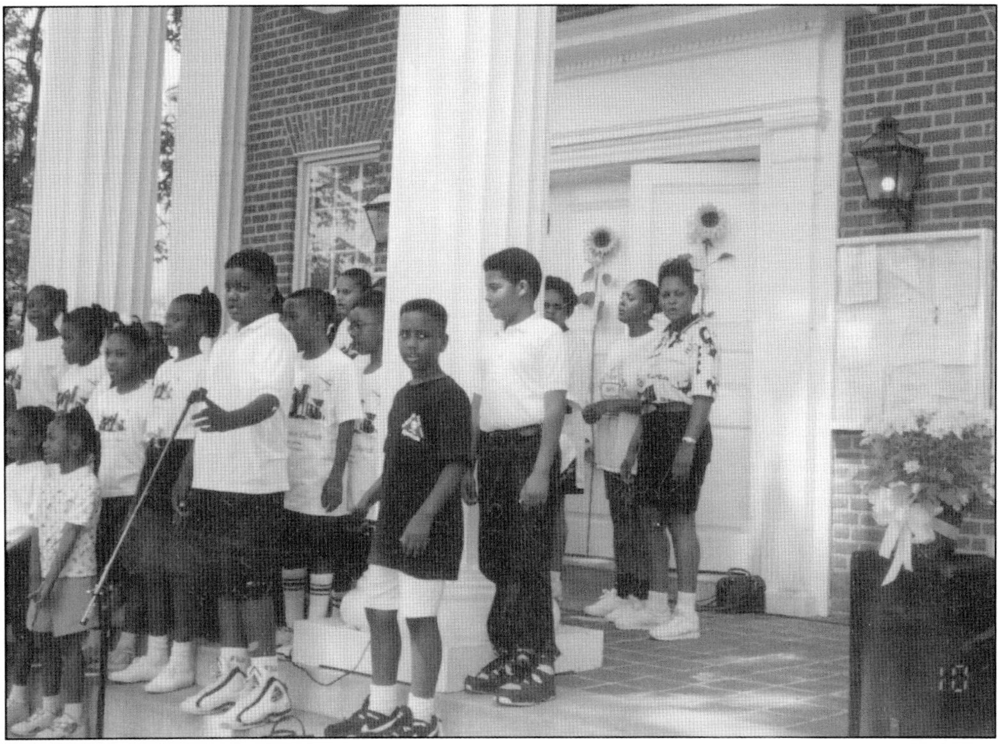

This photograph shows a performance of the Little Angels Children's Choir of the Zion Baptist Church in Tucker Hill.

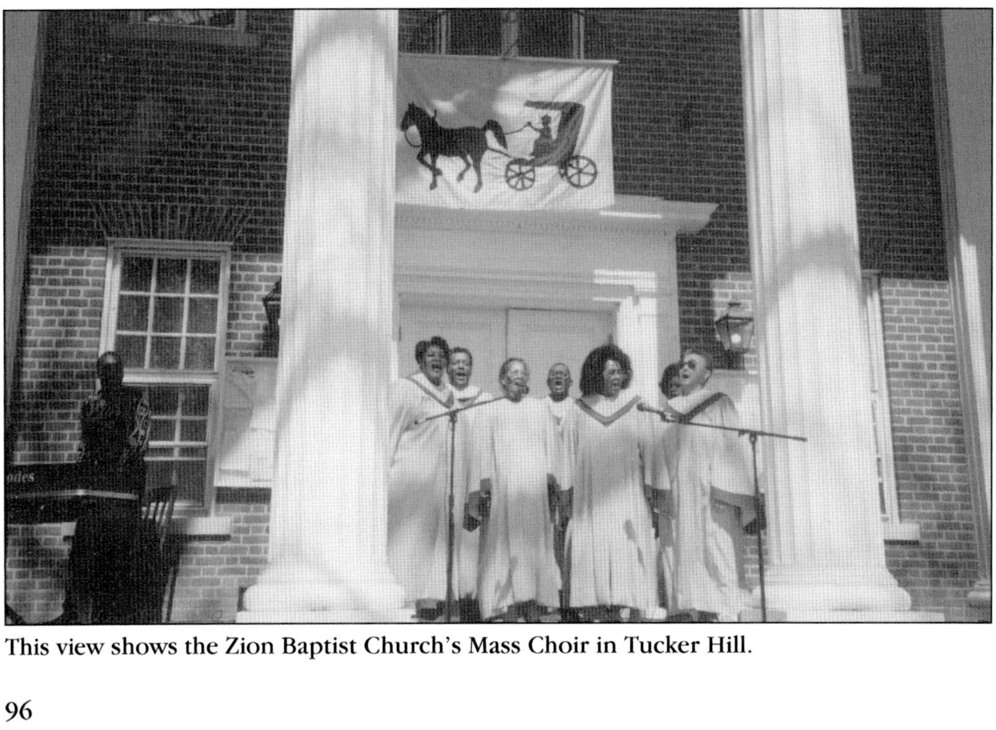

This view shows the Zion Baptist Church's Mass Choir in Tucker Hill.

Five

Moments to Remember

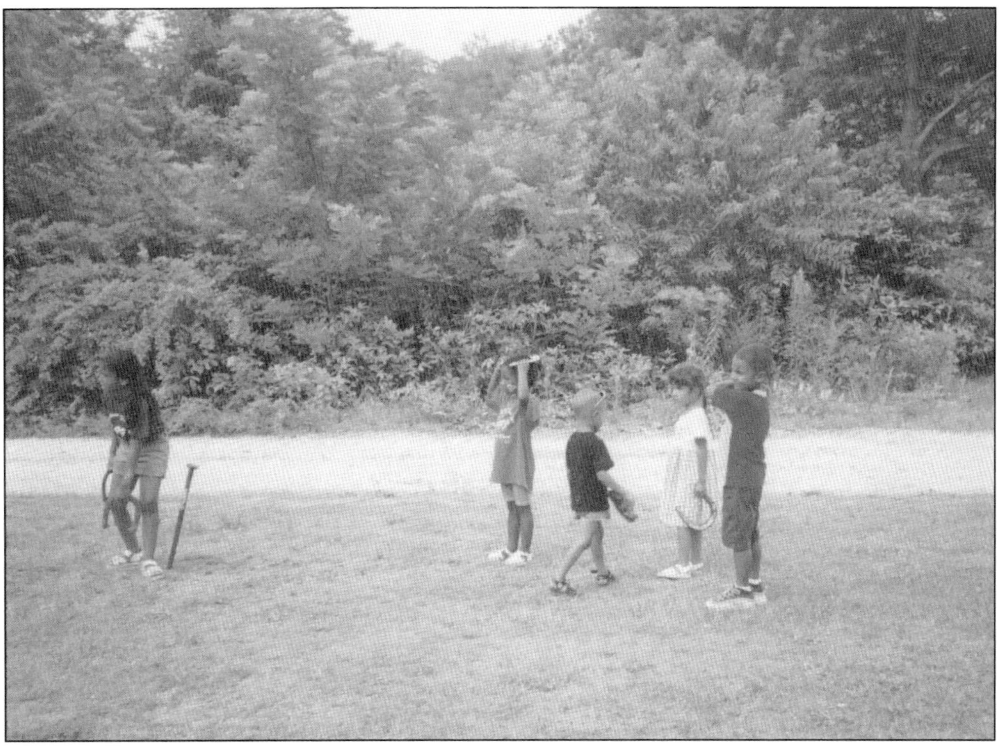

The art of tossing horseshoes is practiced by Leslie Roane, Kristen Miller, John Melendez, Alexis Melendez, and Idris Anderson.

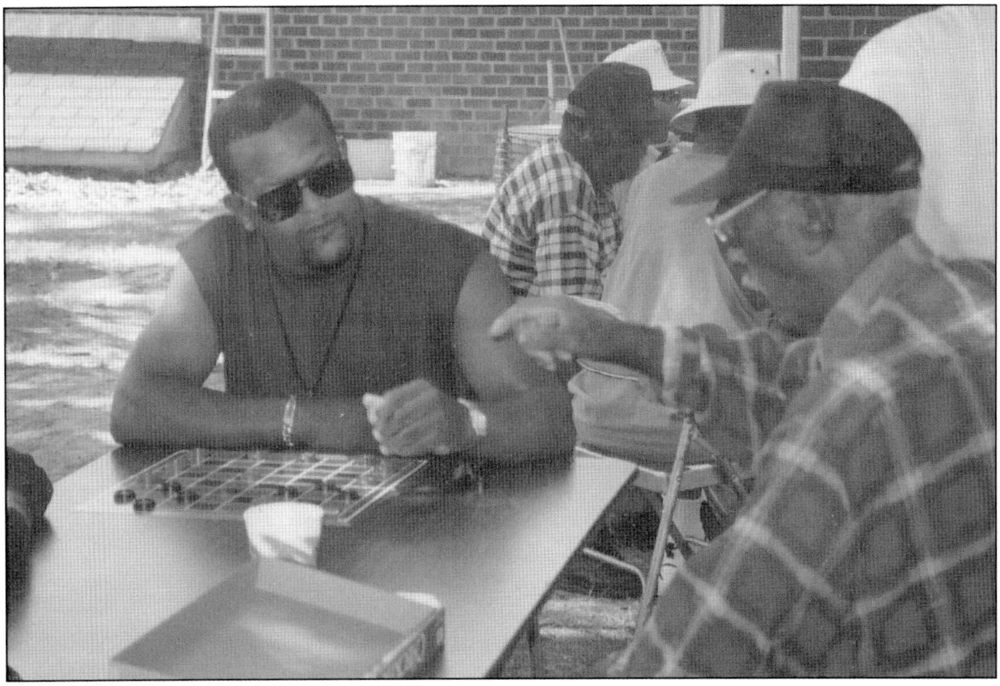

Sylvester Fauntleroy and James "Radio" Thornton are playing checkers under the trees on a hot summer day.

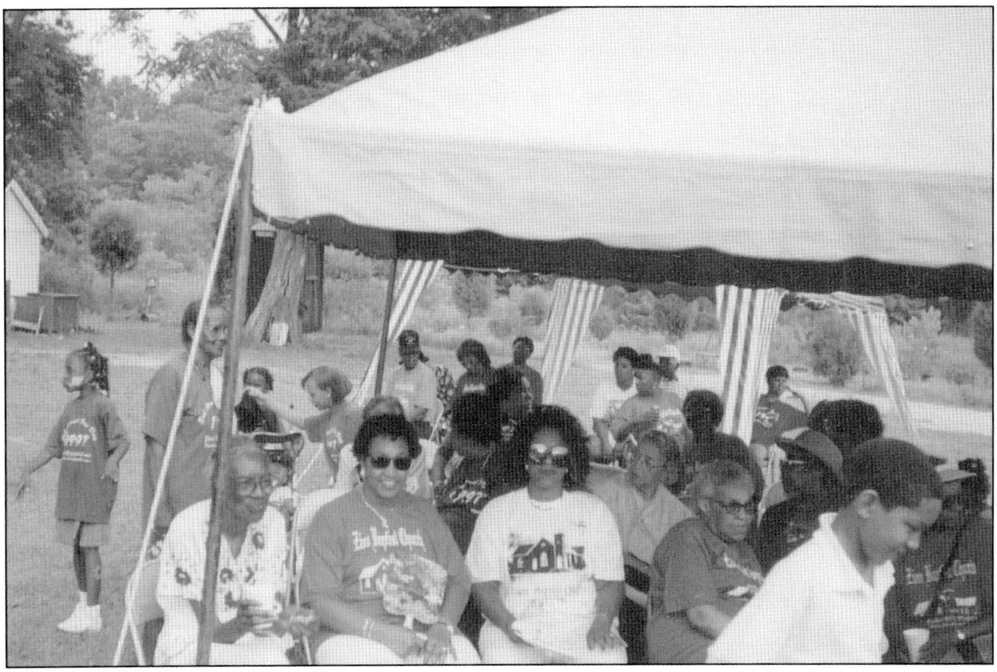

A tent is usually erected to provide shade for those wishing just to be spectators at old-fashioned summertime church events. Some still sit under the trees and enjoy the natural shade.

These children are enjoying games of days gone by sack racing, proving that these old games can still be fun.

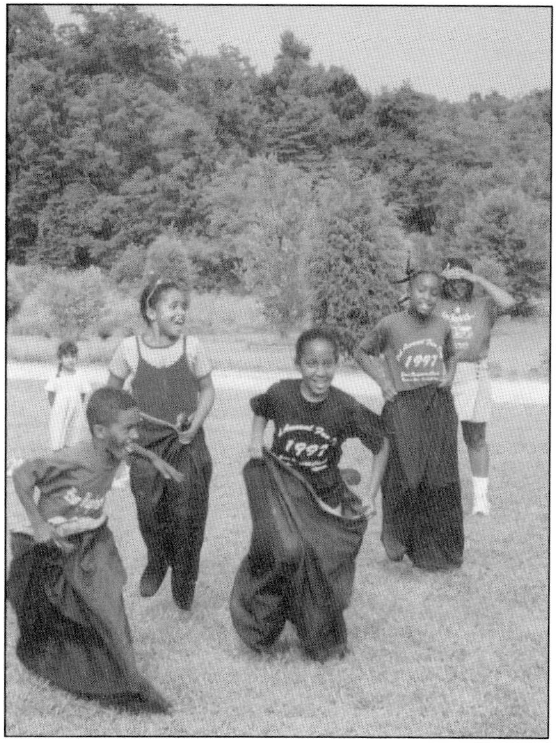

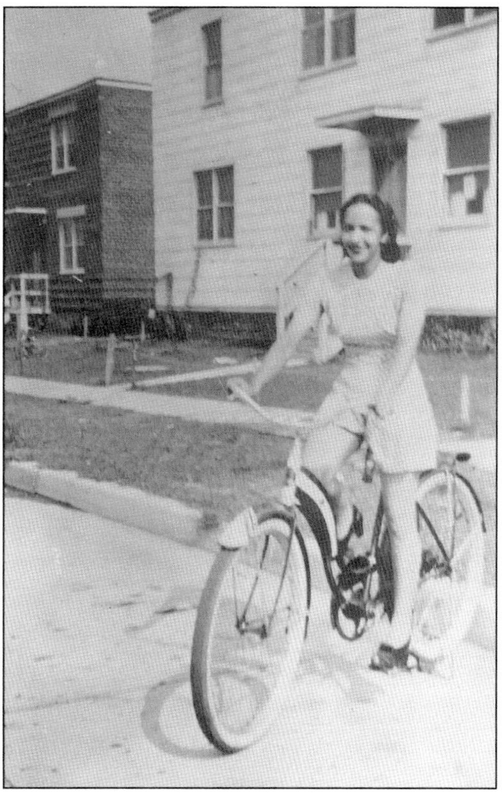

Marie Ashton smiles in this photograph taken of her riding her new bike. (Courtesy of Jacqueline Ashton Wright.)

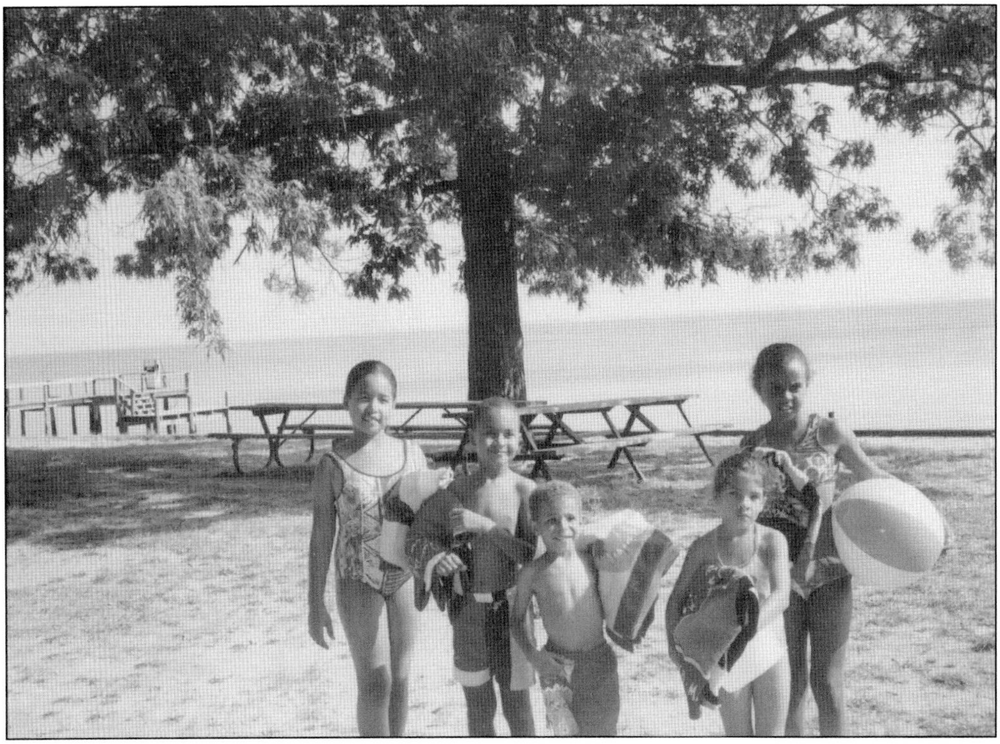

Bathing beauties still find pleasure in gathering on the shores of the Potomac River to frolic. These children are identified, from left to right, as follows: Raven Harris, Idris Anderson, John Melendez, Alexis Melendez, and Ayesha Anderson.

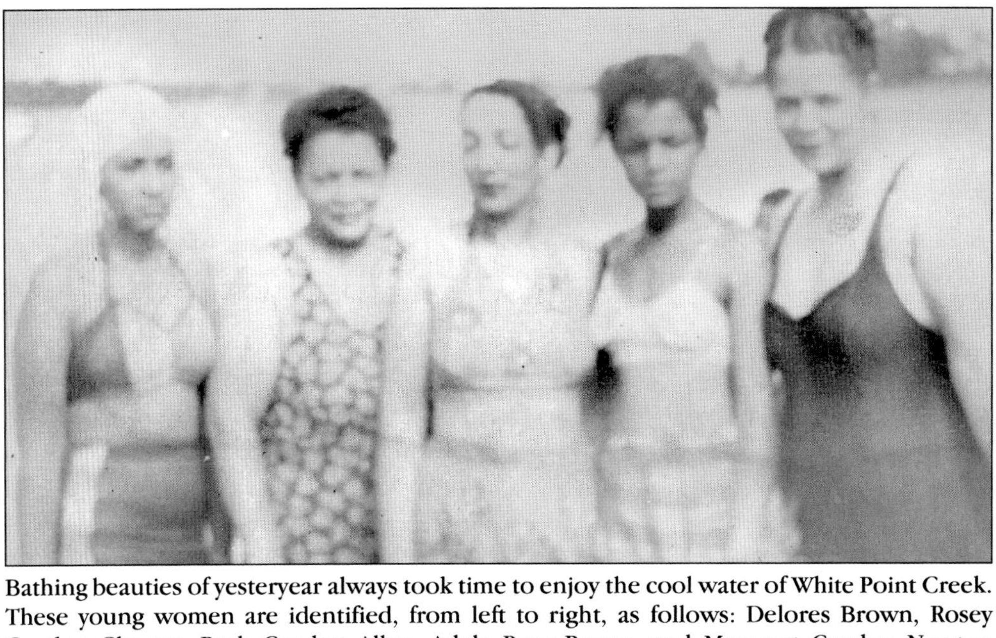

Bathing beauties of yesteryear always took time to enjoy the cool water of White Point Creek. These young women are identified, from left to right, as follows: Delores Brown, Rosey Gordon Clayton, Ruth Gordon Allen, Adele Page Roane, and Margaret Gordon Newton Reed. (Courtesy of Vernell London.)

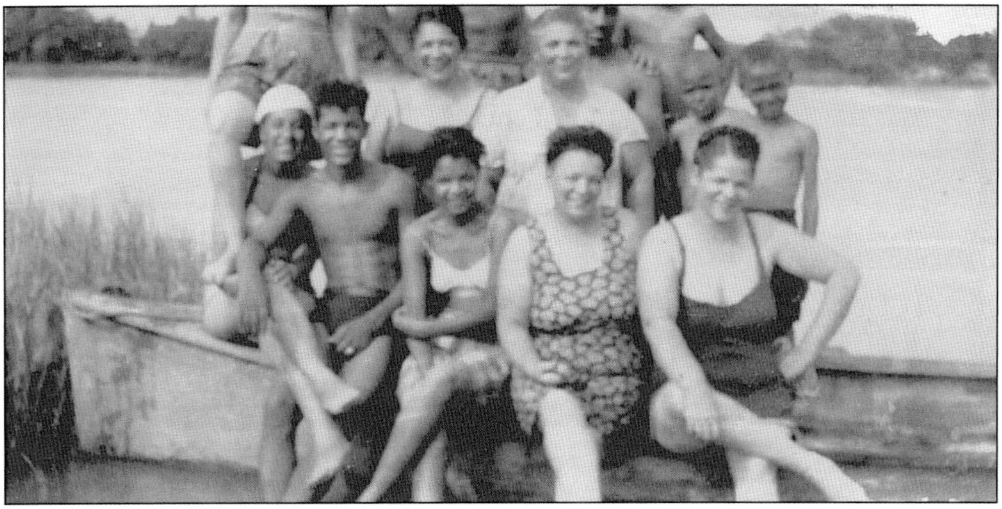

This picture shows Adele Page's boat down at White Point. These "crew members" are identified as follows: Walter Randolph Ball, Bessie Gordon, Helen Gordon Page, Jackson Delores Brown, Shirley Page, Adele Page, Rose Gordon Clayton, and Margaret Gordon Newton Reed.

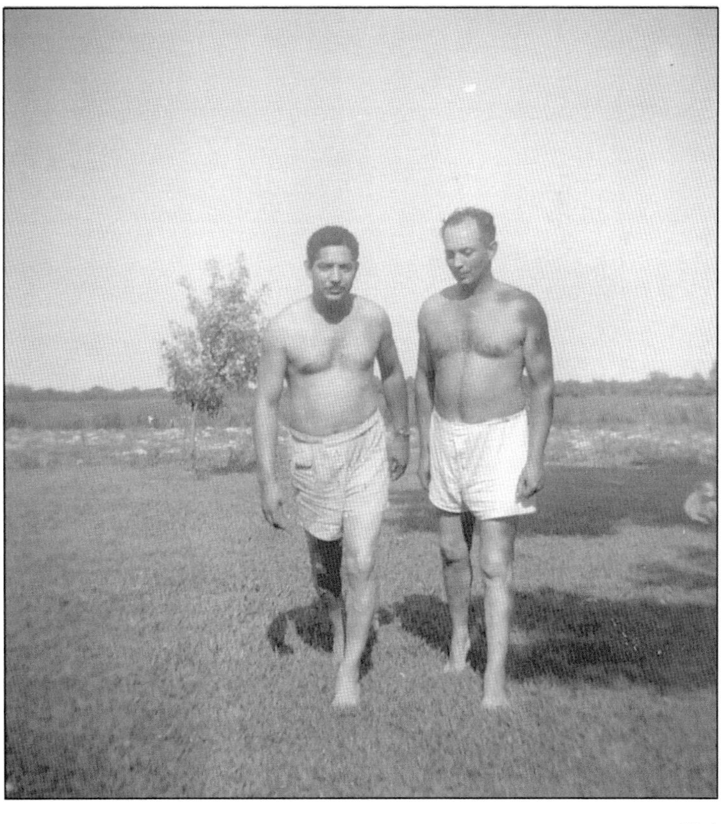

Merrill "Cute" Gordon and Simmuel Gordon are seen here enjoying a day on the water.

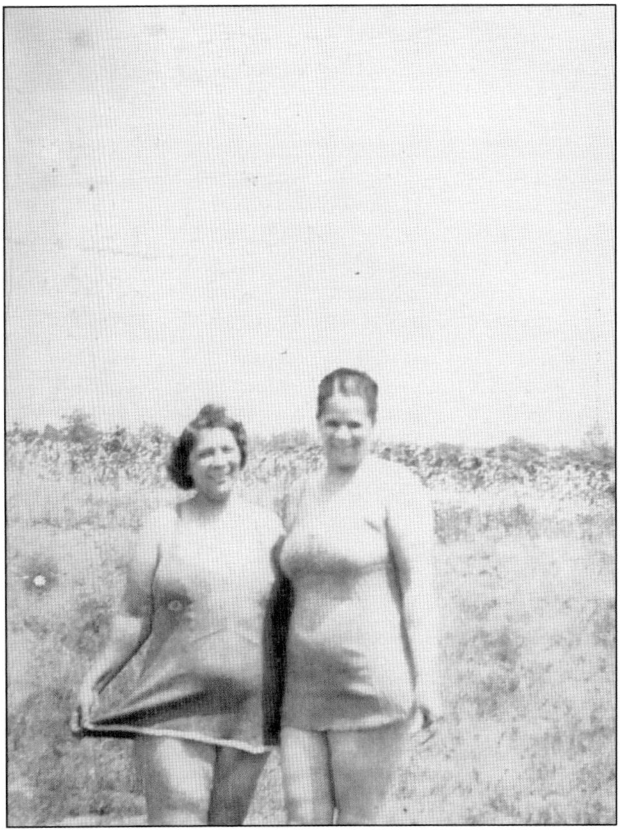

Bessie Gordon and Margaret Gordon Newton Reed are pictured here enjoying the outdoors.

Seen here along one of Westmoreland County's calm waterways are Margaret, Rose Gordon Clayton, Ruth Gordon Allen, Bessie Gordon, and Helen Gordon Page Jackson.

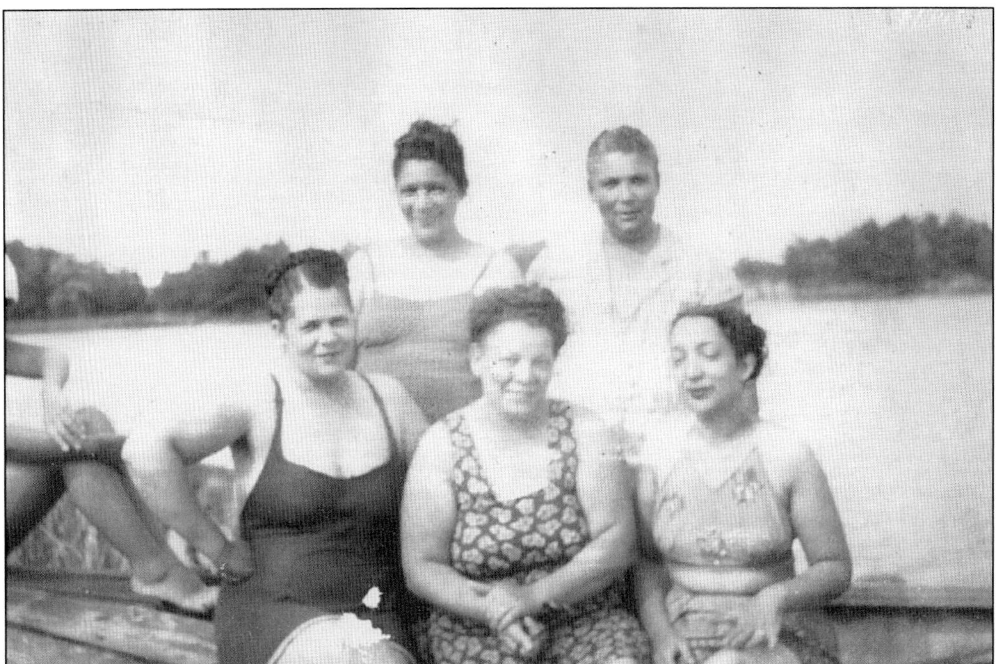

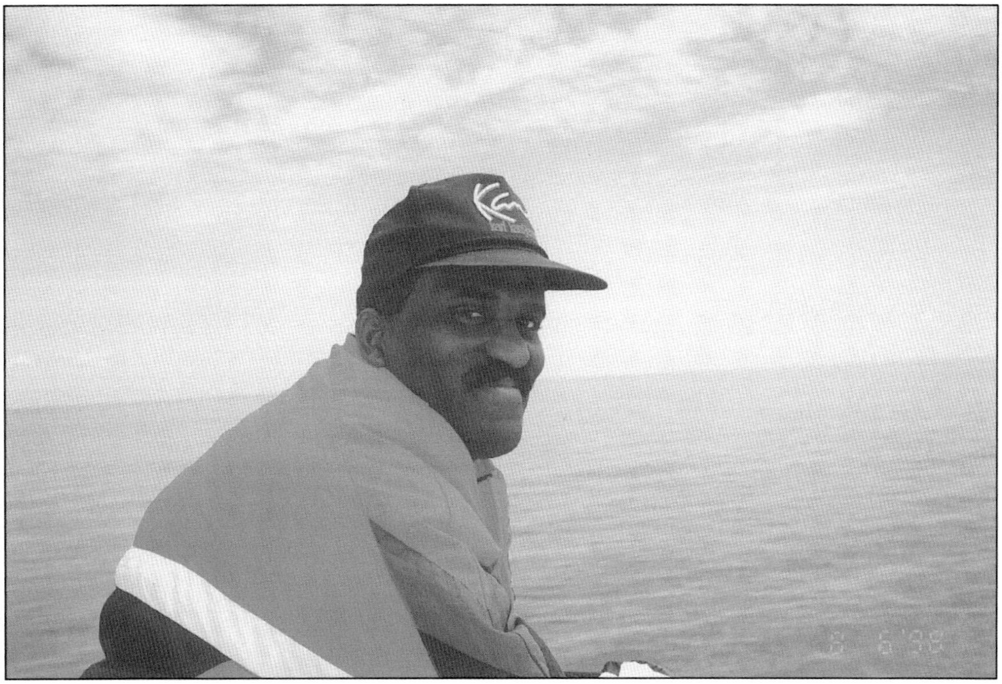

Boating is still a favorite pastime for Marvin Johnson.

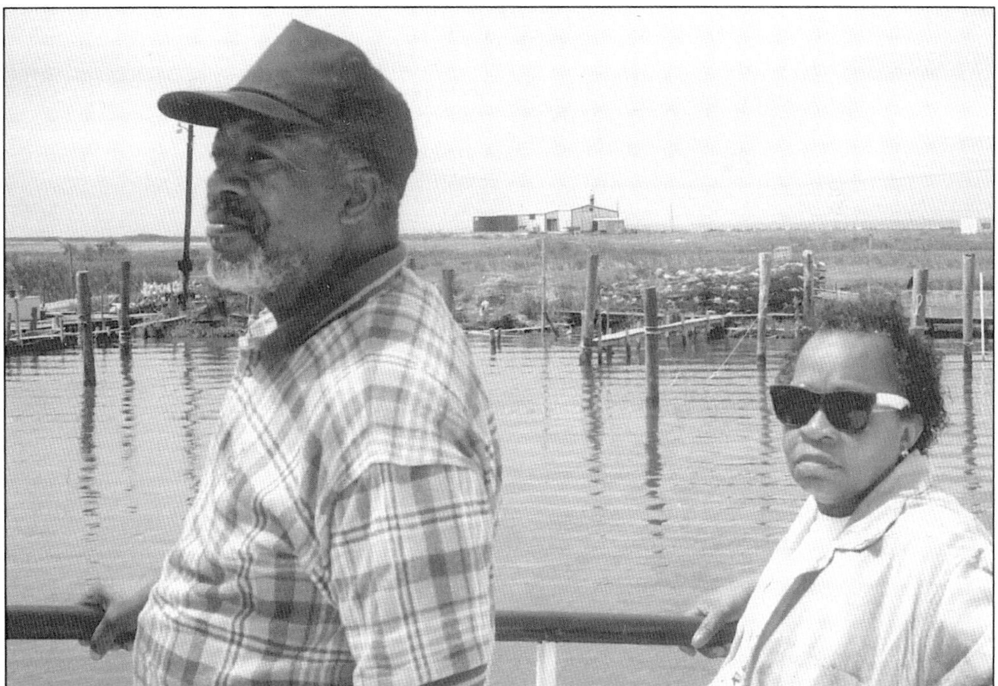

Walker Weldon and Esther Lee are seen here out on the Bay; they, like many Westmorelanders, possess a love of the water that runs deep.

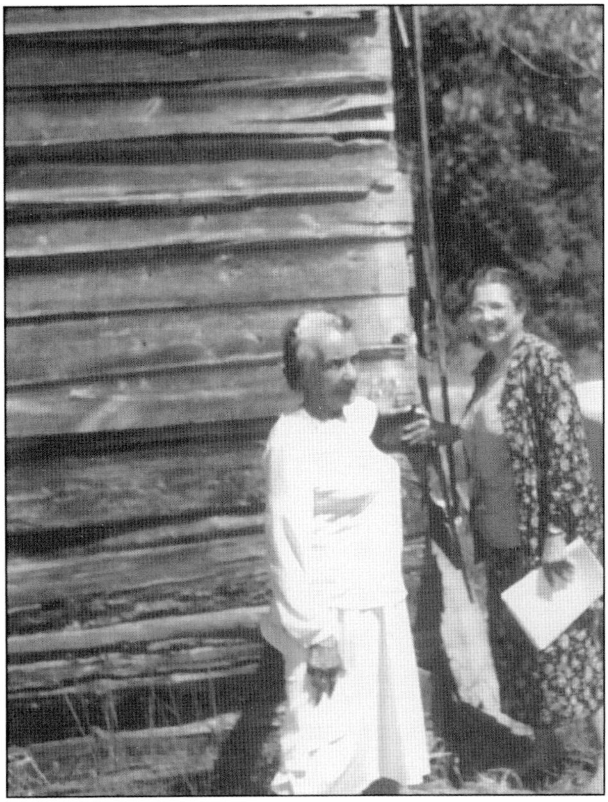

Catherine Fauntleroy Newton, with Ellen Dutton, is seen here visiting the Fauntleroy home place.

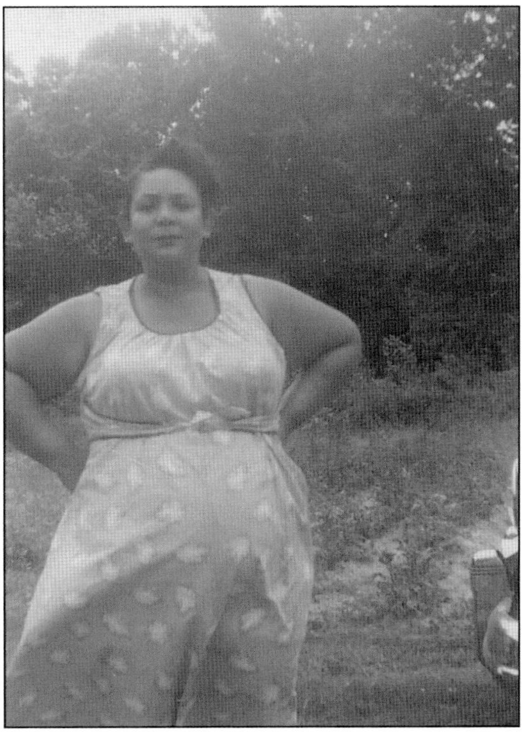

Naomi Gordon Fauntleroy is seen here relaxing on a hot summer day.

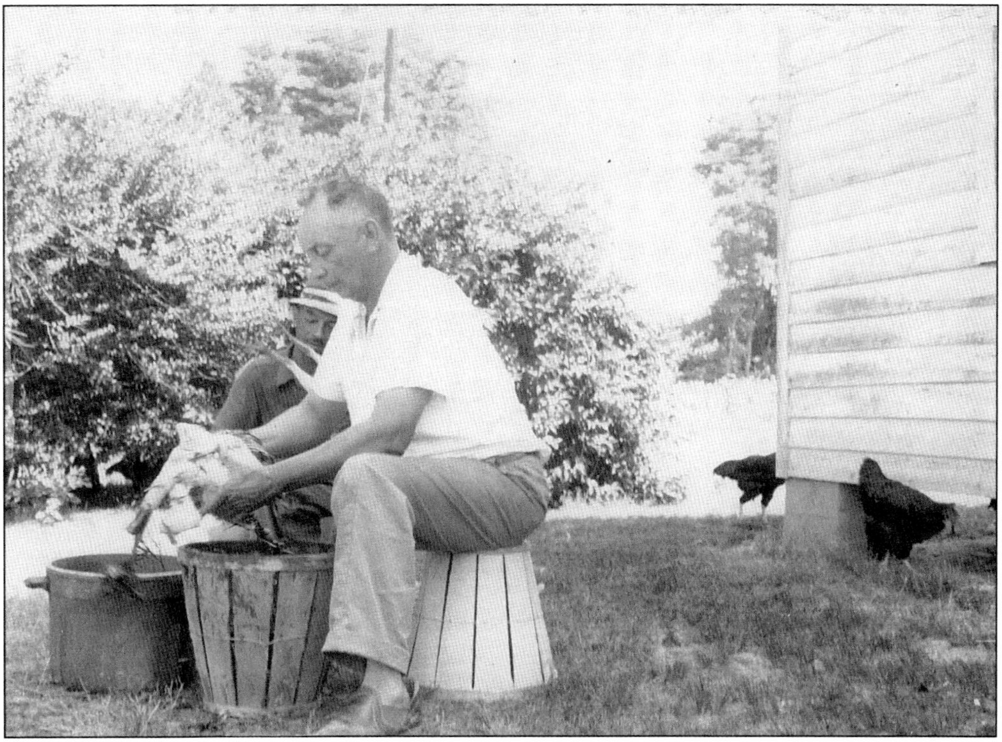

Merrill Gordon is seen here picking chickens for a Sunday dinner—with 22 brothers and sisters, he had a few to pick.

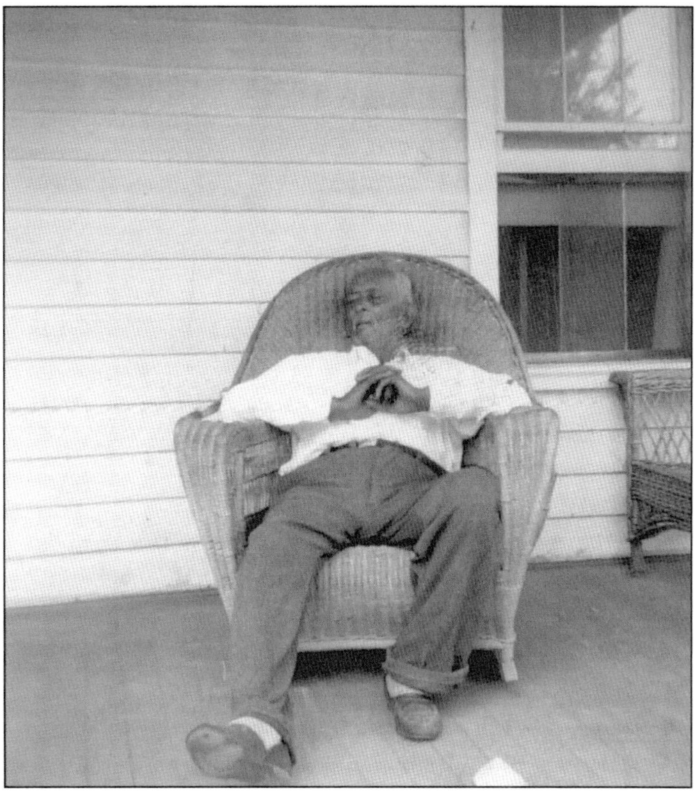

John Gordon is photographed resting on the porch at his home in Hague; he was the father of 22 children, all by the same wife.

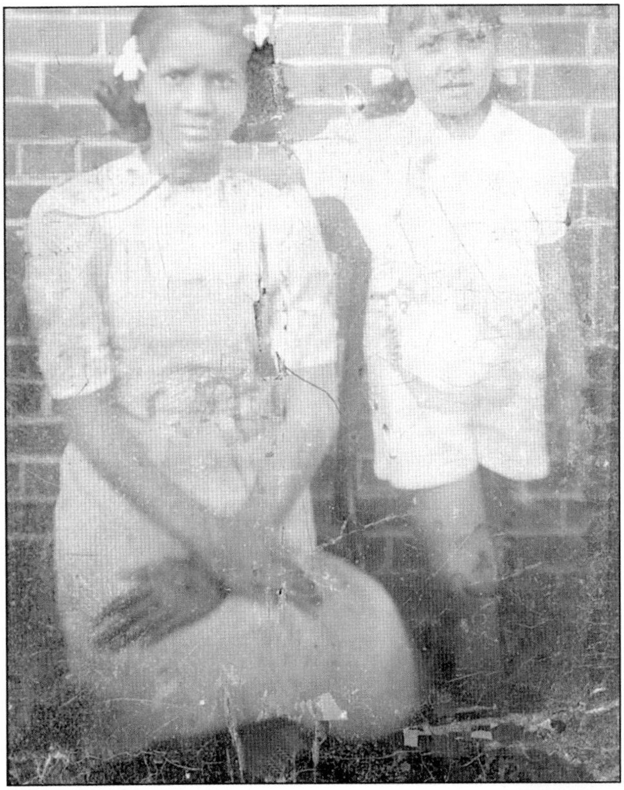

Vernell and Delores Brown were grandchildren of the Gordons.

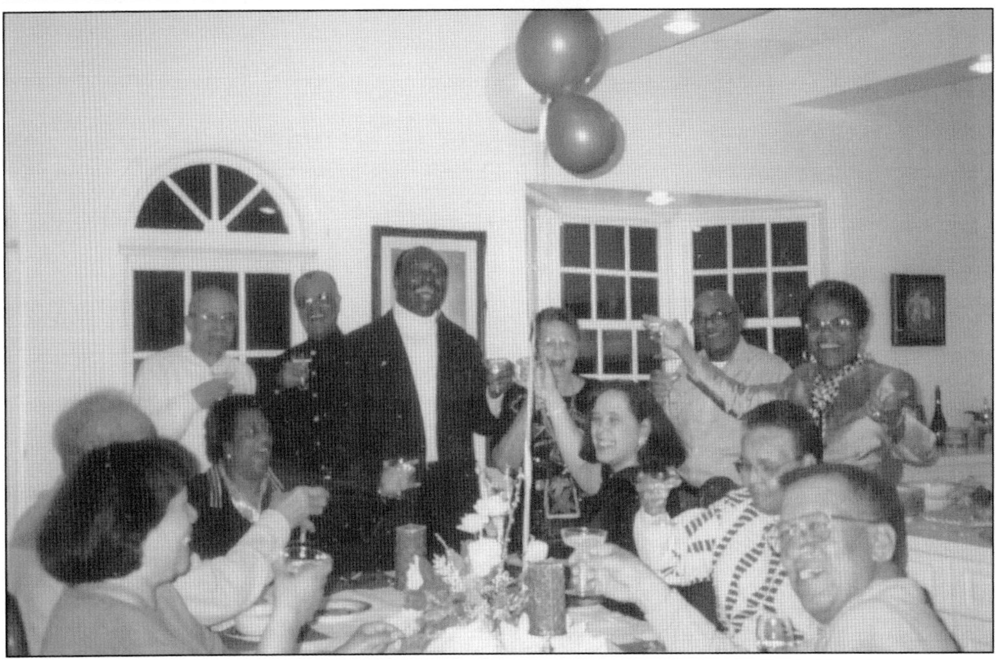

Celebrations with neighbors are special times together. In this photograph, Vondell Mayo, Barbara Eaton, John Roane, John Eaton, Malachi Burton, Bessie Green, Cassandra Burton, Adele Roane, Richard Mayo, and Ivan and Delores Ware enjoy some spirited fellowship.

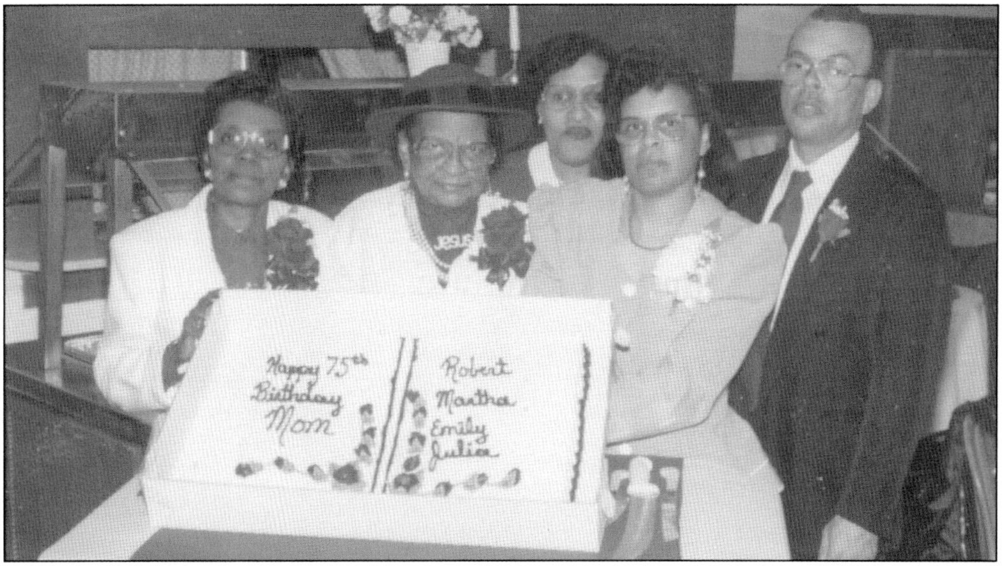

Birthdays with family provide wonderful memories. Eliza Plummer is now 82, and she has resided in Oldhams ever since leaving Tucker Hill in 1924 with her parents, Martha Thomas Plummer and Moses Plummer. Eliza's children are Emily Plummer Tate, Martha Plummer Gray, Julia Plummer Clark, and James R. Plummer. (Courtesy of Reverend Emily Tate.)

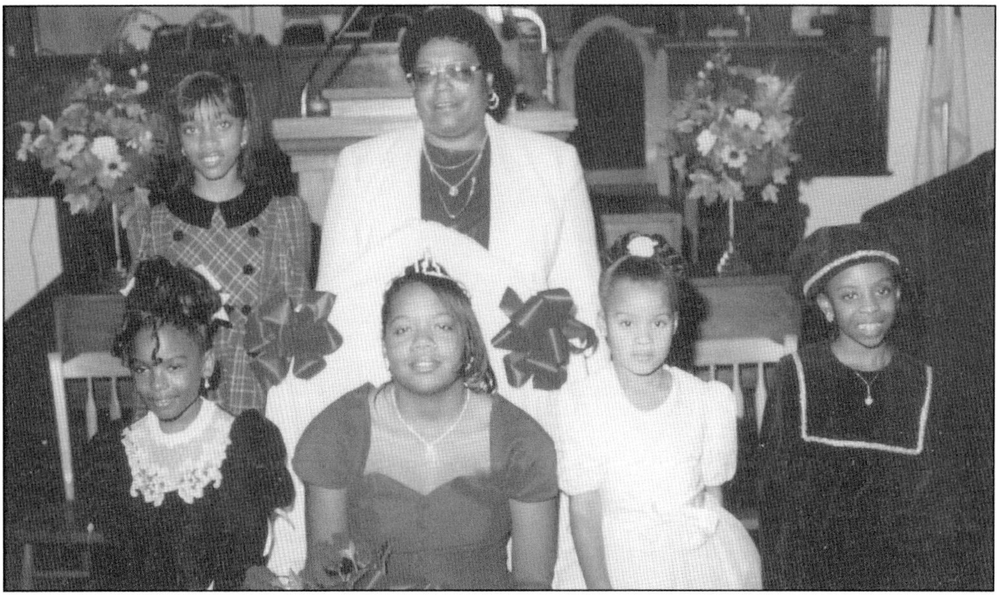

Yearly, the NAACP queen pageant provides local young women an opportunity to represent their church. The poise, grace, and charm of the contestants make the task of the judges quite difficult; however, the girl who succeeds in raising the most money for the organization takes home the crown and title for the next year and is the official county queen. She is then eligible to go onto the State NAACP Queen Contest. Darci Jones, daughter of Jackie Jones and granddaughter of Israel and Evelyn Jones and Gladys Johnson, was crowned queen in 1999. Others participating hopefuls were Rasha Boyd, Briana Henry, Trinesha Shepard, Sherita Day, and Juanita Newman.

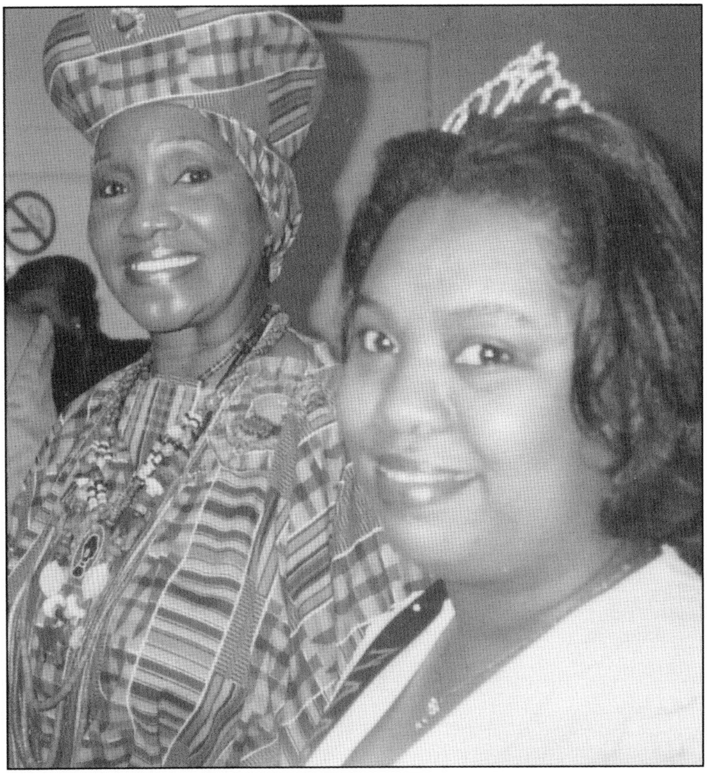

Daisy Howard Douglas (left), author and community leader, is seen her with her daughter, Jewell Douglass, winner of the State of Virginia NAACP Pageant. A George Washington University doctoral candidate and a teacher, Ms. Douglass is also civic minded like her parents, James and Daisy Douglas.

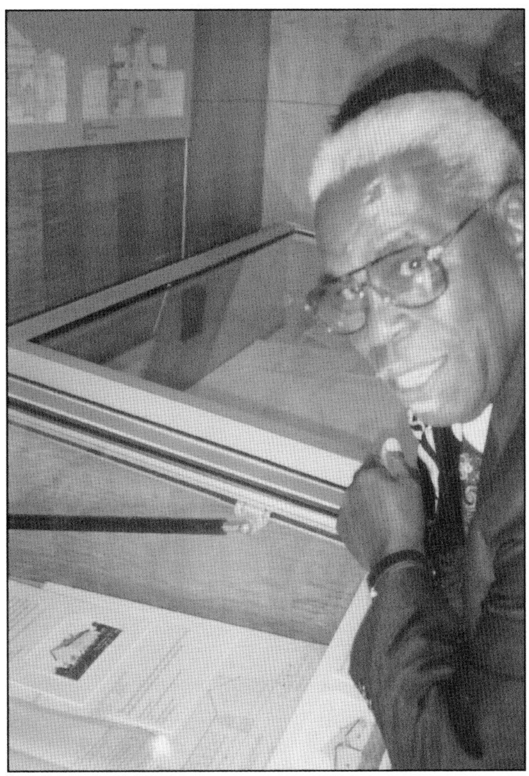

Granville Fisher, seen here at the Library of Virginia in Richmond, is enjoying a display that includes several of Westmoreland County's earlier African-American one-room and two-room schoolhouses. He was still eager to learn more and was proud to see Westmoreland County's inclusion in such a well-done exhibit.

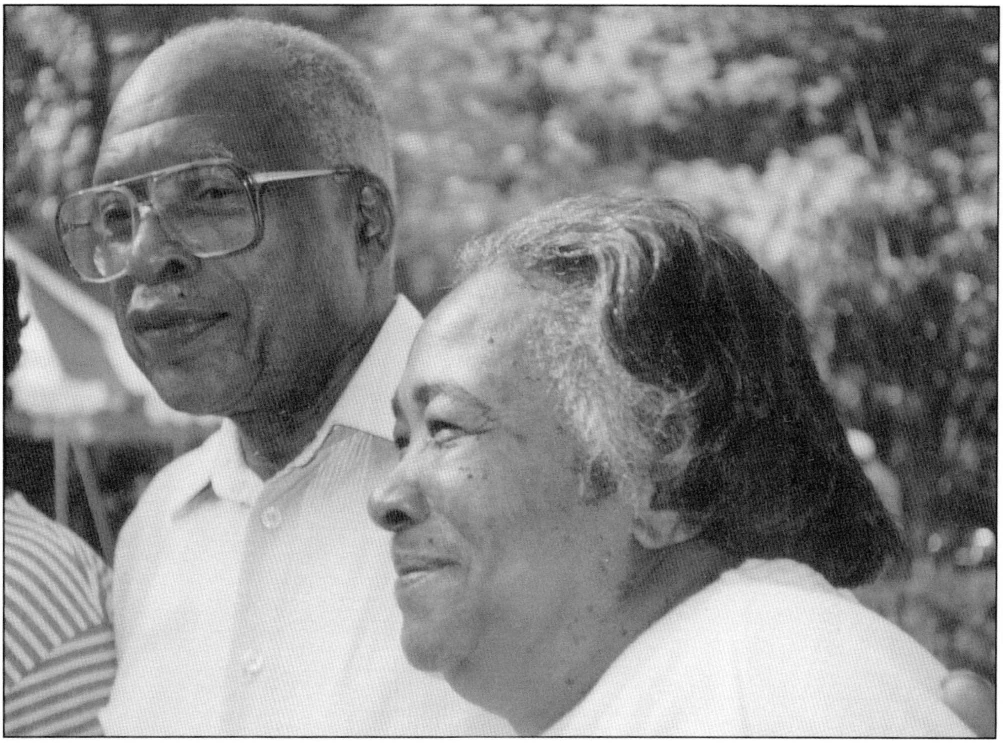

Henry Smith of Hague and his wife, Annie, are enjoying a family reunion they hosted at their home. Bringing many generations together on a portion of what had been the original family farm was no easy task, but the bond of family was the driving force. Family is very important in the black community.

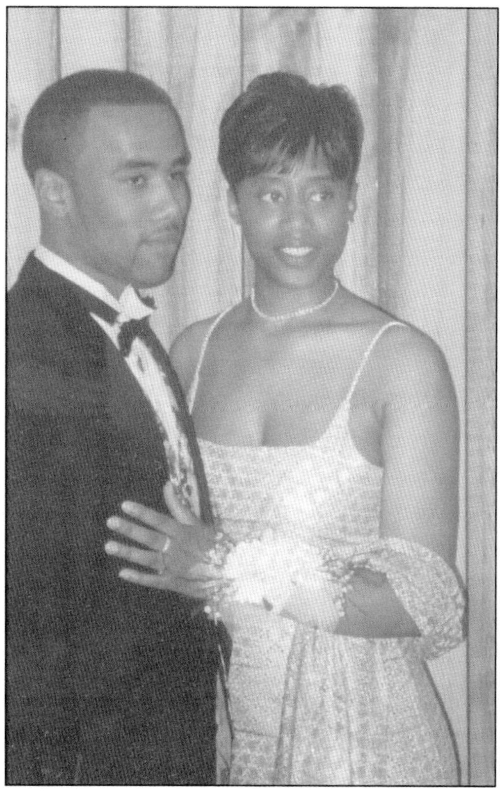

Prom time is always a night to remember, as can be seen in this image of Tiara Jones and Corey Waddy.

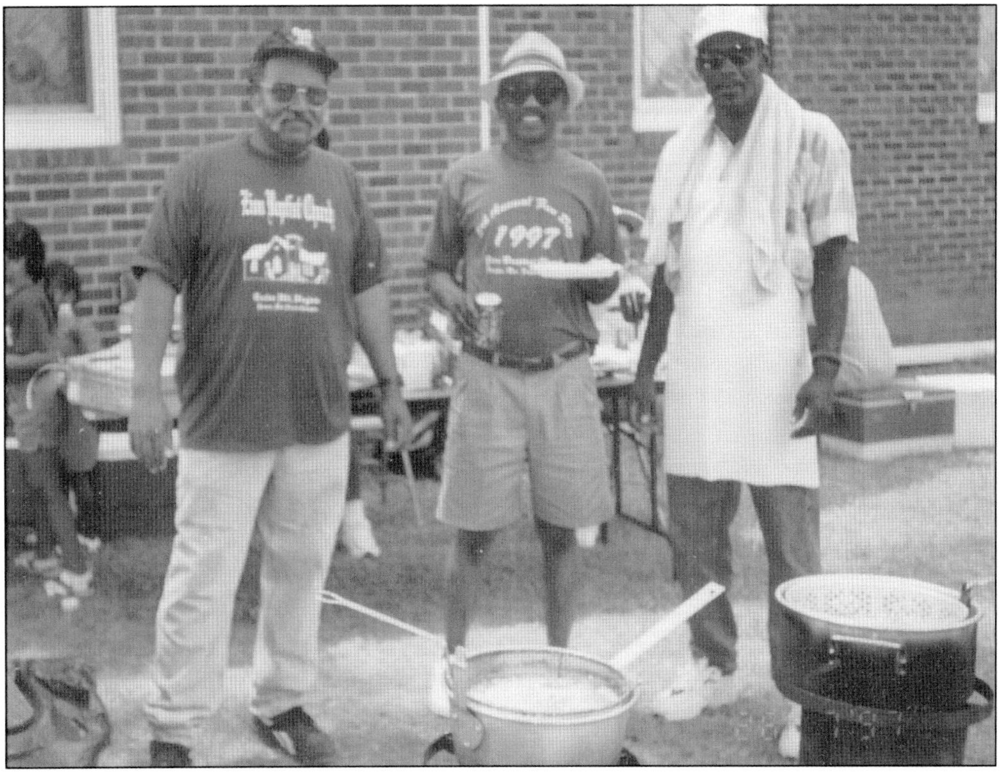

Charles Crabbe, Louis Fauntleroy, and Otho Veney are photographed preparing a fish fry with fish caught fresh from the Potomac and Rappahannock Rivers and the Chesapeake Bay.

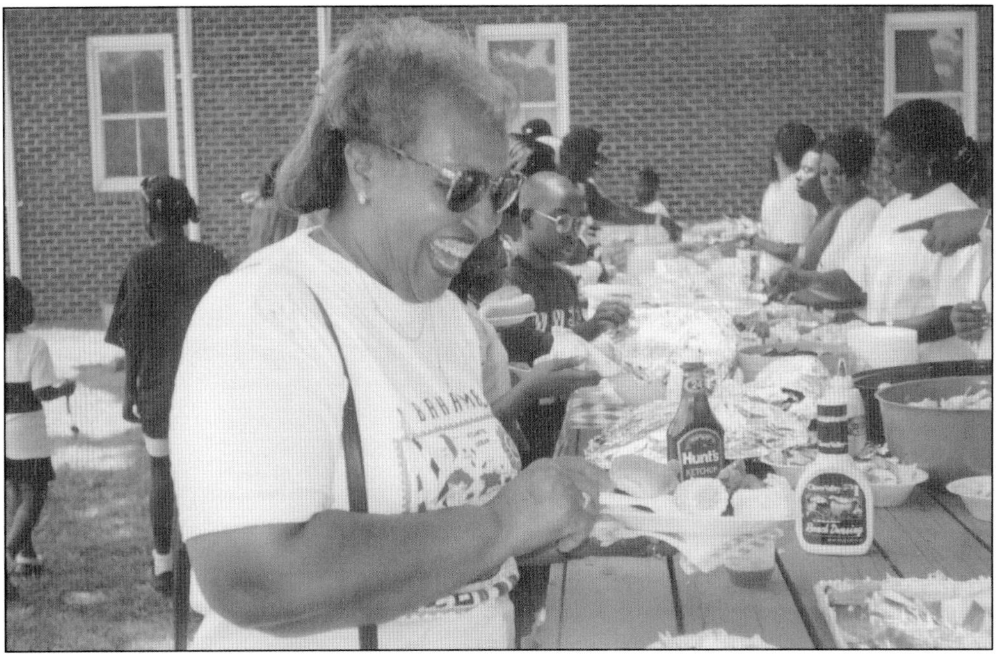

Standing before tables laden with food, Lillian McCoy is enjoying a Zion Church picnic.

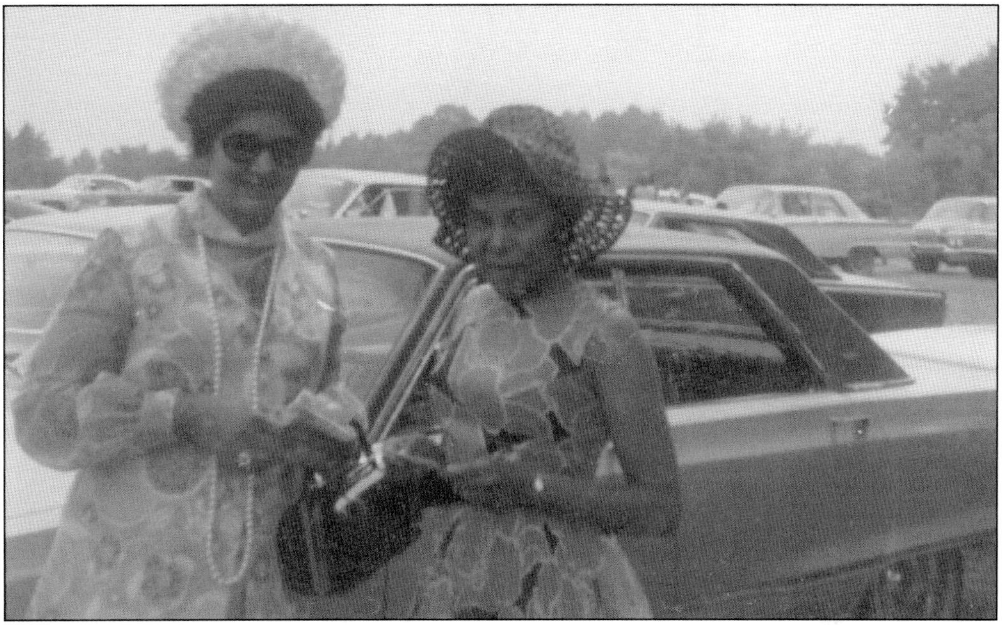

Church meetings every August were very special times. Vernell London is pictured here with friend Sis Thompson. (Courtesy of Vernell London.)

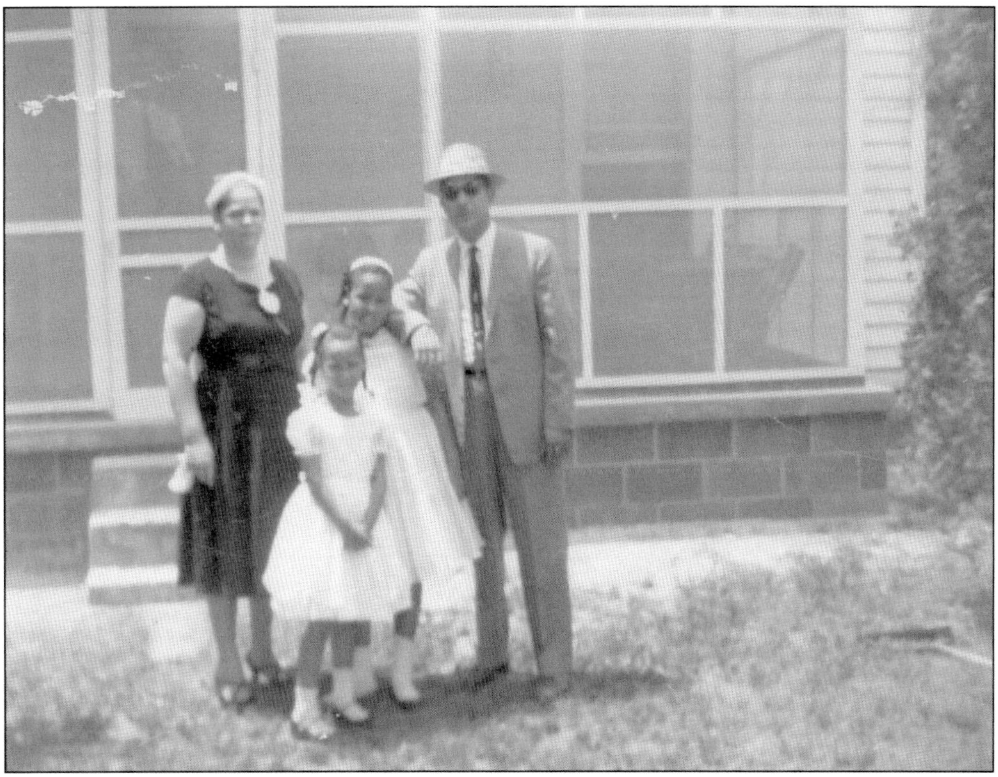

Dressed for church, Margaret Gordon Newton Reed is pictured with her grandchildren, Stanell and Gail London, and Uncle Simmuel Gordon.

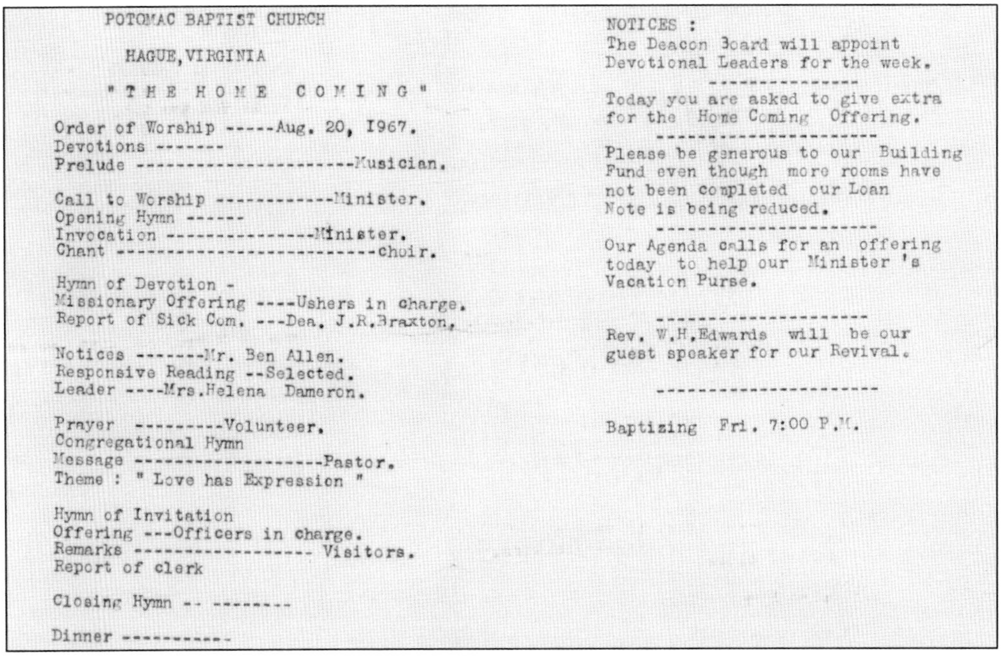

POTOMAC BAPTIST CHURCH

HAGUE, VIRGINIA

" T H E H O M E C O M I N G "

Order of Worship -----Aug. 20, 1967.
Devotions -------
Prelude ----------------------Musician.

Call to Worship ------------Minister.
Opening Hymn ------
Invocation ---------------Minister.
Chant --------------------------choir.

Hymn of Devotion -
Missionary Offering ----Ushers in charge.
Report of Sick Com. ---Dea. J.R.Braxton,

Notices -------Mr. Ben Allen.
Responsive Reading --Selected.
Leader ----Mrs.Helena Dameron.

Prayer ---------Volunteer.
Congregational Hymn
Message -------------------Pastor.
Theme : " Love has Expression "

Hymn of Invitation
Offering ---Officers in charge.
Remarks ----------------- Visitors.
Report of clerk

Closing Hymn -- --------

Dinner -----------

NOTICES :
The Deacon Board will appoint Devotional Leaders for the week.

Today you are asked to give extra for the Home Coming Offering.

Please be generous to our Building Fund even though more rooms have not been completed our Loan Note is being reduced.

Our Agenda calls for an offering today to help our Minister 's Vacation Purse.

Rev. W.H.Edwards will be our guest speaker for our Revival.

Baptizing Fri. 7:00 P.M.

The Home Coming was and still is a special time for many Westmorelanders, who return to the county. Vacations are often planned well in advance to be able to attend the annual event. The entire day is spent in church service, and dinner is served to the parishioners. Some refer to these celebrations as protracted meetings, or revivals, which would last an entire week in August (some now even go into September). Many parishioners use this as a time for spiritual rejuvenation and join the church.

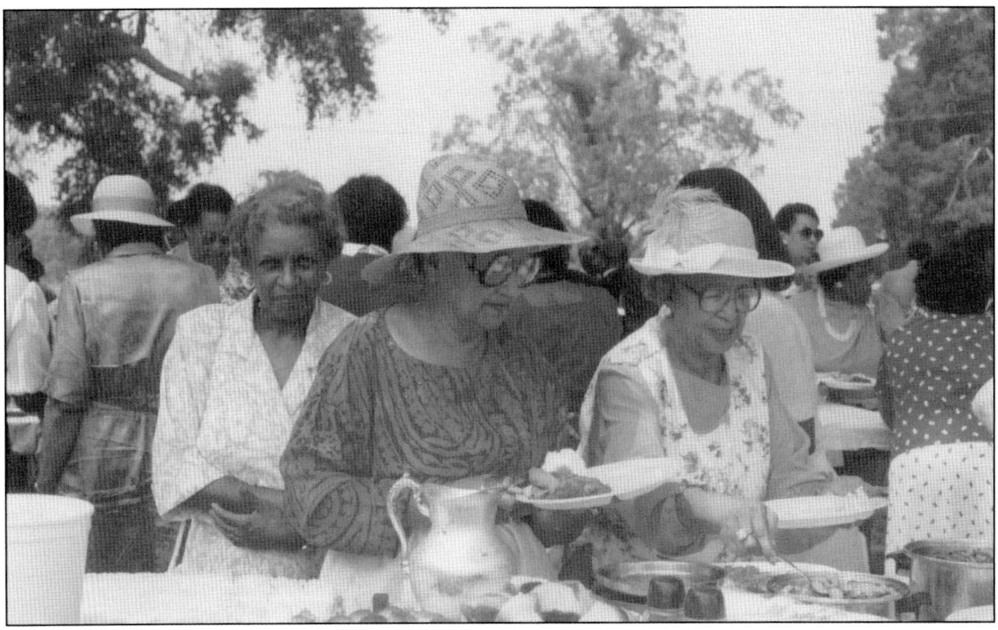

Martha Lowe Jenkins Roane is seen here helping serve at a Home Coming. Women of the church used to take pride making everything, from the good food to new outfits to wear.

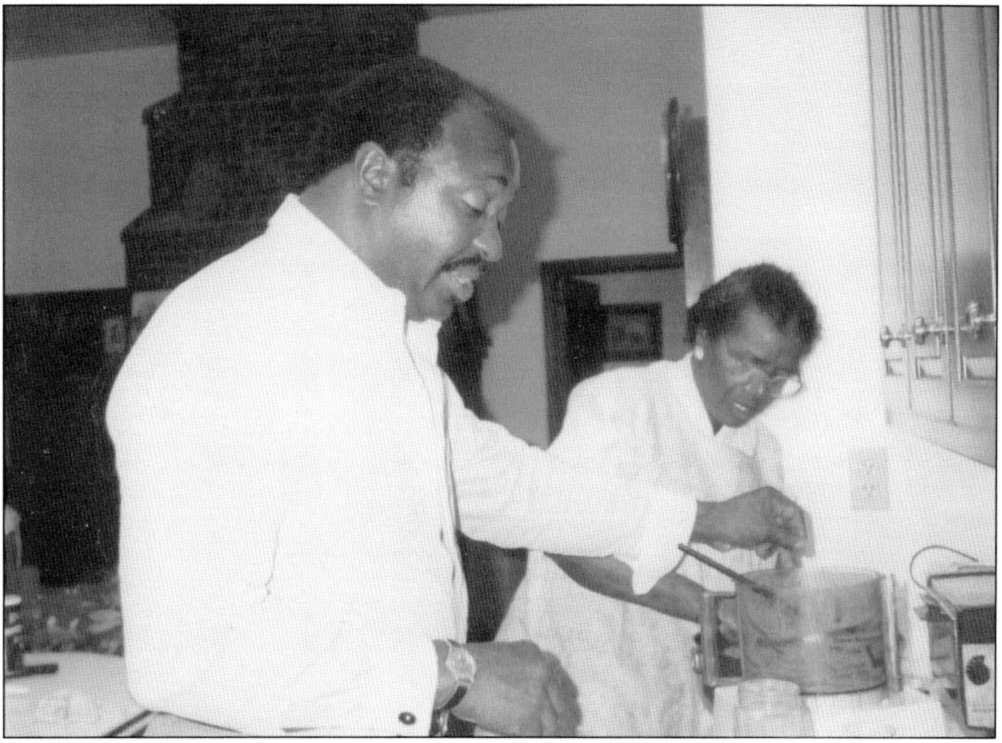

Malachi Burton and Mama Nellie Gaskins are seen here making liver pudding.

Ingredients

1.5 pounds fresh pork liver
1.5 pounds fresh pork jowl or 1.5 pounds unsalted pork middling
1 medium onion
2 cups liver from boiled liver mixture
2 teaspoons salt
.5 teaspoon black pepper
1 teaspoon fresh sage

Directions

1. Place the liver and jowl and onion in a large pot;
2. Cover with water and add 2 inches more of water;
3. Cook on a medium high heat about two hours until tender;
4. Remove the meat and onion and allow to cool;
5. Cut the liver and jowl up, including the skin, into small pieces;
6. Grind up in a grinder or food processor;
7. When ground, add 2 cups of the liquid from the liver mixture;
8. Stir the liver mixture until a very liquid batter and add salt, pepper, and sage;
9. Mix well and bake in a heavy tin pan or 2-quart casserole dish at 250 degrees for two and half hours;
10. Until the pudding is completely dried out, the long cooking is what makes it really good;
11. When cool, place it in the refrigerator.

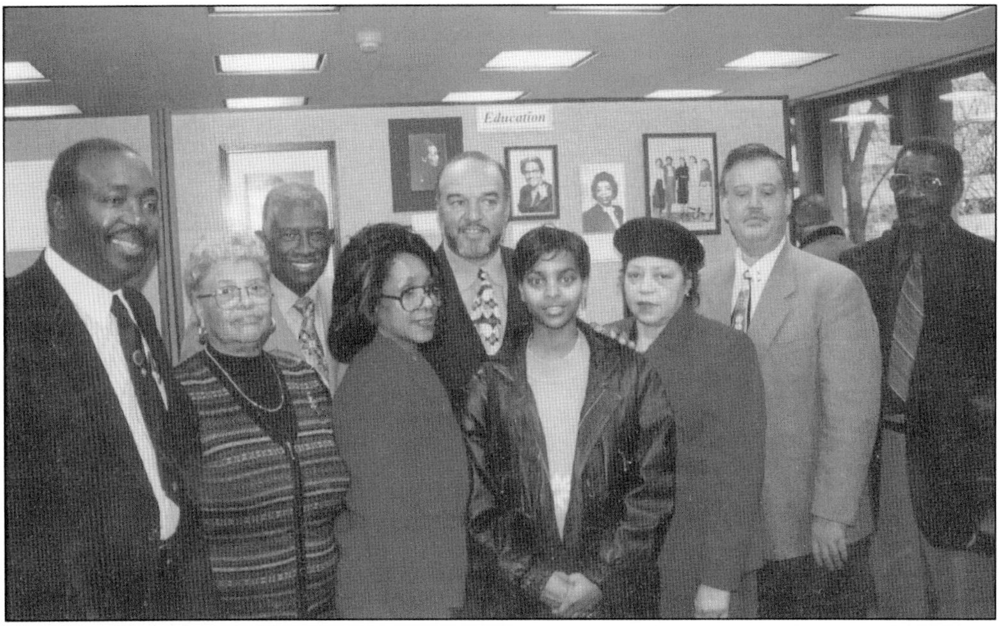

Malachi Burton, Susan Roberts, Ferman Dixon, Gloria Hackett, Robert Cooper, Stephanie Dixon, Margie Peyton, Reverend William B. Scott, and Edward Hall are seen here at an event paying tribute to former Westmoreland County schoolteachers. This special event was a part of a White House Millennium Project at George Washington University.

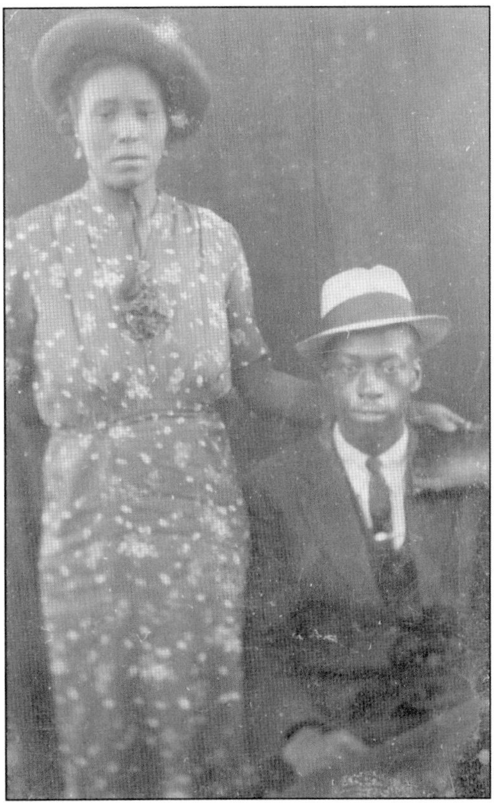

This photograph shows the 1938 wedding of Eliza "Geogeanna" Johnson Lee to Stephen Lee. They are the parents of Calvin Lee, Mary Lee Fulcher, Catherine Conley, and Carolyn Malind Lee.

As seen in this wedding portrait, Lucy Thompson married Moses Wimbish. (Courtesy of Mary Dixon Jones.)

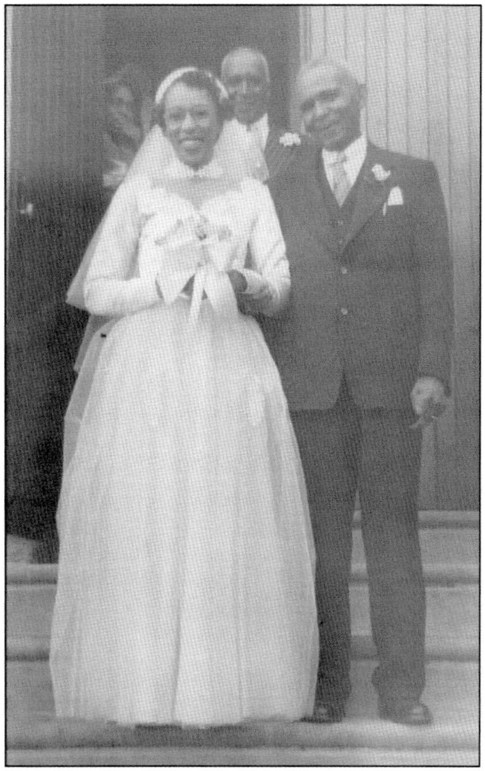

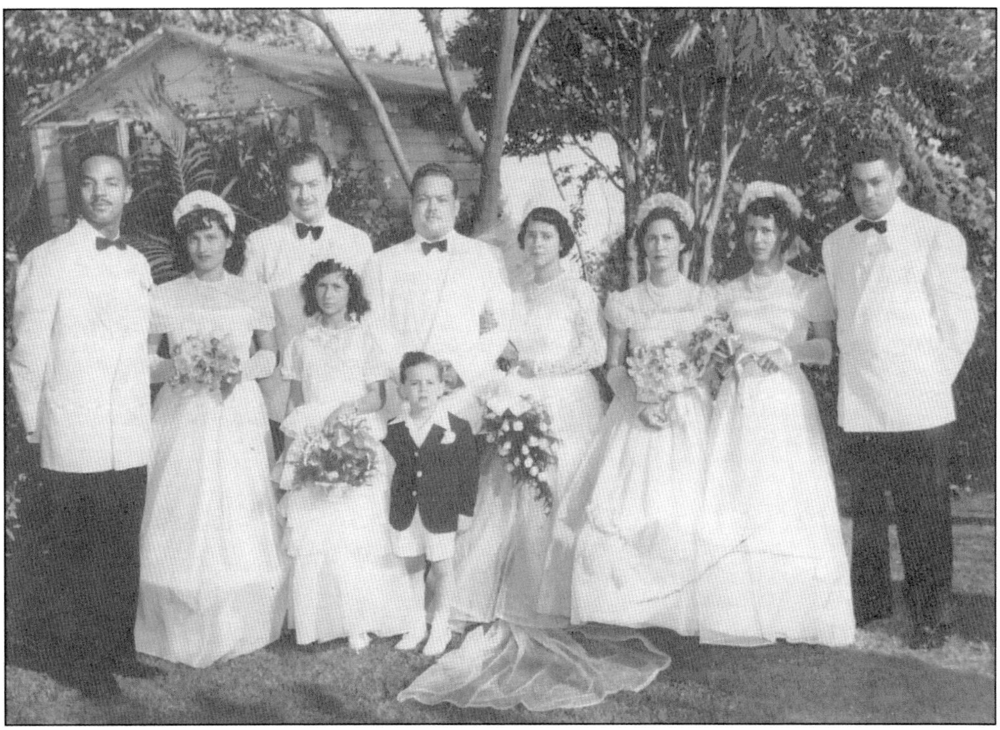

This photograph captures a traditional wedding celebration.

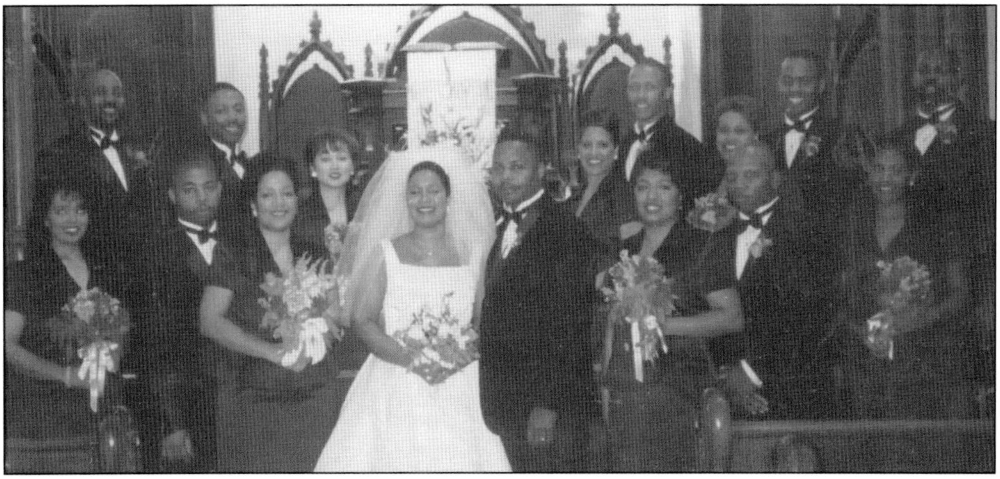

This is the Roane-Blackwell wedding. The participants of the event are identified as follows: Lynnee Roane (maid of honor), Monet Roane (bridesmaid), Towanda Allen (bridesmaid), Mondi Snyder (bridesmaid), Tracey Morton (bridesmaid), Penny Tsao (bridesmaid), Tanya Davis (bridesmaid), Leslie Roane (flowergirl), Kristen Miller (bridesmaid), Elisha Johnson (junior bridesmaid), Jerome Blackwell (best man), Healy LeCator (groomsman), Keith Washington (groomsman), Terry Fortune (groomsman), Michael Maxwell (groomsman), Bernard Leach (groomsmen), Gregory Hatchett (groomsman), and Nathan Mattox (ringbearer).

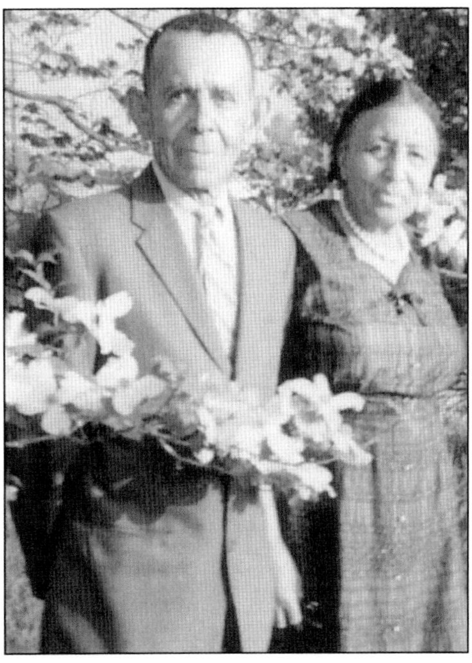

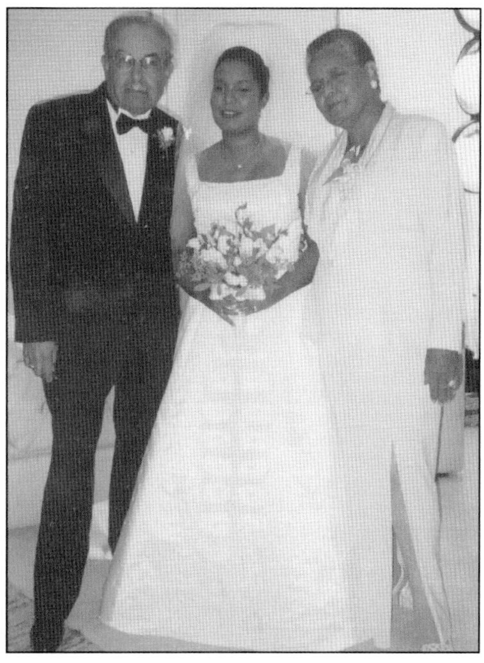

Left: Mr. and Mrs Harrison I. Smith are active in all aspects of the community. A carpenter, Mr. Smith worked on the first community center with Yosif Roane and was also an avid writer, publishing a book called *Birth of a Nation*. He is involved in the political and education process in the county. (Courtesy of Mrs. Philpot.) *Right*: John and Adele Roane pose with their youngest daughter, Rita, on her wedding day.

Prom time was always special at A.T. Johnson High School, as can be seen in this 1940s photograph.

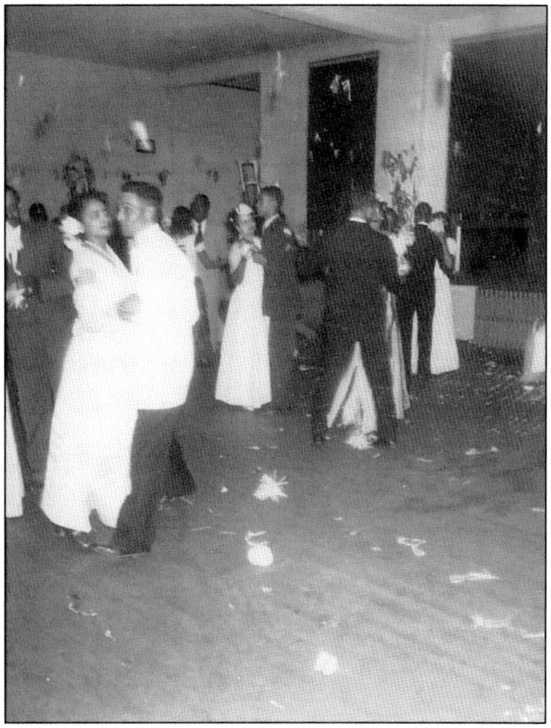

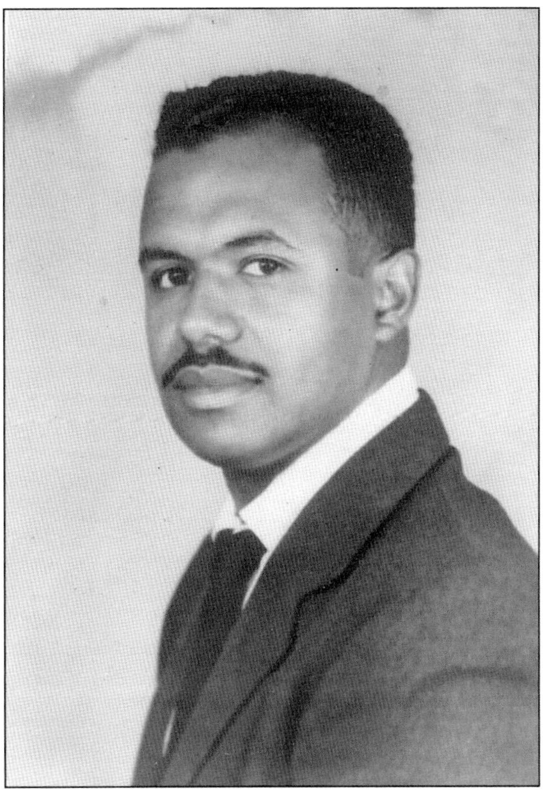

Yosif Roane remembers well the happy memories of prom time at A.T. Johnson High School.

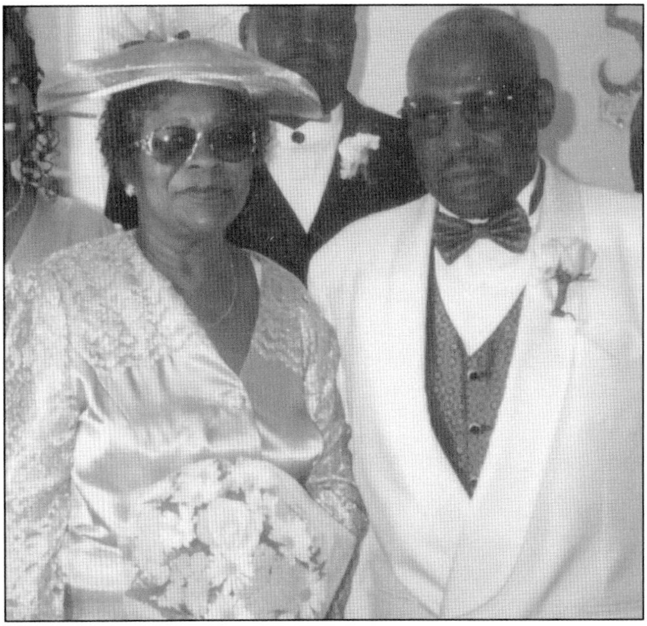

Celebrating their golden anniversary, Mary Brooks White and Paul White did not have a lavish wedding—just a $2 license when they married. However, when they repeated their vows 50 years later, their children hosted a celebration that included granddaughter Tiana Wise and great-granddaughters Jaleque Wise and Demerita Parker tossing flowers. White worked as a farmer and was the last local hog farmer; he and his wife also worked hard to bring up their children: Paul White Jr., Cornelius White, Joyce White Jackson, and Delilah White.

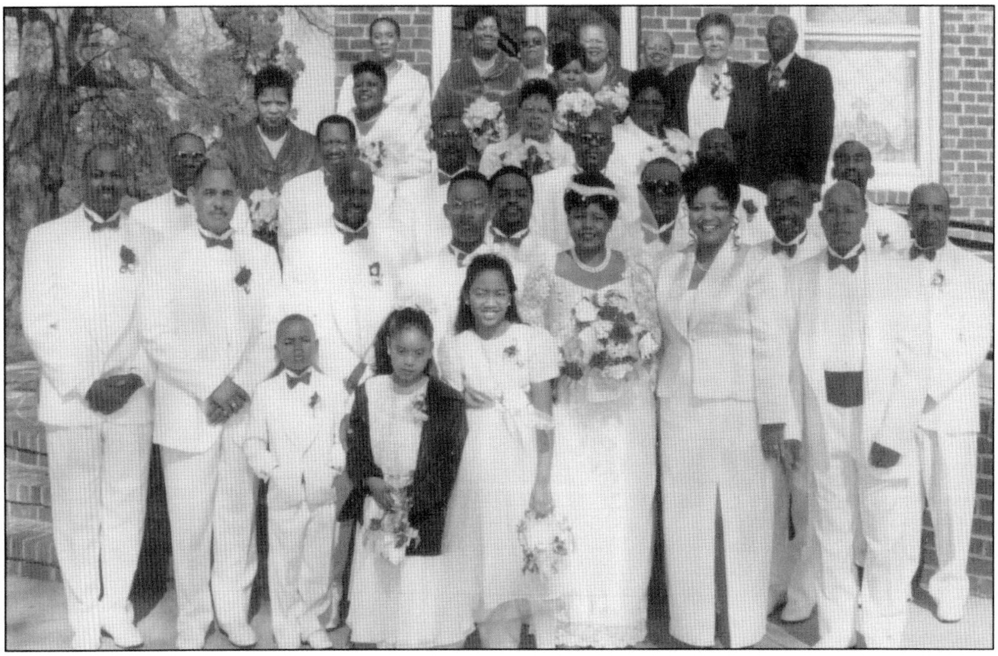

This is a portrait of the Nickens-Fisher wedding party. The wedding party is, from left to right, as follows: (front row) Dantwone Wilson, Shaquanta Thomas, and Leslie Roane; (second row) Gleenwood Hence, Henry Thompson, John Wilson, Reverend Darryl Fisher, Mrs. Carolyn Fisher, Adriane Jones, and Robert Ball; (third row) Marvin Hackett, Ferman Roane, Dexter Monroe, Garfield Johnson Jr., Louis Fauntleroy, Lenwood Tate, Albert Fauntleroy, and Earl Johnson; (fourth row) Rosemary Wilson, Lillian Yerby, Carvletta Fauntleroy, Rosemary Turner, Annette Robinson, Helen Golden, Sarah Wilson, Wanda Fisher, Bessie Brown, Granville Fisher Sr., Sandra L. Jones, and Earnestine Thompson.

Six

HOME GOING

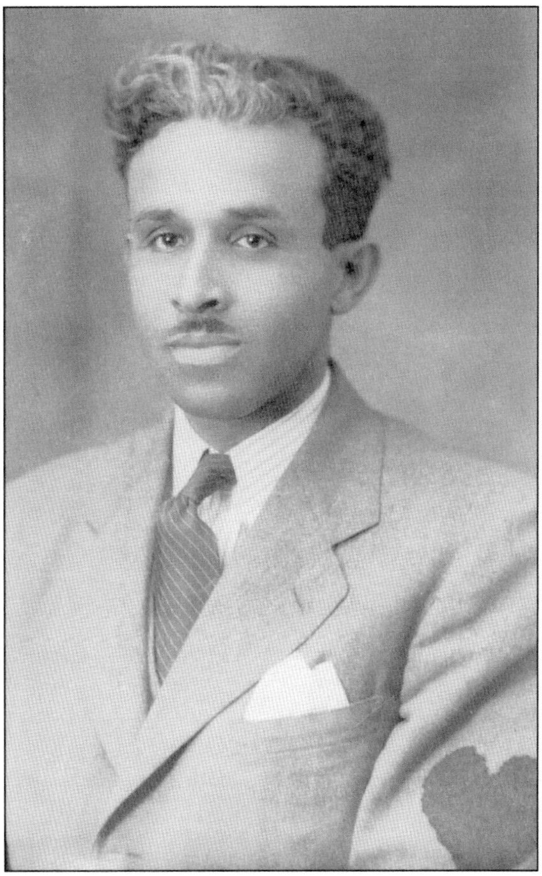

Joseph Roane followed the custom of the times and placed a heart upon his sleeve for his mother's, Virginia E. Griggs Roane, funeral. This was the practice for the male family members. Many members of the family wore black or their Sunday best, as they do today. (Courtesy of Yosif Roane.)

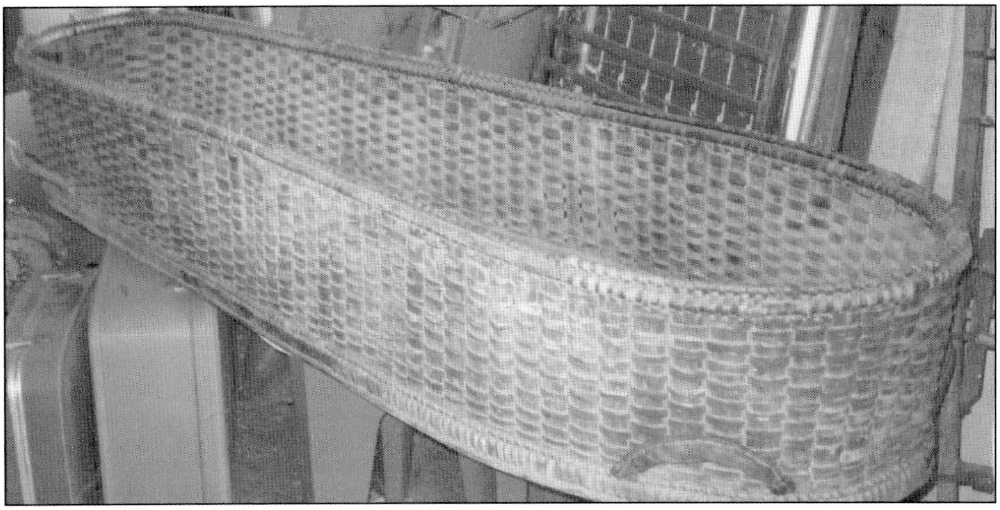

This is a funeral basket made by Willy Jones. Before there were ambulances, when a person died, usually in their home, he or she was taken away by a funeral hearse, which also took ill persons to the hospital. In the earlier days, there were women who would come and wash the dead body. The local Oddfellows chapter would come by horse and buggy to pick up the deceased and prepare the body at the lodge—this was their community service. Once an undertaker became established in the county, he would come to the home with the funeral basket to pick up the body.

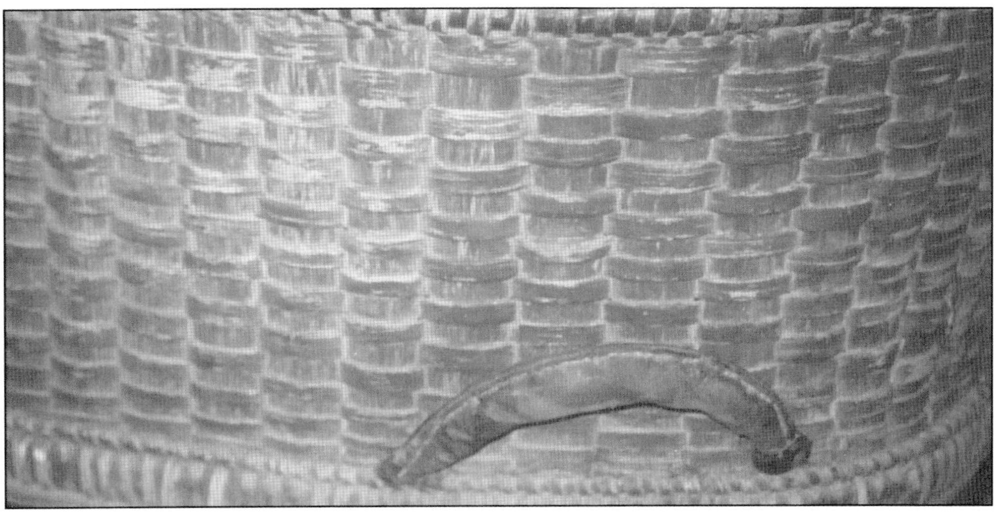

Once the body was prepared, it was returned to the home, where the family would have it placed in the living room, and a member of the family would take turns sitting with the deceased for three days. A funeral wreath was placed upon the door. During the wake, others would come to the home and comfort the family. On the third day, the body was taken to the the church. Today, wakes are not commonly held in the home; the lights at the funeral home signify a deceased person on its premises. The viewing, or wake, is sometimes done at the funeral home, but more people are having it at the church prior to the start of the funeral. In both cases, a funeral guestbook is provided so that the family may acknowledge the many who came. Flowers and cards are traditionally sent to comfort the family. Note the craftsmanship of the basket.

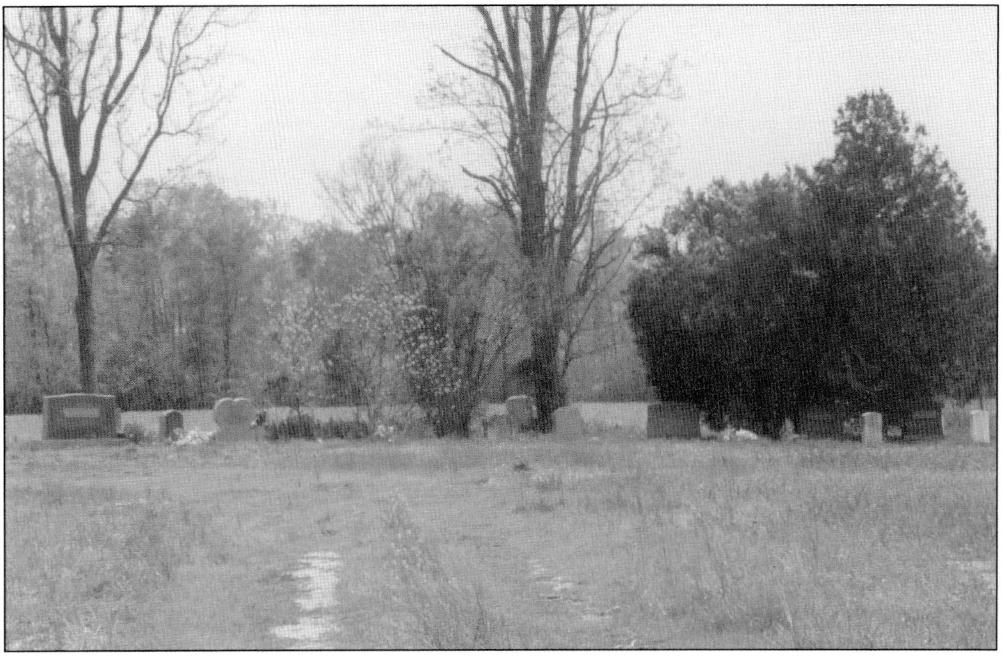

The Roane family has a private family cemetery on their farm.

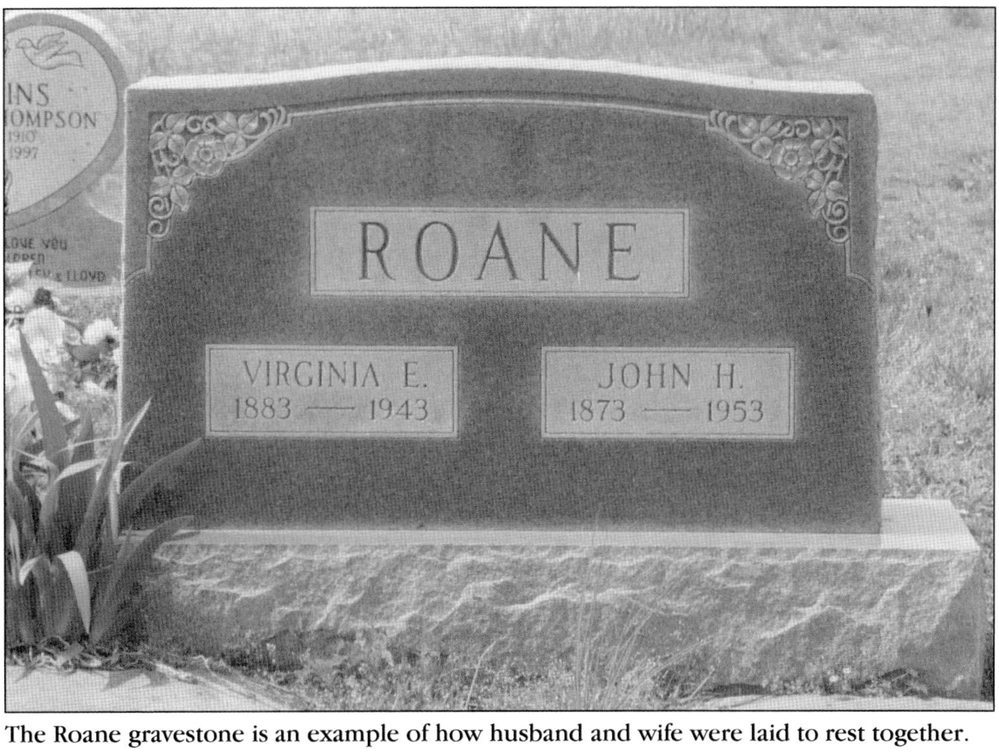

The Roane gravestone is an example of how husband and wife were laid to rest together.

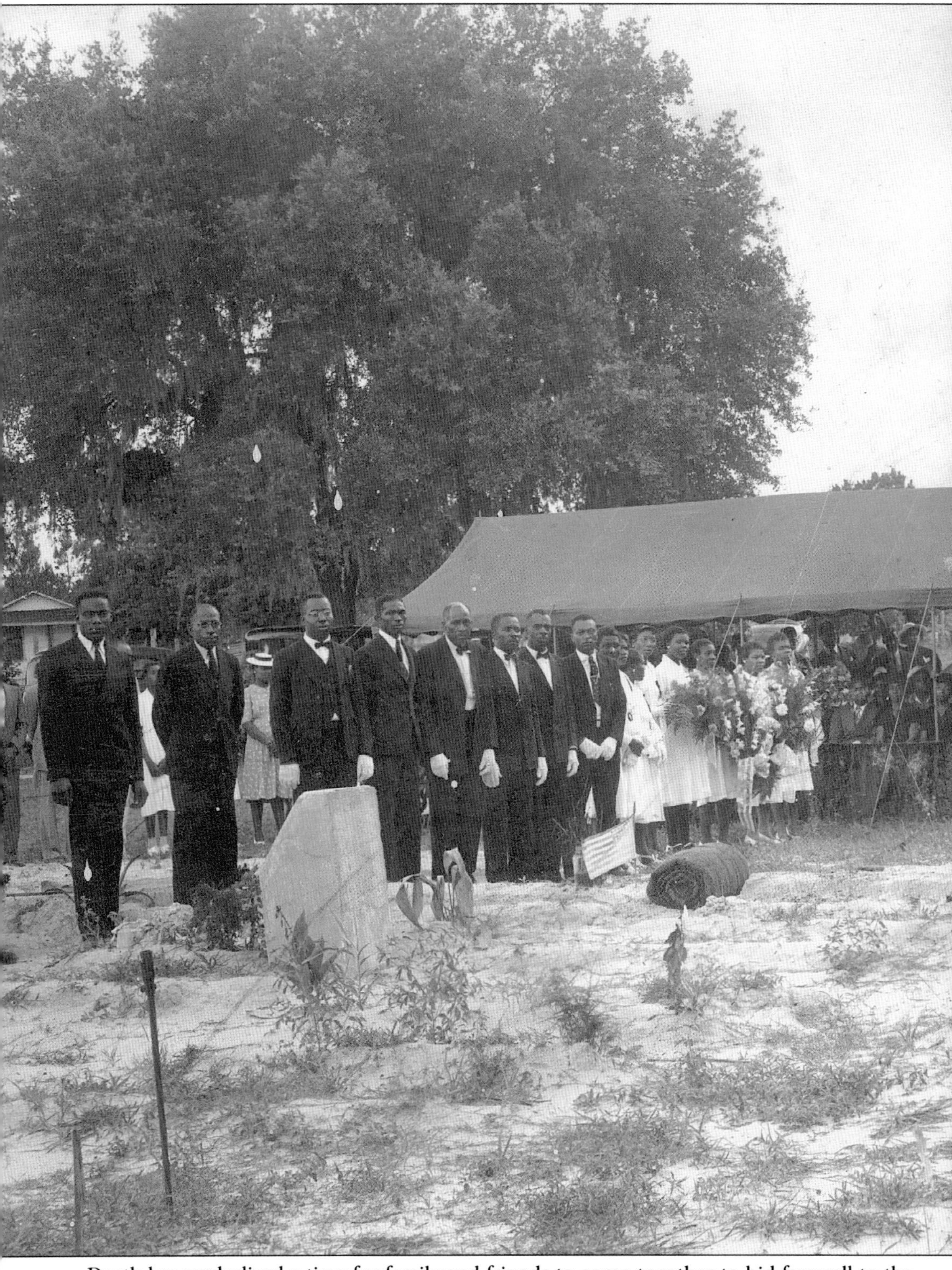

Death has symbolized a time for family and friends to come together to bid farewell to the

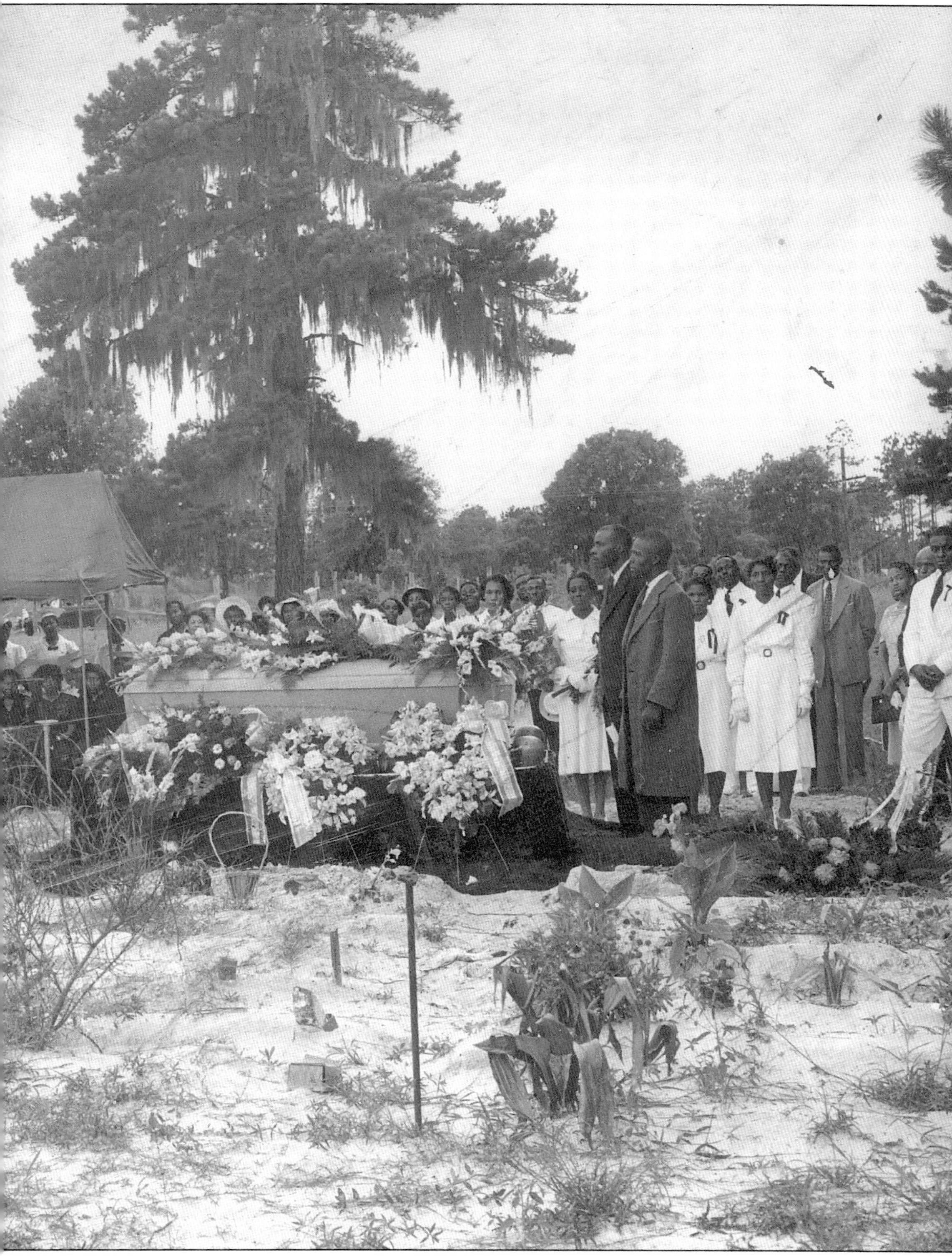

person they had known and to send them on to the "Promised Land."

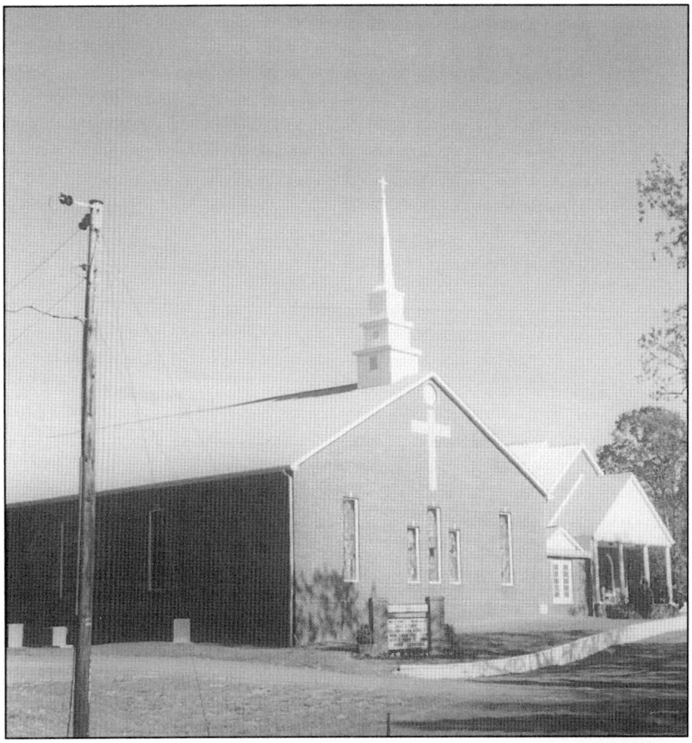

This is Little Zion Baptist Church.

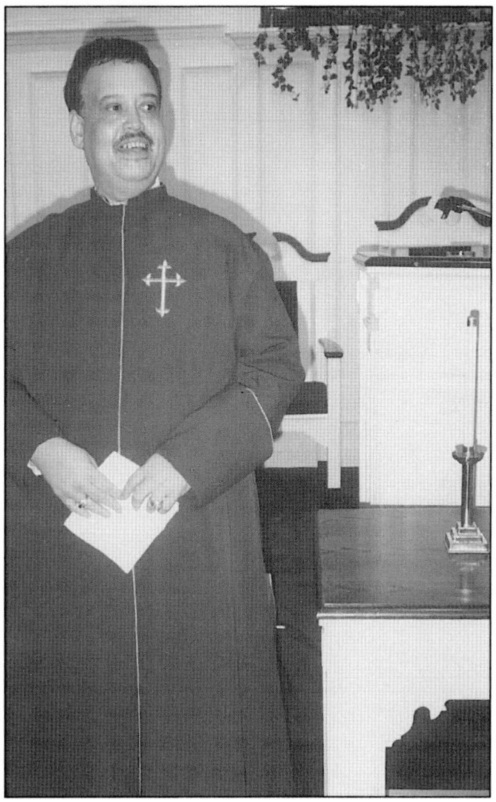

Reverend William B. Scott is the pastor of Little Zion Baptist Church in Oak Grove. He is proud of the new church structure built on the original site of where his members first worshiped in 1866, and he makes his members aware of their history.

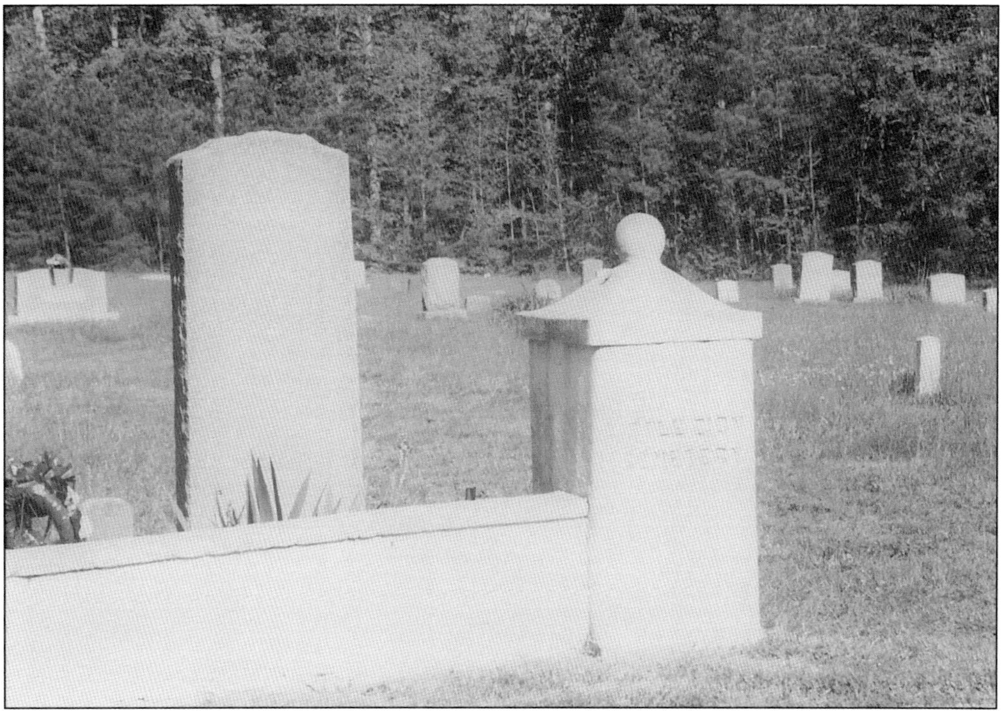

Little Zion has a church cemetery plot of land on the church property.

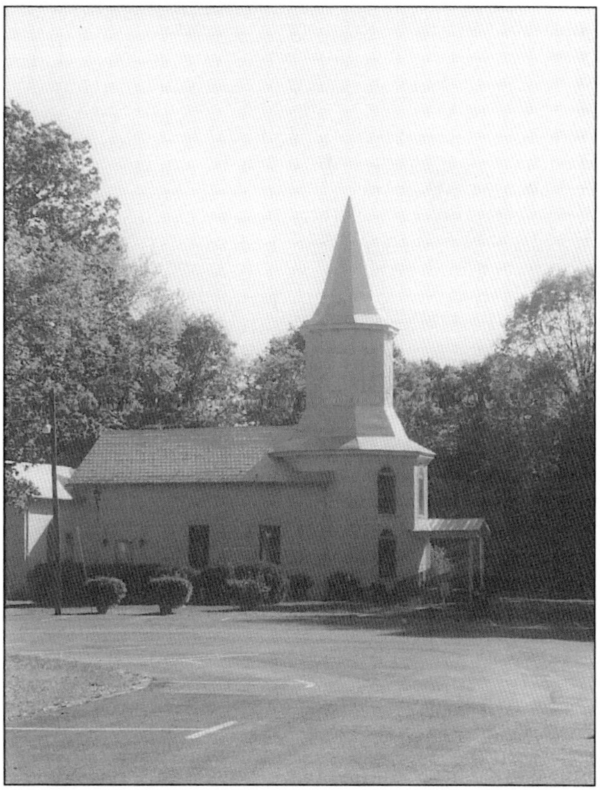

Grant's Hill Baptist Church was founded in 1868. The bell in the the church's tower was given by Susan Howard Johnson.

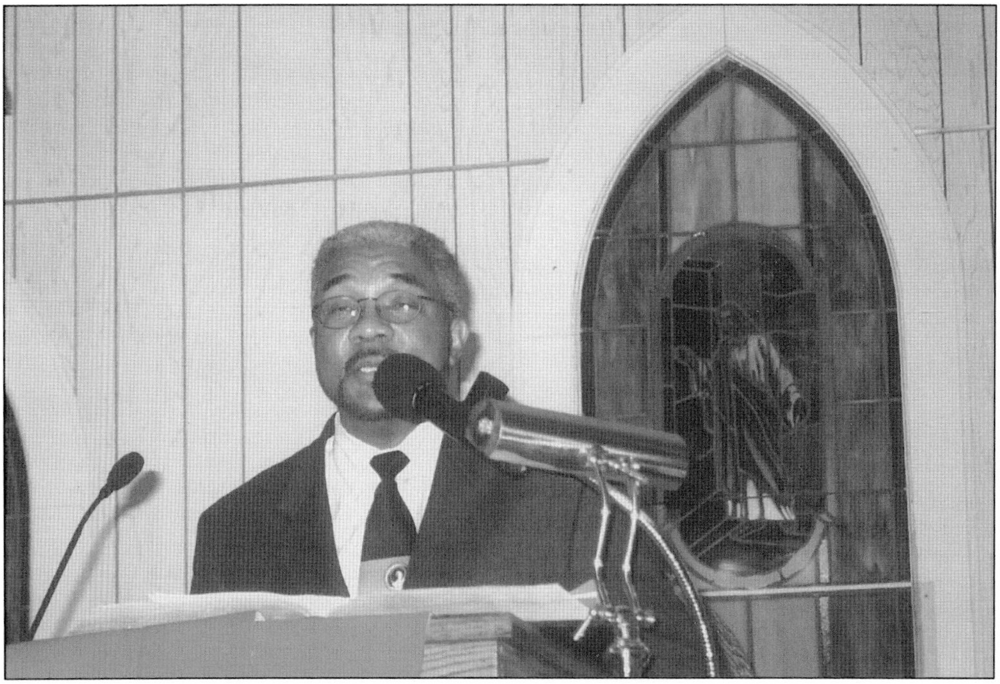

Reverend Lloyd Fox is the pastor at Grant's Hill Baptist Church.

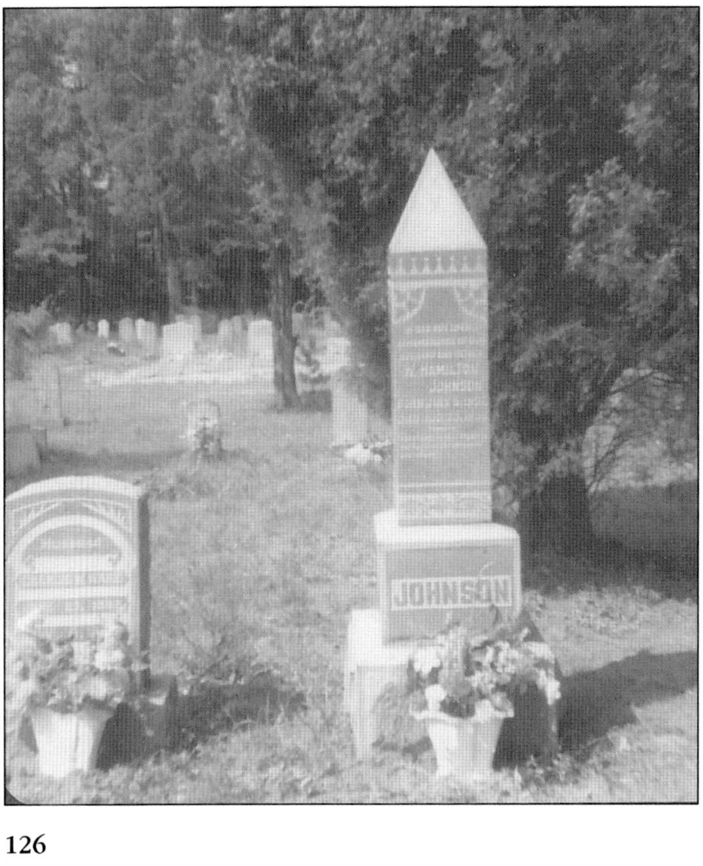

Grant's Hill cemetery plot is located down the road from the church building on a separate parcel of land.

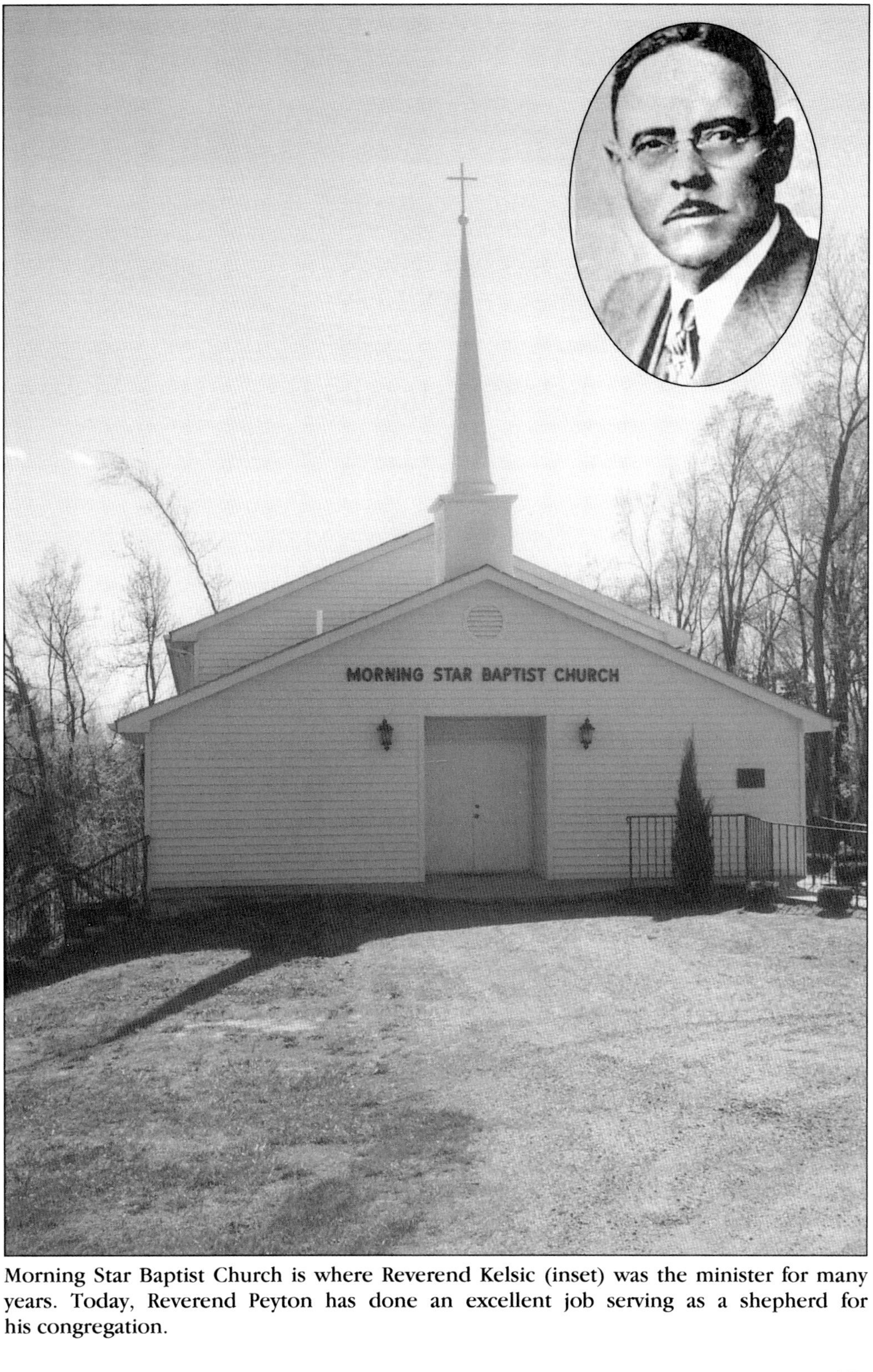

Morning Star Baptist Church is where Reverend Kelsic (inset) was the minister for many years. Today, Reverend Peyton has done an excellent job serving as a shepherd for his congregation.

Believe in Yourself

Whatever I wish . . .
Whatever I dream . . .
Whatever I hope to achieve . . .
Whatever I try for . . .
Whatever I plan . . .
It is mine, if I only believe.

The Last Request

Please don't say that I gave up, just say that I gave in.
Don't say that I lost the battle,
it was God's war to lose or win.
Please don't say how good I was, but that I did my best.
Just say I tried to do what was right,
to give the most I could, not less.
Please don't give me wings or halos,
that's for God to do.
I want no more than I deserve, no extras, just my due.
Don't be concerned about me, know,
I'm well with God, I've made it home.
Don't talk about what could have been,
it's over and it's done!
Just see to all my family's needs,
especially the little ones.
When you draw a picture of me,
don't draw me as a saint.
I've done some good, I've done some wrong
So use your paint, not just the bright and light tones,
use some gray and dark, in fact
don't put me down on canvas, paint me in your heart.
Don't just remember the good times,
but remember all the bad.
For life is full of many things,
some happy and some sad.
But if you must do something, then I have one request,
Forgive me for the wrongs I've done;
with the love that's left,
Thank God for my soul's resting,
Thank God for I've been blessed.
Thank God for all who love me,
Praise God who loved me best.